Prehistorian
A BIOGRAPHY OF V. GORDON CHILDE

SALLY GREEN

Prehistorian

A Biography of V. Gordon Childe

WITH A FOREWORD BY JACK LINDSAY

MOONRAKER PRESS

© 1981 Sally Green
First published in 1981 by
MOONRAKER PRESS
26 St Margaret's Street, Bradford-on-Avon, Wiltshire
SBN 239.00206.7
Text set in 10/12 pt Linotron 202 Plantin
Printed and bound in Great Britain
at The Pitman Press, Bath

Contents

Acknowledgements

The writing of a biography of a man as reserved about his private life as Vere Gordon Childe presents a number of special difficulties. Few of his relatives survive, and none of his intimate friends, if indeed he ever had any who could be described as intimate. He never married, and apparently destroyed all his private papers before his death, and so there is a scarcity of the letters or diaries which usually contribute towards the understanding of a man or woman's personality.

This study of Childe's life and work therefore owes a great deal to the personal recollections and opinions of several of his colleagues, ex-students and friends. Many spent a considerable time talking to me about Childe, and many more engaged in invaluable and often prolonged correspondence. I should like to record my appreciation of the help they have given me and to thank those who kindly gave me their permission to quote from their written reminiscences. The interest and enthusiasm shown in almost every case was most encouraging. I should like to mention in particular: Robin Page Arnot, Paul Ashbee, Sylvia Benton, David Blelloch, R. J. Braidwood, Peggy Burkitt, Humphrey Case, Mary Childe, Lord Chorley, Glyn Daniel, Lady Darwin, H. J. H. Drummond, Peter Gathercole, Margaret Guido, C. F. C. Hawkes, Sinclair Hood, Jack Lindsay, Anne Lloyd, D. J. Mulvaney, Stuart Piggott, Jacquetta Priestley, Nancy Sandars, T. Sulimirski, Celia Topp and Ruth Worsell. The following were especially helpful in obtaining information from Australia on my behalf: Daphne Dobbyn, G. L. Fischer, Ruth Haig, George Munster, Russel Ward and Jean Wall. Several people have assisted me in the course of my research with help and advice, and in addition to those already mentioned my thanks are due to Margaret Deith, Alastair Green and Bruce Trigger.

I am indebted to the Institute of Archaeology and to Professor J. G. D. Clark for permission to quote from Gordon Childe's letters and published works, and to reprint his article 'Valediction' as Appendix I. Professor G. E. Daniel kindly consented to the reprinting of Childe's papers published in *Antiquity*, and Professor Piggott to the publication of his own 'Ballade to a Great Prehistorian'. The contributors (or their heirs) to the B.B.C. radio programme, 'The Archaeologist, no. 58', kindly gave me their permission to use material from the transcript; and the Secretary to the University of Edinburgh allowed me to quote from Lord Abercromby's deed of bequest. I should like to acknowledge a grant from the University of Sheffield Research Fund towards travelling expenses whilst engaged on my research.

My thanks are also due to Lord Zuckerman and the Times Publishing Co. Ltd. for permission to quote from Lord Zuckerman's *From Apes to Warlords* (1978), London: Hamish Hamilton; to Jack Lindsay and the Bodley Head for permission to quote from J. Lindsay's *Life Rarely Tells* (1958), London: the Bodley Head; and to David Higham Associates for permission to quote from J. G. Crowther's *Fifty Years with Science* (1970), London: Barrie and Jenkins.

Foreword

My one claim to write this introduction is that I must be the only surviving person who knew Gordon Childe in his early days in Australia and then later in Britain after he became a famous archaeologist. There is much that is new to me in Sally Green's account. I feel that I would have understood Childe better if I had known what she tells of his childhood and boyhood. The man as he developed emerges clearly from her narrative, while at the same time she summarises effectively his achievement in archaeology and history, setting out succinctly but thoroughly the situation out of which his analyses and reconstructions came and on which they powerfully impacted. Archaeology in the 1920s was maturing and cohering at last as a far-reaching and soundly-based discipline, or at least the bases for such a development were being securely built. Childe's main contribution lay in his capacity to keep on synthesizing and inter-relating the material. Such work was what was needed above all at this decisive phase, to match the continually extended and ever more precise systems of digging at sites. The interpretation and interconnection of the finds called for a rapid and bold expansion of theory, which went beyond the relatively simple systems that had previously attempted to sort out the types of artefacts and the various evidences of social organization.

In the field of excavation, apart from Skara Brae, Childe added little, but on the theoretical side he was a great pathfinder. With his powers of quickly and comprehensively making sense of the complicated and varied evidences brought to light by the digs, he produced much more than a set of useful correlations which helped to give coherence and stimulus to the work being done out in the field. He gave a new force and urgency to that work, which could be seen more and more as providing a picture of the prehistoric past that was understandably human, and clarified the forms of social evolution leading up to the levels where the light of what we call history begins to shine more and more steadily. Childe was not the only scholar contributing to the new breadth of vision, the fuller grasp of how human beings lived and developed in prehistory; but at this important phase of consolidation, clarification and expansion he played the leading role. He went on restlessly seeking to master and use all the new evidence for the construction of large-scale and inclusive systems that by their interconnections revealed the various sites or finds as moments of phases in a continuous human development.

But if we thus merely stress his synthesising powers we fail to bring out anything like the full significance or force of his contribution. To do that we need to consider what we may call the Marxist element in his thinking. What he learned from Marx was that the distinguishing quality of human beings lies in their productive activity, their capacity to take over nature, absorb it, and transform it, and in the process to transform themselves. But he was in no sense a mere adapter of some ideas taken over from Marx. He was a creative Marxist, defining in new fields and relationships the way in which Man the Producer makes Himself, makes history. Hence the far-reaching importance of works like *Man Makes Himself* and *What Happened in History*, which, though largely based on archaeological researches, sought always to realize the material of those researches as human history in the full sense of the term. These and his other books were written in a comparatively short period, a little over three decades: a period, as we noted, in which archaeology and anthropology were both making rapid advances. He was always ready to discard an hypothesis or system of links if new finds undermined it or suggested new and more satisfactory ways of correlating the facts. He never ceased trying to test out the interconnections he had been formulating, and to build on a firmer chronological basis.

It was a misfortune then that he died just as radio-carbon dating was coming effectively on the scene. Its working-out has had many surprising results for the dating and relating of cultures, going a long way to provide the objective basis for the chronological systems that he so much desired. If he had lived another ten or more years he would certainly have eagerly applied the new criteria. But we must be grateful for the valuable correlations which he did achieve, and, beyond any particular points of interpretation, the general outlook and methodology which he brought to bear on the archaeological material. He himself correctly assessed his life-work when he stated that his main contributions to prehistory were 'certainly not novel data rescued by brilliant excavation from the soil or by patient research from dusty museum cases, nor yet well-founded chronological schemes nor freshly defined cultures, but rather interpretative concepts and methods of explanation'. Sally Green's account makes clear just how precise was that estimate of his achievement and how valuable and far-reaching have been its results.

Now I should like to add some details of my friendship with him. Sally Green gives a fairly full narrative of my relations with him in Brisbane in 1919. I should like to add only that he had gravitated to the WEA, an organization which always interested him. In those days in Brisbane it had a very working-class quality. Through it he met Witherby and myself, and I introduced him to a couple of members of the IWW, or Wobblies, one of whom, Jim Quinton, was a striking character, able to set out his ideas with passion, vividly and volubly (I got him to come down and talk at the University one lunch-hour). Later Childe had much to say of the IWW in Australia in *How Labour Governs*. He would in any event have dealt there with the group; but I like to think that it was through Quinton he gained his initial interest in them and in their message to the trade-union movement of the One Big Union and the General Strike, which had a powerful impact around that time.

When I left for England myself in 1926, I had no idea of what had happened to Childe; but about 1928 I heard of his Edinburgh professorship. I thought of contacting him, but was too taken up by my work in London with the Fanfrolico Press to do anything about it; and during the 1930s (as told in my *Fanfrolico and After*) I was mainly in the West Country, very hard up and in difficult circumstances. In 1941 I was called up into Signals and in 1943 by an odd chance became scriptwriter to the Army Theatre of ABCA (the only private in the War Office). In 1945, while still in the army, I at last wrote to Childe, about an anthropological essay on which I was working, and a letter of his dated 27 May has survived among my papers.

Prehistorian

Dear Lindsay Yes Im looking forward to reading your demolition of the Raglanists—it would presumably come to me anyhow editorially [on the *Modern Quarterly*]. Let me say Im very suspicious of psychoanalysis—except as a curative technique & of Freudians even more than Jungians. Totem & Tabu seems to me not a scientific explanation nor yet an historical one but a bad dream—& perhaps that is what its author intended. Electro-encephals [sic] seems to me the hopeful way of getting at those processes. As to John Layard I've just heard he is popping in & out of a Trappist Monastery and leaving his patients to Doris. I shouldn't have read the Maze even had I not read a damning review of it.

Do avoid this woolly stuff Someday we'll understand this in terms of bipoles—Sarkisov's Institute in Moscow is on the fruitful track Meanwhile to hide our ignorance in nebulous imagery is just reactionary

Im coming up this week from Weds to Fri Next week perhaps I'll fly to Moscow. In London Athenaeum will get me. I spent a couple of nights with Bert Evatt last month *Yours Gordon Childe.*

I don't recall what remarks of mine about the Malekulan Maze provoked his rebukes. I could not have praised *Totem and Tabu* since I have never thought of it as anything but a work of sheer fantasy, despite the efforts of anthropologists like Roheim to apply its thesis. On 19 July Childe sent me a card from the University Club, Edinburgh,

I am sure I should have enjoyed your discussion of Superstructure had I been able to get up But I went straight from the Kremlin to the plane & from the plane to train that took me here & stay here till about Aug. 24. USSR was fine. *Gordon Childe.*

The reference here is to a controversial document which I had drawn up and which the Cultural Committee of the Communist Party had arranged to have discussed. The date of the meeting was delayed and Childe was able to attend after all. On 25 October he sent a card:

I gather we are to meet on the battleground somewhere on 2nd at the curious hour of 7.30. Could we feed together somewhere first: As I dont know the place I cant suggest where.

He was interested in the theme of the discussion, particularly as I had prefaced my paper with a quotation from *What Happened in History*, which set the key of the argument. 'The reckoning may be long postponed. An obsolete ideology can hamper an economy and impede its change for longer than Marxists admit.' My paper argued

xii

at length that spirit and consciousness were a necessary element in productive activity, so that 'production is more than a matter of economic mechanism and blind social relations, and Culture is not a *reflection* of productive activity, is *not* determined by it in a mechanist way. . . . In short, production and culture are in a dialectical relation of conflict and unity, and if that is so, then one is being continually transformed into the other.'

On 1 October he had written me a lengthy letter in which he discussed my paper, or rather certain aspects of it. However, without the text of the paper for reference it is not easy to follow his points. I therefore cite here only portions of his letter. He began:

My dear Lindsay When I got here from London yesterday your very interesting paper was awaiting me which your wife kindly sent me on the 23rd the day I left Edinburgh for London. When in town during the summer I often stay here and write from here [the Club] but I dont tell the porter my movements—its too much trouble to explain the details of my travels everywhere I sometimes write a letter. The University & it alone always know my address—to *strangers* I indicate this on top as I have today Funnily enough I did ring you up last Tues.—at least I dialled WEL 2023 but got someone who had never heard of you. I didn't ask if it was 15 Nottingham Pl. but now suspect you have moved hence the address

Well it seems a very useful paper. The collection of relevant passages from M & E are in themselves most valuable. I agree that 'reflection' is not a happy term *umgesetzt und übergesetzt* does not = 'reflected' 'determined' (*bestimmt*) must not be taken in a mechanistic—i.e. transcendentalist—sense.

On examination the points he goes on to raise or question are all found to be connected one way or another with the inner life of human beings, their aesthetic or psychological experiences and developments. Childe does not question my main thesis, and in conversation he agreed with it in general, recognizing fully the importance of ideas within the social whole where the mode of production had the final word. He ends his letter:

Anyhow how would you react to the following approach
    Idea = meaning attached by society to socially approved symbol
    Symbol = any voluntarily produced action (or its result) that stands for something other than itself to a society.
    N.B.: idea (=meaning) is never identical either with the symbol or with the 'things' symbolised But both meaning & symbol are social products. Symbols like ideas are tools of thinking and ∴ 'determine' thought

I don't know whether this helps you any perhaps it doesn't fit in with Gestalt as well as with Behaviourism. By the way Huxley last night made the point I think rightly that both psychoanalysis & introspective psychologies are neglected in USSR in favour of behaviouristic approach.

These remarks are rather disjointed but I send them at once to reach you before the meeting I wish I could attend but by then I'll be in Orkney unless my plans get fog bound. Please thank your wife for her letter *Yours ever Gordon Childe*

His concluding remarks show that he wanted to treat the aesthetic and psychological issues I had raised as questions of epistemology, of the processes of knowledge and its forms of communication. His approach is underlined by the slightly cautious praise of the behaviouristic outlook, which I saw as mechanist.

Behind his positions here I think we can see his revulsion from religion, his personal fear of emotional entanglement. If the questions were treated purely in epistemological terms the complex emotional and psychological issues raised (correctly or incorrectly) by some of my formulations could be set aside. I would argue then that, quite apart from the question as to how validly I had made my points, Childe felt uneasy at their being raised at all. He wanted a Marxism in which questions of the productive base and of a cultural or institutional superstructure were treated solely from the angle of their efficacy in grappling with nature and in achieving a rational basis for action, communication, organization. These questions were those that concerned him in his archaeological work, where he could ignore the aesthetic, psychological, and philosophical issues I had tried to bring into the open in parts of my paper. It might indeed be argued that his positions were the most useful for him in ordering and interpreting the archaeological evidences at the stages then being reached.

I may add that at the discussion he listened with extreme intentness, but said nothing. John Lewis was the main attacker. He insisted that in the beginning was the Deed—just like that—and that I had raised unmeaning problems and created confusion; he denied that Marxists made the over-simplified or mechanistic errors I attributed to many of their formulations. I feel sure that the experience of the evening made Childe more determined than ever not to become involved in Marxist controversies (one person supported me, E. P. Thompson, then a young student).

I should like to cite one more letter from Childe, dated 30 May 1946, Edinburgh; it deals with an essay on the state of anthropology which I had sent him.

Dear Jack Here are some comments as I read your article. p. 2 Surely not 'splitting off' Anthropology articulates itself just [as] Geology etc. do—pa-laeontology petrology etc didn't split off. 18 Sumer—not Sumer*ia*—or Mesopotamia (but *not* Babylonia)

I really think that is all—save perhaps: A hierarchic classification of societies into stages remains subjective and a priori until it can be shown that the stages follow one another in a genuinely historical order. This only archaeology can do: cf. Engels of [?on] arch. evidence in *Der Ursprung* . . . I have just expanded this in an article that I sent the NW Journal of Anthrop. Leslie A. White has been recently writing some quite good articles on Morgan & Diffusion v Evolution in *Amer. Anthrop.*, & *N.W. Journal*. But he doesn't make quite the same points.

Your paper strikes me as very badly needed & a scholarly contribution to the subject. Will you offer it to MQ? I hope to see a good deal of you when I come to town; I believe I have secured a flat in Lawn Road Flats NW3 (I fixed it verbally but have no written confirmation) *Yours Gordon Childe.*

My essay dealt with the limitations of the compilation-methods of Frazer and others, then went on to discuss the need for more fieldwork, with an attempt to analyse the values and methods used in such work. It never reached Childe on the board of the *Modern Quarterly* as John Lewis rejected it at once on the plea that he lacked space.*

An invitation note gives the date of the warming-up party at 18 Lawn Road Flats: 'A Childeish professor invites you to inspect its

---

* I cannot recall what article I asked Childe for in August 1946; he wrote on the 28th, 'In principle I'll be glad to do sort of article you want. But tell me more about it when term starts At the moment Im much preoccupied.' A note of 1 August 1947 verifies what Sally Green says of his attitude to American archaeology. I had written asking about the early horse in America. 'I don't know much about American archaeology. Of course identity of site particularly a cave proves nothing about continuity of culture. The pleistocene horse became extinct I believe (as did camel) but there were pleistocene horses in Old World too. Shall be in London most of August. Let's meet.'

A note of 25 November 1955 runs: 'My dear Jack, Of course I am only too glad to support your application to the Archaeological Institute; you are a most suitable candidate in every respect. Fancy another book on Roman Britain! Yours sincerely, Gordon.'

new nursery and such prehistoric liquors as survive on Thursday, October 3 at 6 p.m.' I saw a fair amount of Childe in the following years. We could now discuss things directly and I can find no letters of interest. In the 1950s I had moved away from London and saw less of him, though we met now and then.

Sally Green refers to the way in which his voice could drop away into an odd mumble. Once the Historians Group of the Communist Party, at my suggestion, asked him to give a talk on the forms of land-tenure in early Sumer. He agreed and we went one evening to the building in Regents Park. He began his talk and went on for a quarter of an hour or so, then made some remarks in an inaudible voice, nodded, and went out. We were surprised, as the talk did not seem to have reached a definite conclusion and we had expected a discussion. After about ten minutes most of the audience wandered off. Then, when only four or five of us were left, Childe returned to ask in surprise what had happened to the meeting. He had told us, he thought, that he was going to the lavatory and would be back after a while.

The last occasion on which we met was at some public gathering. We went aside and talked, and he asked what I was working on. I told him that I projected a book on the Cults of Britain in the fourth century A.D., gathering such evidence as there was for Christian groups and asking if there was something like a pagan revival (e.g. at Lydney and Maiden Castle). He expressed much interest and I said I'd dedicate the book to him. However I never wrote it, turning instead from Roman Britain to Roman Egypt and its papyri. When I completed *Daily Life in Roman Egypt* I dedicated it to Gordon Childe 'in memory', with some lines of verse:

> Now forty years or more I've seen,
> since, climbing up Mount Tambourine,
> by tracks of passionfruit we went
> in a declining argument.
> Careless and caustic still, you trod
> the cart-road and its ruts of red
> that rambled round the mountainside
> while the heat's locusts shrilly cried.
> Demolishing everything I said,
> you smiled like a bland lizard god
> in some Egyptian mystery
> as learned you answered me;

my certainties grew less and less
at your laconic friendliness
until each truth you simply stated
became more oddly complicated.
A wallaby in the bush took flight;
we shared the stark Australian light;
and then, our ancient worlds put by,
at last beneath the topless sky
we came where silver gumtrees grew
amid a lustrous smoke of dew:
great staghorned trees that shining made
a temple of primeval shade—
and no words needed stir the air
of crisp oracular silence there.

This I remembered: when I learned
how to the clear heights you'd returned.
You stood on the sheer rocky edge
of silence, where the stark light burned;
the dialogue with life was ended,
you saw the many-coloured thing
swing out below you, far and splendid;
and you upon the dizzy ledge
let go, went down,
                    went down, and died.
You saw that temple opening wide,
you entered through the shining door
where words weren't needed any more.

When I heard the news of his death, I was sure that it was suicide. I felt that he had reached something like completion in a long arc of work, that he had been very hard hit by the Kruschev revelations of 1956, and that, despite the many friends he had had, he felt his loneliness as something crushing. I learn from Sally Green how his disappointment at the Australia he found further weakened his desire to keep on living.

The impulse to escape and give himself up decisively to the earth he loved proved too strong.

JACK LINDSAY

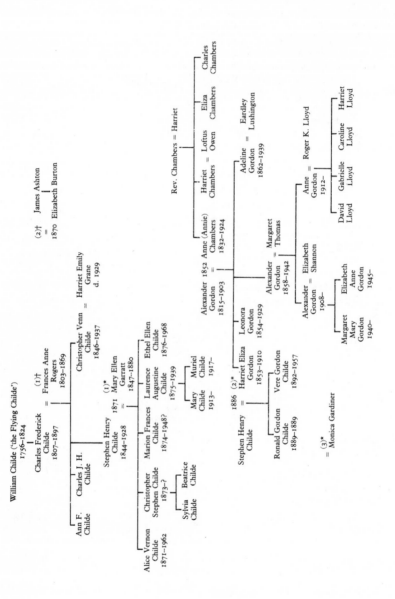

William Childe ('the Flying Childe')
1756–1824

Charles Frederick Childe
1807–1897

(1)† Frances Anne Rogers 1803–1869

(2)† James Ashton = 1870 Elizabeth Burton

Christopher Venn Childe 1846–1937 = Harriet Emily Grane d. 1929

Ann F. Childe

Charles J. H. Childe

Stephen Henry Childe 1844–1928 = 1871 Mary Ellen Garratt 1847–1880

Marion Frances Childe 1874–1948?

Laurence Augustine Childe 1875–1939

Ethel Ellen Childe 1876–1968

Alice Vernon Childe 1871–1962

Christopher Stephen Childe 1873–?

Sylvia Childe

Beatrice Childe

Mary Childe 1913–

Muriel Childe 1917–

Rev. Chambers = Harriet

Harriet Chambers = Loftus Owen

Eliza Chambers

Charles Chambers

Alexander Gordon 1815–1903 = 1852 Anne (Annie) Chambers 1832–1924

Adeline Gordon 1862–1939 = Eardley Lushington

Stephen Henry Childe = 1886 Harriet Eliza Gordon 1853–1910

(2)*

Leonora Gordon 1854–1929

Alexander Gordon 1858–1942 = Margaret Thomas

Ronald Gordon Childe 1889–1889

Vere Gordon Childe 1892–1957

Alexander Gordon 1908– = Elizabeth Shannon

Anne Gordon 1912– = Roger K. Lloyd

(3)* = Monica Gardiner

Margaret Mary Gordon 1940–

Elizabeth Anne Gordon 1945–

David Lloyd

Gabrielle Lloyd

Caroline Lloyd

Harriet Lloyd

Introduction

Although Gordon Childe was not appointed to his first job in the field of prehistoric archaeology until he was 35 years old, and died six months after his sixty-fifth birthday, in 1957, his achievements in a mere three decades earned him general recognition as the most eminent and influential scholar of European prehistory in the twentieth century. An unconventional and genuinely eccentric man, he was dedicated to his chosen study, and had he retired in 1930 would still have been remembered as a pioneer in the study of prehistory. One of his great strengths was his readiness to examine new evidence, see whether it fitted his theories, and if not, freely to admit his errors. The prehistory of Europe absorbed him throughout his life, and he searched with unflagging zeal for the underlying causes which made the civilization of that area unique. In his last book, *The Prehistory of European Society*, published posthumously, he set out what he felt was a satisfactory explanation of the individuality of Europe from the Bronze Age onwards. This explanation would not be acceptable to many prehistorians today, but it is worth remembering that Childe was working largely without the benefit of modern dating techniques; and indeed his own contribution to the building up of a chronology for Europe and the Near East in the days of cross-dating was tremendous.

At the beginning of the century archaeology, and especially prehistoric archaeology, was only just emerging from its infancy. By the time of Childe's death in 1957 it was internationally recognized as a serious scientific discipline, and was also fast gaining popularity with the public. But Gordon Childe never became a well-known figure with the popular appeal of Sir Mortimer Wheeler or Dr Louis Leakey, for example. This was partly because he was not so much an archaeologist as a prehistorian—more of a scholar than a digger—and did not uncover splendid cities or ancient skulls from man's past. However, even in private life Childe was something of a 'loner'; a kindly and generous companion, he had many friends, but no intimates. He never married, and had little contact with his family after he left home as a young man. His deeply-held belief in Marxist philosophy and his sometime naive admiration for Soviet communism also set him apart from many of his colleagues.

If there was one thing of which Childe was always proud, it was being an Australian. Both his parents were actually born in England, but Gordon was born and brought up in New South Wales. He attended school and university in Sydney, showing himself to be academically brilliant, and then travelled to England to continue his training in the classics at Oxford. His father was a clergyman, a man whose word was law in his own home, and from this strict upbringing stemmed Gordon Childe's later anti-clericalism and rationalist beliefs. At Sydney University he read the works of Hegel, Marx and Engels, and thereafter his interest in political philosophy was equalled only by his fascination with prehistoric archaeology. These interests were shared by his great friend at Oxford, the brilliant scholar, R. Palme Dutt, who was later to become a founder member and leading theoretician of the Communist Party of Great Britain.

In spite of his pride in being Australian, Childe never visited his native land between the years 1921 and 1957. This may have been partly due to his shabby treatment at the hands of various Australian officials as he attempted to launch himself on a career. He was effectively dismissed from a teaching post at the University of Sydney in 1918 because of his pacifist views, which were, of course, anathema to the Establishment during the first world war. After further similar experiences he turned from education to Labour politics, and got a job as secretary to the Premier of New South Wales. This post was an eye-opener for the young idealist, and after his dismissal by a change of government he published, in 1923, his first book, *How Labour Governs*, which was a biting indictment of the corruption of Labour politics in Australia.

It was during the mid-1920s that Childe turned his back on a political career, and decided instead to concentrate on prehistoric archaeology. His method of tackling problems in the field of European prehistory was original and of immense importance: he travelled whenever possible all over Central and Eastern Europe, visiting sites and museums, examining the material at first hand, and also reading quantities of papers in obscure foreign languages. Over the next few years he produced in rapid succession several massive and comprehensive volumes on European prehistory. Nothing on such a scale, or with his width of approach, had been attempted before, and these books established his reputation overnight. In 1927 he was appointed the first Abercromby Professor of Archaeology at Edinburgh University, and from that moment on all the unorthodox beliefs in the world could not prevent an outstandingly successful career.

While he is acclaimed by other prehistorians as a brilliant synthesizer of archaeological data, Gordon Childe is best remembered by the general public for his popular books such as *Man Makes Himself* and *What Happened in History*. He always firmly believed that the dichotomy between prehistory and history, so common in the mind of expert and layman alike, was a false one; and his own books illustrate how what is usually accepted as history can be extracted from archaeological material. Childe's most famous excavation, and the only one he apparently enjoyed, was that of Skara Brae, the Neolithic village in the Orkneys. Though often considered an indifferent digger, the painstaking recovery from the sand of the stone houses and furniture of this village argues some technical skill.

In 1946 he became Director of the London University Institute of Archaeology. Though at the peak of his career, he retained all his eccentricities; past students recall the wide-brimmed hat framing his extraordinarily ugly face, and his copy of the *Daily Worker* prominently displayed. It has been said of Childe that he rarely spoke ill of anyone and was incapable of spite; though he could, and did, take real or pretended dislikes to people, movements, countries, and even whole archaeological concepts, on political grounds. However, few of his colleagues realized how deep his involvement with Marxism still was, although he was apparently never a Communist Party member. He rarely spoke of his beliefs to fellow-prehistorians—and this is not surprising when one considers the scathing remarks on this subject made by some reviewers of his later books. Nevertheless, he persisted in his almost childish love of Russia and admiration of Russian archaeological organization, and liked to sign his name in Cyrillic on postcards sent from his many travels.

Childe's death was for many years something of an enigma. He retired in 1956, and the following year returned to Australia for the first time in 35 years. He visited old friends and old haunts, but was bitterly disappointed by what he found in Australian life and politics. Always a keen walker, he was exploring the Blue Mountains west of Sydney when he fell 1,500 feet to his death. Although for over 20 years many of his friends were reluctant to accept that his death was intentional, it is now clear from a remarkable document he wrote in 1957 that it was indeed premeditated suicide.

Prehistorians and archaeologists all over the world were shocked to learn of his early death and believed he could have continued his work for many more years; though Childe himself died satisfied with his achievements, and convinced he had done all he could in his field. His legacy to the study of prehistory was certainly phenomenal for one man; and it was his devotion to scholarship which enabled him to achieve so much. Had he been a more rounded personality he might have had family ties to persuade him that old age was worth living, but prehistoric archaeology might well have been the poorer.

1. Early Years

Vere Gordon Childe was born in Sydney on 14 April 1892, and was the sole surviving offspring of Stephen Henry and Harriet Eliza Childe. Harriet had given birth to another son, named Ronald Gordon, in 1889, but he had lived only one month. Stephen Childe was Rector of St Thomas's Church in North Sydney, and Gordon was brought up in a conventional and deeply religious background. Both his father and mother came from prominent and established British families, and it was perhaps a reaction against his ancestry which contributed to his later atheism and rationalism.

Gordon Childe's grandfather, Charles Frederick Childe, was born on 17 December 1807, the son of William Childe and a member of the well-known Shropshire family, the Childes of Kinlet. He died at Cheltenham on his ninetieth birthday, and it is difficult to believe that he was mourned by many who knew him. By all accounts he was a strict, unbending sort of man, the typical Victorian husband and father. He gained a BA in 1832 and an MA in 1837 from Emmanuel College, Cambridge, although he had originally been admitted to St John's College in November, 1827. He was ordained deacon in 1833 and priest in 1834, holding the post of curate at St Michael's Church, Cambridge, from October 1831, until at least September 1832. It was probably around 1830 that Charles Childe was married to Frances Anne Rogers, and on 10 August 1835 he was appointed curate of Petersfield in Hampshire. The couple already had one daughter, Ann, and a younger son, Charles, when Mr Childe was offered the post of headmaster at Queen Mary's Grammar School in Walsall, Staffordshire.

The Reverend Charles Childe took up his new position as headmaster and minister of the school's chapel, St Paul's, in April 1837. The Queen Mary's Grammar School was an old and established boys' school, founded in 1554, which had a policy of educating local boys to supply the professions and commerce of Walsall. Just prior to Childe's appointment there had been some slackness in maintaining standards at the school, and the Governors, determined this time to leave nothing to chance, had announced in their advertisement that periodical examinations of the boys and reports on the state of the school would take place.

Charles Childe was only 29 when he became headmaster of Queen Mary's, but he had the necessary ability for organization and administration. Six months after his arrival he proposed a new scheme for the school which was accepted by the Governors on 23 September 1837. Learning perhaps from his predecessor's experiences, he ensured the parents' co-operation by requiring them to agree to his provisions before their boys were admitted. Childe's Scheme stated that there were to be two principal schools—the Grammar and the Commercial Schools—and laid down curriculi, regulations, and limits to the number of boys. The new headmaster also availed himself of his right to have four boarders as private pupils, and had it not been for the local policy of the Governors, this right could well have been used to develop Queen Mary's into a public school, as happened at Harrow and Rugby.

There is no doubt that the Rev. Charles Childe threw himself into his duties both as headmaster and as minister of St Paul's with energy and zeal. He had a strong personality and exerted considerable influence on a number of the pupils in his care. However, he ruled the school, and his family, with an iron hand, or, more literally, with 'a stiff stick that looked like a black whale bone',[1] and he was a firm believer in corporal punishment. During his headmastership boys were banned from visiting the nearby meadows where races were held, on pain of expulsion. He may have been a good administrator, but his pupils were more apt to remember him on account of his unbending manner. One boy described the new headmaster as 'an iceberg'. Another later wrote: 'I have never forgotten the hard, red unsympathetic visage of the Rev. Mr. Childe, anything but a face to be revered in the sense of loved. He was a man who, like so many of the cloth, had never a word of kindness or encouragement for the boys.'[2]

Mr Childe could not tolerate unpunctuality, and if his wife was not in her place in time for the family breakfast, she would find her husband's watch on her plate. Their young daughter took some lessons with the boys, and if she was unfortunate enough to answer incorrectly, her imperfections earned her a penetrating look from her father. The second master at Queen Mary's Grammar School at that time was the kindly and approachable Mr Rock, so there was a certain natural reluctance on the part of the boys to progress to the Upper School where Childe awaited them.

Charles Childe's term of office was mercifully short. On 31 January 1839 he resigned to become Principal of the Church Missionary Society's College in Upper Street, Islington. This was a Church of England establishment, founded in 1825, which trained missionaries for abroad, and Mr Childe held the post until 1858, when he became Rector of Holbrook, Suffolk. Whilst they were living in Islington, his wife Frances gave birth to two more sons: Stephen Henry, born on 27 August 1844, and Christopher Venn, two years younger. Frances died at Holbrook on 20 November 1869, aged 63, and Charles was remarried just a year later, on 14 December 1870, at Chorley, to Elizabeth Burton, a widow and daughter of a manufacturer named James Ashton. At Islington, Frances's sons, Charles, Stephen and Christopher, were educated at home by private tuition, under the strict eye of their father. Stephen entered Corpus Christi College, Cambridge, to read theology, and was followed by Christopher, reading law. The youngest brother showed particular brilliance, and began a promising legal career. He was ordained in 1876, and eventually became an Honourable Canon of Gloucester, Honorary Chaplain to the Bishop of London and a Grand Chaplain of the English Freemasons.

Meanwhile Stephen Childe had been ordained in 1867, immediately after obtaining his BA from Cambridge, and became successively curate of Middle Claydon and vicar of St James's, Latchford. On 3 January 1871 he had been married to Mary Ellen Garratt, the daughter of an Ipswich clergyman, and in early 1873 he was appointed Vice-Principal of St Paul's Training College in Cheltenham. St Paul's was a Church of England college which trained teachers, and it was based firmly on Evangelical principles. The Education Act of 1870 had provided elementary education for all children, and so provoked a demand for teachers, and by 1873 St Paul's was a flourishing establishment of high academic standards, whose Principal was the Rev. R. M. Chamney. Stephen Childe had a salary of £300 a year and a residence in college, to which he brought his wife Mary and their young daughter, Alice Vernon. Their second child, Christopher, was born shortly after their arrival. But Stephen Childe did not remain long in Cheltenham, for by October 1873 he had informed Mr Chamney of his intention to vacate the office of Vice-Principal by Christmas.

It is not clear why Stephen Childe stayed so short a time at St Paul's, but it seems likely that he was not sufficiently Evangelical. At that time the College was very strongly of this persuasion—the Principal had said that he intended to make Evangelical 'principles and sympathies' a *sine qua non*, and efficiency in teaching a secondary consideration— whereas Childe had come under the influence of the Oxford or Tractarian Movement, otherwise known as the Catholic Revival. Other possibilities are that he felt the remuneration was too small, or that the College took exception to educational duties he undertook outside the College. Whatever the reason, the Childe family was soon on the move again, this time up to Yorkshire, where Stephen became vicar of various parishes, and where their children, Laurence, Marion and Ethel, were born. Eventually at the end of 1878 the Reverend Stephen Childe left his incumbency in Yorkshire to travel with his wife and children to New South Wales. In April 1879, following the death of the Rector of St Thomas's Church of England Church in North Sydney, Stephen Childe took over this post and became the church's longest-serving, though certainly not its most popular, Rector. The parish was situated north of the river, which was considered in those days a healthier place to live than Sydney itself; but the climate obviously did little for Mary Childe, for she died a mere four months after settling in at the rectory, at the age of thirty-three.

His wife's early death left the Rev. S. H. Childe with five young children to bring up as well as his new parish to attend to. It was not until six years later, in November 1886, that he married for the second time, at Holy Trinity Church, Melbourne. His new wife, Harriet Eliza, was the eldest child of a barrister named Alexander Gordon and his wife Anne. Harriet had been born in Hornsey, London, on 7 July 1853 and had sailed from England with her parents not long afterwards. So Harriet grew up in Australia, and her younger siblings were born there.

Harriet's mother, Annie (née Chambers), was the daughter of a Protestant Irish clergyman, and for many years Annie was brought up in India where her father was a missionary. She was a public-spirited and religious woman, and soon became well-known in Sydney, where she founded the local branch of the Girls Friendly Society. The Gordons had a smallholding in the town, keeping a few livestock for their needs; Harriet's brother Alexander (later a well-known High Court Judge) and her sisters Leonora and Adeline were born there. In later years her parents returned to England and settled at Pucklechurch, Gloucestershire, where her mother died in 1924 at the age of ninety-two.

On their father's side the Gordon children could trace their ancestry back to the Lords Kenmure of Kenmure Castle, Kirkcud-brightshire; and even (though various offspring born on the wrong side of the blanket) to the English royal family. A tale which lingered on in family tradition was that of the Lord Kenmure who was beheaded after the uprising of 1715. Alexander Gordon, the barrister, had a brother William who was MP for Chelsea from 1874 to 1880. Alexander and Annie were married in 1852, and their daughter Harriet, known to the family and friends as Haddy, was born the following year.

Harriet's family were less than pleased over her marriage. They disliked Stephen Childe, and had nothing to do with him after Harriet's death. They were convinced he was generally no good and a womanizer who treated Harriet badly. Harriet herself was a religious and public-spirited woman like her mother, and took on a greater share of the parish duties than her husband. Her position as new wife of the Rector of St Thomas's must have been a difficult one. Not only had she to get used to married life and to her duties in the parish, but also to coping with her husband's five children, now ranging in age from 10 to 15 years. Harriet herself was 33 years old at the time of her marriage, and was provided for by the terms of her marriage settlement under which she received a few thousand pounds.

It was also her money which financed the palatial home, named the Chalet Fontenelle, which the family owned at Wentworth Falls, in the spectacular Blue Mountains west of Sydney. Harriet Childe was very fond of this country house, which was built right at the Falls on the edge of the Jamison valley and commanded a magni-ficent view of the surrounding scenery. As her young son Gordon grew up, he too enjoyed the time they spent there, and he loved walking in the Blue Mountains. Before a railway was built across the

Blue Mountains in the later 1860s few people lived there apart from innkeepers providing accommodation for travellers to the better country and towns to the west. The railway made access much easier, and after it was constructed many Sydney people bought land in the Mountains to build holiday or retirement homes. By the turn of the century the area was becoming gradually more residential in character, and less of a holiday resort.

The parish of St Thomas's in North Sydney was large and semi-rural, though during Mr Childe's ministry the area became gradually more built up, and the Diocesan Authority whittled away at the parish boundaries. In 1880 the township consisted of two distinct classes: the officials and business men who built homes on the ridges of North Sydney overlooking the harbour, and the workers of the waterfront industries, whose houses crowded along the harbour front. Plans for building a new, much larger church for St Thomas's had begun in 1870 and this work continued under the Rev. S. H. Childe. However, Stephen Childe seems to have been an unpopular minister, and this undoubtedly had some effect on the formation of his son's character.

One cause of Mr Childe's unpopularity was his introduction of a different style of worship; he had been influenced by the Tractarians and placed emphasis on the mystical and ritualistic approach to church teaching and worship. During Childe's 33 years as minister of St Thomas's, the church was plagued by numerous rows and resignations; influential benefactors severed their connections with the parish, and church income and attendance fell dramatically every year. A note written by a JP associated with St Thomas's from 1897–1904 sheds some light on further causes of Stephen Childe's unpopularity: 'it is perhaps regrettable to record that the Rev. S. Childe was the subject of some ribald mirth among the young fry due to an impediment in his speech, nor was he very popular among his parishioners by reason of his aloofness.'[3] The young Gordon, listening to his father's sermons, cannot have failed to notice this 'ribald mirth', nor to be affected by it. Stephen Childe had a defective palate and it is possible that his son's rather indistinct speech in later life had an hereditary origin.

The Rev. S. Childe's 'aloofness', if taken to mean some difficulty in communicating with his fellows, also showed itself later in his son. However, in the case of the father, this aloofness went hand in hand with a lack of consideration for others. He refused to take the churchwardens into his confidence, and it was not uncommon for a warden to arrive at the church one Sunday to find to his surprise a *locum tenens* conducting the service because the minister had taken an unannounced holiday. Stephen Childe was Rural Dean of North Sydney from 1901 to 1906, and it was later said of him: 'Some of his friends, as well as his critics, often commented that he was a great "Rural" Dean—so rural that he almost lived in the rural surroundings of Wentworth Falls. He was there more often, they said, than at St. Thomas'.'[4]

It was against this background of his father's unpopularity and frequent absenteeism that Gordon Childe grew up. His five half-brothers and sisters were all considerably older than he was, and it seems probable that Gordon was very much of a 'loner' even at an early age. He was a sickly boy and for some years was taught at home, and then at a private school in North Sydney run by a Miss Chisford, so he had few opportunities to meet friends of his own age. However it would be incorrect to think that he had an unhappy childhood. The family was a close-knit one, held together by the awe, which amounted almost to reverence, with which the children regarded their father. The three sisters adored Gordon and as he was so much the youngest they spoilt him and felt protective towards him. He in turn loved them and was very kind to them all his life, making special provision for Ethel, who was considered delicate. His parents and sisters obviously brought him up carefully to be a 'gentleman' for he had beautiful manners and always appreciated good manners in others. The household was a very musical one; Christopher became a professional organist, Laurence was a talented amateur violinist, and Ethel, who later taught music, used to play the drums when the church orchestra and choir performed 'The Messiah'. Gordon fully shared the family's appreciation of music; but as he grew up he began to realize he could not share their involvement with Christianity. This alone set him apart in a family of actively religious individuals, and as he approached adulthood a further divisive influence began to make itself felt in the sphere of politics. A family as conservative as the Childes eyed with horror anyone who even considered that there could be anything worthwhile in Labour politics; that the renegade should be their beloved Gordon hurt them deeply. The whole family disapproved but especially his father, who, no doubt, had few scruples about expressing his feelings on the subject. In youth as in later life Gordon Childe avoided giving pain where possible; it is difficult to imagine that he quarrelled with his father and probably he withdrew into himself and did not discuss with his relatives those controversial beliefs which became more and more important to him.

In July 1907, at the age of 15, Gordon left Miss Chisford's private school and entered the Sydney Church of England Gammar School in North Sydney. He achieved his Junior Matriculation two years later, and his Senior Matriculation in 1910. He took ancient history, French, Greek, Latin, geometry, algebra and trigonometry, and passed well in all, though excelling in Latin. Gordon Childe must inevitably have suffered at the hands of his school-fellows on account of his extraordinary looks. He had, especially in his younger days, a very odd face, not helped by his thick spectacles and gingery hair, together with a thin frame and awkward movements. He was always extremely sensitive, and his unfortunate physique can only have contributed to the reserve and detachment from his fellow human beings which characterized him throughout his life.

On 26 July 1910, Harriet Childe died at Wentworth Falls at the age of 57. It is impossible to say how much his mother's death affected Gordon, who was then aged 18, but it seems likely that he was much closer to her than to his strict father, and that Harriet was very fond of her only son. From that moment on Gordon rarely visited his father, especially after the latter's marriage to his third wife, Monica Gardiner. In later years he seldom mentioned anything to do with his childhood, but he did once admit that he had disliked his stepmother. She was, he said, a harsh and very limited woman; one thing which particularly impressed him in his youth was her habit of covering all the mirrors and steel knives in the house in a thunderstorm.

In 1913 the tensions between the Rev. Stephen Childe and his parish came to a head, and the rector agreed to resign, on condition that he was paid £85 a year as a retiring allowance in addition to his pension. The parish obviously felt this a small price to pay for his removal, and Stephen Childe retired to Wentworth Falls, where he continued to receive his allowance until his death in 1928. After Harriet's death Stephen Childe had sold the Chalet Fontenelle, in which he had a life interest under the terms of her will, and built a new house, named 'Coronel', to which he and Monica retired. Coronel was on the opposite side of Wentworth Falls, on a mountain ridge between deep valleys, and had to be constructed with solid and expensive foundations to cope with the difficulties of the hillside site. As Stephen's much younger wife was likely to survive him, their plan was that she would be able to make a living by taking paying guests in the large house. However this scheme proved to be a white elephant, for in the 'Twenties and 'Thirties, as the family car became more popular, Sydney people were less restricted in their choice of holiday and the stream of guests to Wentworth Falls dried up. On his father's death in 1928 Gordon inherited Coronel under his mother's will, but when Monica wrote to her stepson about his plans for the property he replied that she could do as she liked with it. Shortly afterwards she sold the house and returned to England to live with her sisters.

At the beginning of 1911 Gordon Childe entered Sydney University to read for a Classics degree. As a new student, his knowledge of ancient civilizations would have been gleaned mainly from the classical authors and their writings. His contact with prehistoric archaeology probably came mainly from such popular descriptive works as Layard's *Nineveh and its Remains* and Schuchhardt's account of Schliemann's excavations of Troy and Mycenae. The 1890s and early twentieth century were a period when many archaeological expeditions set out for classical lands, sending back reports of their discoveries which were eagerly read by the public. In 1900 Sir Arthur Evans had begun his work at Knossos, which was to become world-famous as the centre of the Minoan civilization. In the years preceding the first world war it must have seemed to the young Gordon Childe that fresh discoveries bearing out the writings of the classical authors were being made every day.

At Sydney University Childe was an exceptional scholar. He studied not only classics and philosophy but also, in his first year, geometry, algebra, trigonometry and geology. On 4 April 1914 he graduated with first class honours in Latin, Greek and philosophy, and gained the University Medal for Classics as well as Professor Francis Anderson's Prize for a Philosophy essay. He had received the Cooper Scholarship for proficiency in the Classics in both 1911 and 1912. He later said that his life-long interest in philosophy stemmed from these early studies. He was also active in the University Debating Society, and in the light of his future beliefs it is interesting to note that he spoke in favour of the motion that 'socialism is desirable', but against the motion that 'compulsory military training is an unjustifiable interference with the liberty of the individual'.

Whilst at Sydney University Gordon Childe certainly studied the works of Hegel, Marx and Engels, and came under the influence of the first Challis Professor of Logic and Mental Philosophy, Francis Anderson, a Scottish Hegelian. Professor (later Sir Francis) Anderson had been born in Glasgow, but spent most of his life as a well-known philosopher and educationalist in Sydney, and was a keen supporter of tutorial classes and the Workers' Educational Association. An earlier Sydney student, the great Australian educationalist, Gerald Vere 'Gerry' Portus, recalled that Anderson was a small neat man, a polished and inspiring orator, and always dressed in a grey morning suit and tall grey hat. The legend went that he had once bought all the tall grey hats of his size from the stock of a bankrupt Glasgow hatter. Portus recalled that Anderson's lecturing 'ranged over a much wider field than could be covered even by that elastic term "philosophy". In my day he lectured on logic, ethics, metaphysics, and the history of philosophy. These might fairly be regarded as coming within the scope of his Chair; but to them he added courses on education and economics which were not then taught elsewhere in the University. . . . Anderson's was the first and only lecture room that I found in my undergraduate days at Sydney where questions were asked and discussion was encouraged. The other lecturers used to keep the rostrum to themselves, and leave to us the business of writing down what we could. But Anderson would dictate a few sentences to us slowly, and then begin to walk about elaborating his points, popping questions to us, encouraging our replies, and trying to get as many of us as he could to join in the discussion. This at least helped us to think and roused our interest. To how many generations of students was that lecture room of his, right up in the Tower, a refreshment after arid mornings of note-taking in other lectures?'[5]

One student who benefited from that refreshment was Gordon Childe, for such teaching methods suited his enquiring mind, and spurred him on to read the original works of Hegel, Marx, and many other philosophers. He was firmly anti-clerical, probably as a result of reaction against his father and his upbringing, and a rationalist philosophy appealed to him. A fellow-student of Marx at Sydney University was Herbert Vere Evatt, a slightly younger and also brilliant man, who followed Childe in receiving Professor Francis Anderson's prize for Philosophy in 1914. Evatt later read law, and eventually became leader of the Australian Labour Party; he and his wife, Mary Alice, remained life-long friends of Childe's. The two men were both somewhat unconventional undergraduates in the Sydney of the day—to begin with, their exceptional ability set them apart, and apparently the other students complained that any prize Evatt entered for he won; the same could have been said of Childe. Both were also masters in the art of dressing shabbily, and Evatt's biographer tells the story that the two friends had a contest to see who could wear his hat the longest: Gordon Childe won with twenty years!

Whilst he was attending university Childe did not live at home with his father. Instead he boarded with his uncle, his mother's younger brother, Alexander Gordon, at Elizabeth Bay, Sydney. Alexander Gordon, born in Australia in 1858, followed in his father's footsteps and became an eminent lawyer; he was later knighted for his services to the High Court. Alexander was married fairly late in life to Margaret Thomas, a Welsh singer, and by 1912 the couple had two young children, Alexander and Anne. When Gordon Childe stayed at Elizabeth Bay however, his aunt and cousins were away in England. His uncle Alexander Gordon somewhat disapproved of his nephew's freely-expressed radical views, for he felt they put him, as a public figure, in a difficult position.

During Childe's final year at Sydney, extra-mural education received a boost with the arrival of Albert Mansbridge to found an Australian Workers' Educational Association. The first discussion groups were held at the Friends Meeting House in Devonshire Street, Sydney, and Gordon Childe was a keen and talkative attender, remembered still for his typical 'radical student' attitudes and his interest in peace and public affairs. The very first class held by the WEA was on 'The History of the Balkan States'—an area whose prehistory Childe was later to study with special interest.

A favourite meeting place and general centre of socialist activity in Sydney in those days was Bertha McNamara's bookshop. H. V.

Evatt's biographer described the scene: 'a shabby little place in Castlereagh Street, where she sold inflammatory pamphlets, revolutionary literature, and cigarettes in small numbers so that men in lodging down the lane could afford them, you met international socialists like Tom Mann, anarchists, IWW men: Bertha welcomed them all. She was Polish, fiery, warm-hearted.'[6] Bertha McNamara's son, Bill, was at the university a couple of years behind Childe, and was in later years a good friend of Bert Evatt's.

Gordon Childe finished his studies at Sydney University at the end of 1913, and was awarded the Cooper Graduate Scholarship in Classics—worth £200 p.a.—which enabled him to continue his education at Queen's College, Oxford. At Sydney he had studied under the Greek scholar, Professor Woodhouse, who possessed great teaching skill and aroused his pupil's curiosity about the people and patterns of human behaviour in past civilizations. It was Professor Woodhouse who advised Childe to take his research degree at Oxford University. Owing to the difference in the academic year between Australia and England, he now had about nine months to fill in, and he used this time to earn his living by teaching. He obtained a post as teacher under the headmastership of Mr H. S. Moss at the New England Grammar School at Glen Innes, a town a few hundred miles north of Sydney. Here it soon became obvious that the well-educated and brilliant young classics scholar was not the ideal teacher for the 40 or so boys at the school. Most of the pupils were sons of local farmers, with perhaps a handful of the sons of business or professional townspeople. Many were expected to milk cows or feed horses before breakfast, and not surprisingly, were too tired to absorb much at school. In any case, they and their parents considered a basic grasp of the three R's to be entirely sufficient for their needs, and any further years at school a waste of time. So they were unsympathetic to the efforts of their new and odd-looking teacher, who, when he failed to make his point with the class, would angrily pound the chalk with his clenched fist.

More to Childe's taste, and less frustrating for one keen to impart knowledge, was another post which he undertook at the same time. He was engaged as tutor to the delicate child of George M. Simpson, a wealthy squatter who owned Stonehenge Station, some 15 miles south of Glen Innes. Young Harold Simpson, brought up by well-educated parents and with his future assured, was more receptive to Childe's teaching than the poorer boys at the New England Grammar School, and the hours he spent at the sheep station were much happier than those at the school. The company of the squatter and his wife would have been more congenial to him; and like many teachers, he was always more at ease with a small number of pupils than with a class.

In May 1914 Childe learnt that he had been allotted a free return passage by sea from Australia to England. Under a scheme inaugurated in 1909 by Sir Kenneth Anderson, the Orient Line Company allotted to Australian universities a number of such free passages, valid for three years but available only in the 'off' passenger seasons. The Senate of each university selected students who wished to continue their studies abroad, but were debarred by the expense involved. Presumably then there was a provision in Harriet Childe's will whereby her son could not use her money until he attained a certain age. In any case, Gordon Childe was selected to receive one of the free passages, and sailed for England in August 1914.

2. Oxford during the First World War

Childe's years at Oxford during the first world war were formative in many ways. They were productive academically, and stimulated his interest in archaeology as a method of gaining knowledge of past societies. The friendships he formed at this time were also to have considerable influence upon him.

Gordon Childe was 22 years old when he entered Queen's College in October 1914, to take the Diploma in Classical Archaeology followed by a B.Litt. He had been guided to Oxford by Professor Woodhouse of Sydney, but it is possible he chose Queen's because of its association with A. H. Sayce, Professor of Assyriology, who had tackled problems of comparative philology. The only other student entered for the Diploma in 1914 was Joan (later Dame) Evans, daughter of the great nineteenth century antiquarian, Sir John Evans, and young half-sister of the archaeologist Arthur Evans. However the two had little in common apart from their studies and did not become friends.

Childe never completed the requirements for the Diploma, but he spent the best part of a year on the course, under the tuition of J. D. Beazley, J. L. Myres and Marcus Tod. Beazley was at that time a young Christchurch tutor of 30, but he later became Oxford's Professor of Classical Archaeology. Marcus Tod had been for some years closely connected with the British School of Archaeology at Athens, and in 1914 was lecturing in Greek epigraphy. During Childe's period of study the Professor of Classical Archaeology was Percy Gardner, 'a tall upstanding figure,' wrote a later student, who 'lectured in a frock coat and winged collar of a type which must have gone back to the 1860s. He gave us of his incomparable store of learning with a permanently bored expression, in a monotone that somehow contrived to rivet our attention.'[1] Under the tuition of these men, Childe became familiar with the ancient remains uncovered from the classical civilizations of Greece and Rome. In an autobiographical review written in 1957 and entitled 'Retrospect', he wrote: 'My Oxford training was in the Classical tradition to which bronzes, terracottas and pottery (at least if painted) were respectable while stone and bone tools were banausic.'[2]

He was lucky to have as supervisors for his B.Litt. Professor (later Sir John) Myres, holder of the Wykeham Chair in Ancient History, and also Sir Arthur Evans. Myres had an agile mind and wide range of knowledge, and admired these same qualities in Childe. Though absent in the Aegean for much of the first world war, he continued to take an active interest in his pupil in later years. He was closely connected with the Royal Anthropological Institute, and his influence there was to be of immense benefit to his former student in ten years' time. Joan Evans later wrote of Myres: 'he was accustomed to teaching people who were reasonably accomplished classical scholars, and instinctively approached Aegean archaeology by way of Homer.'[3] Such an approach was ideal for Childe with his classical education; and he found Myres an inspiring teacher.

Sir Arthur Evans was a very different man: a Progressive who supported the examination and simplification of University legislation, the promotion of research, and the establishment of a Chair in Northern Archaeology. He had a natural sympathy for the underdog, and became something of an embarrassment to the British Government over his involvement with political events in Bosnia. Evans was also deeply concerned, as Childe was later to be, that political differences should not limit the exchange of scholarship between countries. In an address given to the Society of Antiquaries in 1916 he said: 'that there should be a serious and prolonged estrangement of the peoples of the British Commonwealth from those of the German Empire has become inevitable. But . . . it is incumbent on us to do nothing which would shut the door to mutual intercourse in subjects like our own, which lie apart from the domain of human passions, in the silent avenues of the past.'[4]

Sir Arthur Evans had been for many years a respected scholar and archaeologist, but it was his excavations from 1900 to 1908 at the site of Knossos on Crete which brought him public acclaim. His work not only revealed a Bronze Age civilization—the Minoan—which pre-dated Schliemann's Mycenaean and was its ancestor, but also laid bare earlier Neolithic levels. This meant that the Mycenaean and Minoan civilizations could be seen in an historical perspective for the first time; and by cross-dating objects found at Knossos which were Egyptian imports, Evans was able to synchronize the Minoan periods with corresponding Egyptian dynasties. The finds at Knossos were rich and spectacular—beautiful frescoes of boys and girls leaping over bulls, and rows and rows of huge storage jars or *pithoi*. It seemed that Evans had discovered the palace of King Minos and brought to life the legend of the Minotaur and the Labyrinth; something to catch the imagination of an Australian schoolboy when published in R. M. Burrows' popular version, *The Discoveries of Crete*.

Now that prehistoric archaeology is a recognized and familiar scientific discipline it is difficult to remember that the situation even only 50 or 60 years ago was very different. Whilst Gordon Childe was growing up archaeology was also in its infancy, and by the time he arrived at Oxford it was just becoming recognized as a distinct branch of learning with its own unique contribution to make to the study of man's past. Its roots lay in the antiquarianism of the eighteenth century, when the collection of antiquities from abroad became a fashionable pastime of the wealthy. The upsurge of the Romantic Movement brought archaeology to a wider audience when scholars turned away from classical ideals and romanticized the rugged remains of the Ancient Britons and Druids. Monuments attributed to these prehistoric ancestors—great stone circles like Stonehenge, and megalithic tombs—caught the imagination of many who could not afford to travel to classical lands. William Stukeley (1687–1755) was an important British archaeologist of the Romantic era, who differed from many eighteenth- and nineteenth-century antiquarians in that his field work was methodical and his excavations carefully recorded.

The late eighteenth century had seen a quickening of interest in the study of natural history, but the important advances in geology which heralded the real birth of prehistoric archaeology took place in the nineteenth century. Lyell's doctrine of uniformitarianism, set forth in his *Principles of Geology* (1830–33), provided a theory which explained the geological record. It also enabled archaeologists such as Pengelly and Boucher de Perthes to demonstrate the great antiquity of man by proving the contemporaneity of man and extinct animals. Before this, in 1819, C. J. Thomsen had arranged the Danish National Museum on the Three Age System, and shown that artefacts from man's past could be classified chronologically by the material from which they were made—Stone, Bronze and Iron. The originality of his approach lay in the fact that following the criteria used in the study of numismatics, he established a developmental sequence for tool types. Though the Three Age System needed much modification and refinement, it was a first and extremely important attempt to introduce some sort of chronological order, independent of written documents, into the study of antiquities.

During the Victorian age, archaeologists and geologists found their belief in man's great antiquity bringing them into direct opposition with traditional religious ideas; Bishop Lightfoot had claimed that man was created at nine o'clock in the morning on 23 October 4004 B.C.! The publication of Darwin's *The Origin of Species* in 1859 brought fresh outcries, but the doctrine of evolution, together with Lyell's uniformitarianism, gradually gained adherents and brought about the acceptance of the antiquity of man.

In 1914 less than 100 years had passed since the inception of these revolutionary ideas, and many of Childe's parents' generation still clung to the old belief in the Creation. Archaeological techniques had slowly developed during those years, as men like Pitt-Rivers brought order and method to excavation. At the same time the greatly increased study of contemporary primitive peoples seemed to offer parallels to prehistoric societies. Archaeological research spread gradually to many lands, and a vast mass of facts about prehistoric man was being accumulated. Gordon Childe saw that the task now confronting prehistorians was to collect this scattered data together and examine it as a whole. He was soon to be acclaimed as a great synthesizer of archaeological data, and even during his Oxford days he had a remarkable knowledge of the material. He published his first paper, 'On the Date and Origin of Minyan Ware', in the *Journal of Hellenic Studies* in 1915. It is clear from this article that he had already visited the Mediterranean (possibly on his way from Australia) and studied at first hand the Minyan pottery on sites and in museums. This practice of personal examination of little-known data was to be characteristic of his career, together with an astounding memory which enabled him to recall almost every artefact.

He had always had a facility for and fascination with languages, and comparative philology played a large part in his B.Litt. thesis of 1916, entitled 'The Influence of Indo-Europeans in Prehistoric Greece'. Unfortunately it appears that no copy of this survives; possibly Childe destroyed his own copy when the Indo-European theories gained disreputable connotations with the rise of Nazism, and it was not at that time compulsory for theses to be deposited at Oxford University. He studied the problem of the origins of the Indo-European speaking peoples, and his search for their homeland led him to archaeology in the hope of discovering archaeological links between prehistoric Thessaly and areas north of the Balkans which might lead to Iran and India. It was first recognized in 1786 that nearly all modern European languages, as well as the Sanskrit group, are descended from the Indo-European group of languages. It was believed that an Indo-European people had spread into Europe, the Near East, Iran and India in the second millennium B.C., possibly from a region in the steppes or from northwest Europe. The linguistic and palaeontological evidence was too vague to support either theory exclusively, hence the importance of archaeological data. Nowadays the term 'Indo-European' is used only in a linguistic sense, for there is little evidence to correlate it with a culture or race. Although Childe's search of the archaeological data failed to reveal the links he had hoped for, he became acquainted, through the libraries of Oxford and London, with pre-Mycenaean pottery and its analogues in Central and Eastern Europe. At the same time he studied for 'Greats'—Classics and Philosophy—and obtained a First Class in *literae humaniores* in 1917.

Gordon Childe gained more than an education in the classics during his years at Oxford University; the friendships he formed in these early years had a profound influence on the development of his political philosophy. When he first moved into his ground floor corner room in Queen's back quad, the young Australian was already fascinated by the theories of Marx, and their application not only to economics but to the study of history. Most of the friends he made at Queen's and at University societies shared his extreme Left-wing views, and some (including Childe himself) were unpopular with the University authorities for that reason.

Not long after his arrival he joined the Oxford University Fabian Society; amongst the fellow-members with whom he became friendly were R. Palme Dutt, David Blelloch, the lawyer Robert (later Lord) Chorley, and Raymond Postgate, Socialist journalist and later of *The Good Food Guide* fame. In 1914, when Childe joined, the University Fabian Societies were enjoying their maximum membership; in that year there were—at least on paper—101 members at Oxford alone. The University Fabian Societies were formed essentially by and for undergraduates and their success depended to a large extent on the personality and influence of their members. At this time both the Oxford and Cambridge Societies had a number of exceptionally dedicated members, many of whom later became influential and respected Socialists in various professions. At Oxford University the Fabian Society was particularly strong, owing to considerable continued support from older members in permanent residence, such as Sidney Ball at St John's College. In 1912 the national Fabian Society had set up a research department, which gradually moved further away from the society and by the end of 1918 emerged as the Labour Research Department; later still it became closely associated with the Communist Party. Childe was a frequent visitor to the Department's offices in London, where he was on friendly terms with such leading lights of the Socialist fraternity as Robin Page Arnot, William Mellor, Alan Kaye, Margaret Postgate (sister of Raymond) and her future husband, G. D. H. Cole.

In 1915 the Oxford University Fabian Society became the Oxford University Socialist Society (OUSS) when its president, G. D. H. Cole, an advocate of Guild Socialism, disaffiliated it from the Fabian Society. Childe continued to play an active part in the Society's activities, and often spoke at its meetings. He was a mature student compared to the undergraduate majority there, and could put his point of view across well to an audience. He became quite well-known as a speaker, especially amongst the much depleted numbers of students at Oxford during the war, and earned the nickname of 'Handsome Childe'. This nickname, whether used affectionately or not, emphasized the fact that Gordon Childe was, particularly in his younger days, a man who caught the eye on first meeting because of his odd looks. However this ugliness, which was, interestingly enough, more often noted by men than by his women friends, was soon forgotten in comparison with his great kindness and gentleness and delightful companionship. Although in many ways a lonely man, for he lived largely for scholarship and was timid of anything touching the emotions, Childe loved company. He never married, and indeed there is no hint of any deep relationship with a woman in his life; but equally there is no suggestion of any homosexual tendency. The main effect was of someone withdrawn, who greatly enjoyed the company of both men and women, but purely on the level of friendly acquaintance. Throughout his life he had many friends, but, it appears, no intimates. Anyone who tried to penetrate the invisible barrier Childe erected between himself and other human beings found him kind and friendly, but always enigmatic. Especially as a young man he was rather awkward and uncouth, without any social graces, and many acquaintances found it difficult to converse with him on everyday topics. Most of his time at Oxford was spent in study or in Socialist activities, and he was not a great asset at social gatherings. He played tennis occasionally, rather ineffectually, and was very fond of bridge, a game he continued to enjoy all his life, although apparently his skill was not as great as he liked to believe. In later years he seemed to derive great satisfaction from being accepted at a bridge party as Childe the bridge-player rather than Childe the prehistorian.

Although he was happier in the company of his like-minded friends in Oxford and London, he did not forget his family ties. In England for the first time, he probably took the opportunity to visit the Childe family estates in Shropshire—Cleobury Mortimer, and Kinlet itself, where many illustrious members of the family are buried. In June 1915 he certainly visited his relative, Mrs Frances Baldwyn Childe, who lived at Kyre Park on the Shropshire/Worcestershire border, another ancestral home of the Childes of Kinlet. The name Baldwyn was annexed to Childe in the eighteenth century when the heiress to the estates, Catherine Childe, married Charles Baldwyn of Aqualate and Bockleton, MP for Shropshire. Their eldest son William assumed the name of Childe on his mother's death in 1770, and became renowned as a sportsman and agriculturalist under the nickname of 'the Flying Childe'. He and his wife Annabella had one son, the long-lived Sir William Lacon Childe (1786–1880), who was MP for Wenlock from 1820 to 1826. Frances Baldwyn Childe, whom Gordon described as his aunt, was the widow of Sir William Lacon Childe's son, Edward George Baldwyn Childe. However, the exact relationship of Gordon's immediate family to the Childes of Kinlet remains uncertain; though there is evidence that his grandfather, Charles Frederick Childe, was an illegitimate son of 'the Flying Childe'. No doubt the young Gordon would have heard tales of his aristocratic ancestors from his father, and whilst keeping quiet about them in the presence of his Left-wing Oxford friends, would naturally have been interested to meet Frances Baldwyn Childe, who was a keen family historian. Her home, Kyre Park, was a well-known beauty spot with gardens landscaped by Capability Brown surrounding a house dating back in part to the fourteenth century. Gordon had promised his family in Australia photographs of Kyre Park, and in a letter to his father he described his impression of the grounds: 'Kyre is quite as lovely as I expected. To the S of the house there is a lake covered with yellow waterlilies and white swans. This is backed by a little garden brilliant with flowers of every hue and behind it rich green trees and a wooden slope beyond. To the W. the land slopes away more steeply. At the foot of a steep grass slope there is another sheet of water. Beyond this you get a delicious view of green fields rolling hills and dark apple orchards. The hill is even steep to the N. and the view wider . . . I came back home through the wood down the famous avenue of alternate oaks and beeches all of enormous girth and great age.'[5]

Gordon Childe's closest friend at Oxford was Rajani Palme Dutt, half-Indian and half-Swede, who was later a founder member and leading theoretician of the British Communist Party. Palme Dutt's college was Balliol, but the two friends moved out of college in 1916–17 to share digs in Richmond Road at the joint cost of 25 shillings a week for full board, lodging and laundry. For this remarkably cheap price the students each had a small bedroom and shared a tiny sitting room where they ate, worked and entertained their friends. Raji Palme Dutt was an outstandingly brilliant scholar, and a convinced Marxist, who was expelled from the University in 1917 for the propaganda of Marxism; sharing rooms with him was an experience with lasting effects for Childe. The two friends often enjoyed prolonged debates into the early hours, pursuing their favourite themes of Hegel, Marx, the Bronze Age and Mycenaean civilization. Palme Dutt was another devoted scholar to whom small talk did not come easily, and he and Childe found great pleasure in working together on these subjects in which both had such interest.

However it was not all work and no play, and Palme Dutt later recalled one of their lighter moments: 'On one occasion we had been celebrating, I think his First in Greats, or someone's 21st birthday, and returned in the small hours, each determined to prove that our heads at any rate were perfectly steady, as we sat down busily pulling at our pipes to clear up a knotty point in phenomenology or whatnot.

'Only when I discovered that the pipe at which I was vigorously puffing had no tobacco in it did I suspect that my command of my faculties was not as complete as I had wished to imagine and that I must yield pride of place to Childe.'[6]

In 1917 the National Secretary of the University Socialist Federation was the historian of mining trade unions, Scotsman Robin Page Arnot. He later recalled that at that time both Palme Dutt and Gordon Childe were already well-read in Hegel and Marx; though Dame Margaret Cole remembered that Childe was rather more interested in the materialist conception of history than in Marx's economic theories. Page Arnot travelled to Oxford in June of that year to visit the OUSS, and he also ran into Childe and Palme Dutt at a drunken party after the latter's finals. This time Childe's good head for alcohol was not so much in evidence, and Page Arnot was obliged to take the suffering reveller outside and hold his head as he sobered up; only to find that every time the two met in later years, Childe referred to Arnot's excessive kindness on that occasion.

When Childe left the shores of Australia in 1914 war had just been declared. His entire stay at Oxford was spent against a background of the first world war, and one effect of this was that of the few students who remained at university during the whole of that time, a high proportion were the hard-core anti-conscriptionists or pacifists who were prepared to be imprisoned rather than fight.

Childe was apparently not anti-war when he arrived at Oxford in 1914. An entry in the books of Queen's College records that he was 'Drilling with civilians'. Under the Australian Defence Acts of 1909 and 1910 he was a year too old to be compelled to take part in the universal military training scheme in force before the war; and military conscription was never adopted in Australia during the 1914–18 war. It is quite probable that Childe's poor eyesight and physique would have in any case exempted him from service.

The situation for many of his friends at Oxford was quite different. Conscription was introduced for the first time in Britain early in 1916, and unless exempt for health or other reasons, conscientious objectors were arrested, tried at tribunals, and often spent the rest of the war in gaol. In trouble for his anti-conscriptionist views, Childe wrote in 1918:

The authorities of Queen's College, Oxon, have been fully cognisant of my opinions ever since I was reluctantly convinced in 1915 that, for me, orthodoxy was impossible intellectually.[7]

Presumably he had come round to anti-war views as a result of the persuasions of his Socialist friends, many of whom were members of the No-Conscription Fellowship and were imprisoned or on the run during the period 1916–18. The viewpoint of the Socialists was that capitalists and the ruling classes made wars and expected the working class to fight them. They were not necessarily pacifists, but believed that national wars were unimportant, as only class war was significant. Their belief that blame for the war was not entirely on the side of the Germans enraged the majority of the public; this extract from an official history of the Great War shows the hatred with which they were generally regarded:

... the field was left open for pro-German agitators of the pseudo-Socialistic or the falsely pacifist school continually to suggest, with an increasing virulence of expression, that the movement towards compulsory military service in our country was the consummation of a great plot to reduce the working classes to impotence after the war and make it impossible for them ever to come out on strike, no matter how just were their grievances. The pro-German agitators also went on to develop the still wilder and more fantastic theme that military conscription was only a step to industrial conscription, and that when the war ended the employing class would have the working class reduced to a condition worse than that of ancient serfs.[8]

Childe was fully in agreement with these 'pro-German agitators' and staunchly supported his friends when they got into trouble over their beliefs. In the early months of 1916 a number of them, including David Blelloch and the secretary of the OUSS, P. T. Davies, were arrested as deserters under the Military Service Act, following their failure to report for duty after receiving their call-up papers. Other conscientious objectors also arrested in this way included such famous figures as Bertrand Russell and Lytton Strachey. The usual procedure for the anti-war Socialists was to put forward a plea for absolute exemption as a CO. Often they were determined to display their principles and expose the iniquity of the system, and the scene could become farcical, as it did when the case of Raji Palme Dutt was being heard before a tribunal at Oxford Town Hall on 26 May 1916. Palme Dutt put forward the usual plea for absolute exemption, whereupon the Military Representative, Captain W. Baldry, jumped to his feet and said, 'We don't want this man. He's Indian, and the India Office wouldn't let us take him.'

This attitude did not suit Palme Dutt at all, who was British born, the son of an Indian doctor practising in Cambridge, and a Swedish mother. So he flourished his copy of the Military Service Act, which he had thoughtfully brought with him, and read out the opening words: '"Every male, British subject . . ." I am male, I am British and I am a subject: it therefore applies to me.' In the end the obvious logic of Palme Dutt's case was recognized and in due course his heroic stand had its reward when he was arrested and sent to Cowley Barracks. Accompanying him on the journey to the barracks was the equally fervent anti-conscriptionist, Gordon Childe. Palme Dutt was imprisoned and spent a few months in Aldershot, Winchester and Wormwood Scrubs before being released on 18 August to continue his studies.

Childe's lot was easier, but it still took considerable courage to stand up to the taunts and vilification of the majority; and he believed in expressing his views in no uncertain terms. In March 1917 he wrote to the Australian High Commissioner in London:

Having now finished my studies at this university, I may want to return to Australia in June after my finals. I have however, heard a rumour to the effect that to obtain a passport one has to give an undertaking to join the army on arrival in Australia. As I could under no circumstances give any pledge which might involve my helping, however indirectly, in a war which I believe to be destructive to civilisation and true liberty instead of working for immediate peace, I should be glad to know if I have been rightly informed.

If so it will be useless to attempt to go home and I must make other plans.[9]

This letter was later to have unpleasant consequences for Childe, but he obtained the required assurance that he was not compelled to enlist, and made plans for his departure. Raymond Postgate, who, together with his fiancée Daisy, daughter of the radical politician

George Lansbury, were good friends of Childe's, arranged a farewell party for him in June. The venue was a small restaurant in Soho frequented by the Scottish Socialist politician, Ramsay MacDonald. At that time the Allied armies were preparing for a further attack on the German lines, and the group of young extremists who attended the party drank to the failure of the coming offensive. With such committed anti-war sentiments ringing in his ears, the young scholar set sail for Australia.

3. Australia: Politics and Prejudice

When Gordon Childe arrived back in Australia after his three-year absence he began looking for a job in the field of education. He still hoped to continue his study of European prehistory when the war ended and he could visit museums closed or inaccessible during the fighting. He was very highly qualified for a teaching or tutoring post, and already recognized as a brilliant scholar. Nevertheless he was to suffer not only dislike and contempt for his radical views, but also to experience several instances of attempts to block his career. In 1917, as Australia was now at war, different provisions of the Defence Acts of 1909 and 1910 applied to service obligations. On Childe's return he would probably have been called on to enlist; and as he never did so, apparently he fell into one of the categories of exemption. Possibly he was deemed medically unfit, but it seems more likely that he claimed conscientious objection to bearing arms, for like other CO's he was kept under surveillance by the Department of Defence and had his mail censored.

The first job he obtained after his return was as a Latin teacher at the Maryborough Grammar School in Queensland. This school had been founded in 1881, and by 1917 was experiencing difficulties, with frequent disintegration of discipline and its restoration by drastic measures. There were few competent teachers on the staff, and Childe had little chance of proving his own ability under the difficult circumstances. Coming to the school as an avowed anti-conscriptionist with the war still in progress, he would have met a hostile atmosphere. The Headmaster was a strong Conservative and uncompromising patriot who probably regarded the radical young man with misgivings, if not actual dislike. Childe's abilities were obviously not appreciated by his pupils either. A former schoolboy at Maryborough recalled: 'Whatever scholarship Childe brought with him was obliterated in the pandemonium that attended his classes. The climax came one day when a class all armed with peashooters launched a concerted attack on him.'

Childe left Maryborough Grammar School at the end of the school year. In November 1917 he had accepted the post of Senior Resident Tutor at St Andrew's College, Sydney University, and he took up this appointment when the new term began in early 1918. This post, with older students and a scholarly atmosphere, suited him well; and he was glad too that his friend Bert Evatt had been awarded a scholarship to St Andrew's in 1913. Evatt was still living there in 1918 as he completed his final year of law studies, and eventually he graduated with First Class Honours and a University Medal.

Whilst he was living in Sydney Childe was in an ideal position to take part in the Left-wing and anti-conscription activities centred in that city. When Prime Minister Billy Hughes had attempted to introduce military conscription in Australia in 1916 the issue split the Labour Party down the middle. Australian Labour opinion was on the whole anti-conscription, and they were actually supported by those volunteering for overseas service. Two popular referenda were held, and in both the conscription proposals were thrown out by a majority of the voters. Billy Hughes, who by this time had become anathema to the extreme Left in both Britain and Australia, remained in power by allying with the Liberals to form a new National Party, which defeated Labour in the elections of 1917. In early 1918, with the war responsible for the lives of thousands of Australian soldiers, conscription was still a vital issue, and anti-war meetings were held by societies which united both pacifists and Socialists under one banner. In June 1916 the Australian Union of Democratic Control for the Avoidance of War had been founded, and advocated among other things democratic control of foreign policy and the total abolition of conscription and compulsory military training. Childe was assistant secretary and an active member of this group, and this was to give the Sydney University authorities a lever by means of which they could remove the radical tutor from their midst.

At Easter 1918 the Third Inter-State Peace Conference, convened by the Australian Union of Democratic Control, was held in the Friends' Meeting House in Sydney. It was attended by over 100 delegates from peace groups, the Australian Labour Party, the

Society of Friends and some trade unions. Also present was Peter Simonoff, the Soviet Consul-General for Australia, and the conference passed a motion calling for his official recognition. The Peace Conference had a large contingent of radical extremists present, and its report stated that 'it is realized that only by the abolition of the Capitalist System can justice be secured and the fundamental causes of international friction be permanently removed.' Childe was of course entirely in sympathy with such sentiments, and indeed he was one of the speakers at the conference.

Shortly after this meeting, at the end of April, news of Childe's participation was brought to the attention of the Principal of St Andrew's College, Dr Harper. Dr Harper also spoke to the Warden of the University, Mr Barff, who showed him the letter written by Childe to the High Commissioner for Australia in March 1917, in which he had so clearly expressed his views on the war. The Warden left Dr Harper with the strong impression that the University had no intention of employing the young radical; which placed the Principal in a difficult position. He talked the matter over with Childe, and asked him whether he would like to anticipate the probable outcome of bringing the matter before the College Council by resigning the tutorship. Apart from his political views, Dr Harper was careful to point out, he had no fault whatever to find with Childe's fulfilment of his official duties.

Childe was of course outraged by such a request, but he realized that the matter was effectively out of Dr Harper's hands, and after some hesitation he sent the Principal the following strongly worded letter of resignation and protest:

Since I accepted the appointment of Senior Resident Tutor which the Council offered me on your recommendation, I have discovered that the University authorities have taken an attitude of very pronounced hostility towards me on account of my political views. In view of this fact I have begun to fear lest my position here may prejudice the college in its dealing with the University. As I am unwilling to do anything to hurt the College in any way, I am prepared to offer my resignation to take effect from June 1st or such later date as you may determine, if in the opinion of the Council and yourself my retention of this post for the full term of my appointment might be damaging to the College.

This must not be taken to imply an admission of the principle that the private political or philosophical views of a public teacher are any just disqualification, or that penalisation for such views is anything but the gravest menace to the whole intellectual life of society.

I hope, however, that the Council and yourself may not think it desirable that I should sever my connection with this institution whose service as this letter shows, is my central aim. In case, however this cannot be, I think it would be only just in the event of the Council desiring to accept my resignation, that my salary should be paid up at least to October 1st next.[1]

The Council of St Andrew's College met on 31 May and accepted both his resignation and his suggestion about his salary. Although the affair of Childe's effective dismissal met with some opposition within the College and the University, many members of the public approved wholeheartedly of such measures. The words 'pacifist' and 'conscientious objector' were widely regarded as synonymous with 'pro-German' and 'traitor'. 'To my way of thinking', wrote a Glen Innes reader in the *Sydney Morning Herald* of 1 July 1916, 'the first shot from each and every soldier's rifle should find its home in a conscientious objector'. Such sentiments were far from uncommon during the years of the Great War, and the public part played by Childe in the Sydney peace efforts demonstrated considerable bravery.

However he did have sympathizers, amongst them William McKell, a New South Wales Labour minister of his own age, who rose from being a boilermaker to become eventually Governor-General of Australia. McKell tabled a parliamentary question about Childe's case which he asked the Minister of Public Instruction before the Legislative Assembly on 27 June. The Minister claimed that no religious or political tests, as opposed to tests of academic fitness, were ever applied in the selection of teachers for the University of Sydney; and that he had no authority over appointments to St Andrew's College.

This was not to be the end of the harassment of Childe over his political convictions. In March the University had considered informally the possibility of employing him as a tutor in Ancient History in the Department of Tutorial Classes, but decided not to make any recommendation until they had evidence of his teaching ability. Shortly afterwards the local Workers' Educational Association formed for Childe a class in Political Philosophy, and asked G. V. Portus, who was then assistant director of tutorial classes, to inspect it. In July Childe made a formal application for the appointment as tutor, and a Joint Committee Meeting of the Department of Tutorial Classes, which consisted of university staff and WEA representatives, was held.

The outcome of this meeting could not be held up as a shining example of democracy at work. G. V. Portus reported that he had inspected Childe's WEA class and found him a satisfactory tutor, and it soon became obvious that the committee members, with one exception, intended to vote for the appointment. Professor Todd, Assistant Professor of Latin, outlined his objections to Childe, and drew warm protest from three WEA representatives and from the chairman, Professor Francis Anderson, for concerning himself with the political opinions of the applicant. Finally the application was approved by six votes to one; but Childe was never offered the post. The dissenting Professor Todd wrote to the Chancellor of the University, Chief Justice Sir William Cullen, outlining his point of view. He objected strongly to the proposal to place in a University teaching post a man whose opinions were, as he believed, opposed to the national interest. He was particularly concerned in case the appointment should afford Childe an opportunity to indoctrinate his students. Todd's plea fell on sympathetic ears, and the University Senate refused to sanction Childe's appointment.

Many people were horrified at this second blatant act of prejudice on the part of the educational authorities. Amongst them were H. V. Evatt, who was Associate of the Chief Justice at the time, and Bill McKell, the New South Wales Labour minister. Once more McKell, as well as a Mr T. J. Smith, questioned the Minister of Public Instruction on the circumstances surrounding Childe's case. Mr Smith said: 'Mr Childe's academic record is a distinguished one, yet the Senate of the University, which is supposed to be composed of cultured men who should be tolerant and broadminded, simply because Mr Childe holds certain political opinions which are not recognised as orthodox, refused to sanction his appointment. I very much regret it, because it means that Mr Childe will leave the State and we shall lose a man we can ill afford to spare. We have not too many men of distinction, particularly in the science of archaeology. I have analysed the position disinterestedly and it makes my blood boil to think that such an outrage should be perpetrated on a citizen of this state by the Senate of the University.'[2] Both McKell and Smith were given short shrift by the Minister, who was obviously anxious to avoid involvement in the issue, and claimed that administrative matters were dealt with entirely by the Senate.

Childe himself reacted with characteristic vigour to the Senate's decision. This second deplorable episode at the hands of the University authorities spurred him on to retaliation, and he wrote immediately to the Chancellor:

As the University of Sydney has set its face against the freedom of the teacher and ignoring academic merits, enquires into the private views on politics of its professors and teachers, you will be relieved to hear that the enclosed section of my will whereby the University stood to gain about £2,500 has been cancelled in favor of a more enlightened body.

An account of the systematic attempt to prevent the most brilliant classical student ever turned out by the University of Sydney from employing his gifts for the benefits of his native State has also been sent to those educationalists in England who having enjoyed the freedom of education that men like Sidgewick vindicated for the ancient Universities of that country know how to appreciate its worth.[3]

Considering his treatment by the Chancellor it is easy to forgive Childe the immodest tone of this letter. The 'more enlightened body' which was to benefit by his will was none other than the Labour Council of New South Wales, and he specified that the money should be used for educational propaganda; thereby confirming the worst suspicions of Sir William Cullen and Professor Todd!

The alteration of his will was indicative of a turning point in Gordon Childe's life. He had returned to Australia in the hope and expectation of embarking on an academic career; now he found his path made so difficult by his adherence to unorthodox political views that he decided to try turning his difficulties to advantage and seek a job in Socialist politics. Shortly after the despicable action of the Sydney University Senate, he left his native State and travelled to Brisbane, in Queensland. Childe had been of great help to Bill McKell when the ex-boilermaker was studying for the bar, and McKell hoped to repay his friend's kindness by assisting him in finding a job in politics. He retailed the sorry story of Childe's harassment to his friend, E. G. Theodore, nicknamed 'Red Ted', who was at that time Deputy Leader of the Queensland Labour Party, and succeeded T. J. Ryan as Premier of the State in 1919. Theodore managed to secure for Childe a clerical job in one of the State Government Departments, and although the job was routine and gave no scope to his abilities, it sufficed to keep body and soul together.

As soon as he arrived in Brisbane, Childe made contact with the local WEA, which was run by a remarkable man called Witherby. He also became friendly with the Socialist and writer Jack Lindsay, who was at that time reading Classics at the University of Queens-

31

land, and also giving a series of English Literature lectures for the WEA.

Witherby, whom Childe soon grew to know and like, was a clergyman and an eccentric, who never spoke of religion and enjoyed shocking respectable people. Tall and gaunt, he was a born teacher, with the gift of awakening interest and developing enthusiasm for a subject. A man of integrity, with definite beliefs in human dignity and freedom, his opinions were always open to change as a result of new experiences. Jack Lindsay, remembering him in an autobiographical book, wrote: 'He had a foible of liking to shock any highly respectable and pious company, and could not resist using the basic Australian adjective *bloody* at the Bishop's table—asking in his extremely aristocratic accents, made even more drawlingly polished for the occasion, "Will you please pass me the blood-ay jam?" Once, bored at a meal with two women in a restaurant, he got under the table and started reading. He did just what occurred to him as the most sensible and pleasant thing to do, and with a courteous smile ignored all conventions.'[4] On one occasion Lindsay heard Witherby speak at a public meeting organized by supporters of the Russian Revolution: 'I was astonished to find how powerfully and passionately the smilingly aloof English gentleman could express himself. After defending the Revolution as the achievement at last of a truly human society, he declared, "I believe in Lenin because I believe in Christ."'[5]

During his months at Brisbane Gordon Childe had opportunities for exploring the Queensland scenery with his friends. Fifty miles south of Brisbane on the coast stood Mount Tambourine, 1,800 feet high and set among the luxurious rainforest of the area. Near the top of the mountain, built on the edge of a precipice, Witherby owned a precarious shack commanding a magnificent view. Childe and Lindsay used to spend weekends there, and have long discussions on politics and the ancient world. Jack Lindsay found Childe an interesting companion, with a wide knowledge of classical civilizations, who listened patiently to the enthusiasms of his younger friend. In a later account of those days he recalled:

He always listened patiently to my divigatory outpourings, sometimes correcting facts or pointing to facts that had been omitted, sometimes nodding in assent, but also often waiting for the best moment to interpose one of his amiably withering comments, after which I would feel shiveringly bared of all pretensions to understanding of the Greeks. In those days the only way to reach the mountain-top, unless one was the unlikely owner of a car, was to walk across the flats to the slopes and then wind one's way up. I recall particularly one day when he had let me ramble on about my conception of Periklean Athens all the way over the paddocks and the rutted roads, and then, as we began climbing up a rocky track lined with trailing vines of purple passion-fruit, he demolished my whole picture with some nicely-chosen details of the real nature of Greek society and its inner struggles.'[6]

Since his shabby treatment in the academic world, Childe's main interests were political, but Lindsay found that his friend's deep-rooted irony, which included a refusal to take himself seriously, prevented him from making any direct declaration of faith: 'I remember him in those days solely as a bubble-pricker, a mildly caustic iconoclast, whose glasses took on an unholy glitter as he demolished somebody's illusions with sardonic kindliness. He was the most detached person I knew, and yet one felt all the while that there was a warm core to his gently-spoken and deadly sarcasm.'[7]

This detachment, noted by Jack Lindsay in 1919, was to characterize Childe throughout his life. Although the two friends had much in common, and greatly enjoyed their long walks in the mountains, Lindsay never felt very close to him: 'I was never quite sure if he guarded his detachment as a defence against the bruises which a brutish world could so easily inflict on his too-tender sensibilities, or if he wanted to break through it, but halted the moment he felt the cold wind blowing in through a fissure. His odd though likeable face, I felt certain, contributed to his refusal to come too far out of his inner refuge.'[8] Something of this feeling of detachment from his fellow human beings comes across in the poem which Jack Lindsay later dedicated to Childe's memory and published in his book *Daily Life in Roman Egypt* (see *Foreword*).

Childe remained less than a year in Brisbane, for in August 1919 he had the chance of a more responsible position, as private secretary to the leader of the Labour opposition in New South Wales, John Storey. He did not leave Queensland without bitter memories however, for on 14 August he had applied for a post as lecturer in Classics at the University of Queensland. Though there is no definite evidence that on this occasion political prejudice was brought to bear, the fact remains that another man of far less outstanding qualifications was appointed to the lectureship. The reporter of the local Labour paper, the *Daily Standard*, had no doubts about the circumstances of the case, and took full advantage of the opportunity offered to present the Senate of the University in a bad light:

> . . . the senate had the opportunity of appointing one of the most brilliant classical scholars in Australia. . . . But Mr. Childe, besides being a man of learning, whom Queensland can ill afford to lose, does not share the political views of the reactionaries who, despite a Labor government, control the affairs of the University. Mr. Childe is in fact a Laborite, an exponent of Guild Socialism, and generally a man of progressive ideas. Although the purpose of a university is supposed to be intellectual progress, our Queensland Institution does not want men of Mr. Childe's views, no matter how great his special qualities may be.
>
> There is good reason for believing that, when the vacancy occurred in the department of classics, instead of attempting to secure Mr. Childe's services, arrangements were surreptitiously made to get someone else, politically less objectionable, and when the senate met the matter had already been settled. Every effort was made to keep Mr. Childe in the dark about the vacancy.[9]

Whatever the truth of this affair, it was clear to Childe that his exceptional qualifications and ability once again seemed to carry no weight with the university authorities, so he was glad of the chance to return to New South Wales and a job in the field of politics.

At the turn of the century the Australian labour movement was internationally regarded as one of the most advanced in the world, though in fact its reputation rested more on its fortuitous success in raising living standards and reducing hours of work, and on its dramatic political advances, than on the extent of its industrial organization. Nevertheless Australia had developed state socialism of a welfare kind and state arbitration in industrial disputes well before European countries. Left-wingers of the early years of the century had high hopes for Australia's future as a more virile and socially egalitarian extension of Britain. However the more radical wing of the Australian Labour Party was held in check by the industrial interests of many members; by the strong Catholic labour movement; and by its inability to secure the necessary majority for constitutional revision. Under the leadership of William Hughes the Australian Labour Party developed into an imperialist movement, but it became more moderate after his defection to form the new National Party.

From his experiences in Storey's secretariat Childe had excellent opportunities for discovering the gap between the theory and practice of Labour government. He was bitterly disillusioned by many aspects of Australian politics, and frequently assured his friend Bert Evatt that Labour men would always move away from their party when a conflict arose between their beliefs and their personal interests. 'Honest John Storey' was a moderate in politics, opposed to conscription, and a very hardworking and conscientious man. During this period Childe was also working closely with J. T. Lang, a much more controversial Labour figure, nicknamed the 'Big Feller' because of his size and political aggressiveness. He later became Labour Premier of New South Wales twice, but was eventually dismissed from office in 1932 on a point arising from his refusal to allow the state to pay interest on its public debts.

Gordon Childe's new duties included drafting speeches for Storey, who became Premier of the State in April 1920, forming a government with a precarious majority of one. During the elections in March of that year Storey concentrated his main attacks on the administrative record of the Nationalist government. This was a telling move, for Holman, the Nationalist leader, had recently been accused of corrupt practices, and became a favourite target for the Press. H. V. Evatt later wrote of this election: 'Storey happened to have as his secretary one of Australia's greatest scholars—Gordon Childe—and the concentrated pungency of Storey's daily comments on the Government strongly suggested the brain of the classical scholar.'[10]

Childe's position as secretary to the new Premier began formally on 14 April 1920, his 28th birthday, at a salary of £394 p.a., an increase of £82 p.a. on his previous one. It also meant that he was very closely involved with all political events and policies over the next couple of years. Characteristically, he applied himself to the study of the Labour Movement in Australia and soon had an unrivalled grasp of its structure and history. In 1921 he began to write a book on the political and industrial organization of the Labour Movement since 1900, which was later published under the title *How Labour Governs*. He also planned a second book on the work and policy of Labour governments, but this was never written.

One movement with which Childe had particular sympathy, and in whose struggle he was particularly involved, was the Industrial Workers of the World. In 1907 IWW clubs spread beyond the United States and began to appear in Australia. Closely affiliated at first to the Socialist Labour Party, they soon launched out on their own and formed 'locals'. The philosophy of the IWW was Marxist, but also anarchist; their most constructive contribution lay in their belief in the One Big Union, whose purpose was to fight Capitalism and after its defeat carry on production. Childe wrote: 'No body has exercised a more profound influence on the whole outlook of labour in Australia.'[11] The membership of the IWW was never large, but the 'Wobblies', as they were known, did exert a much greater influence than their numbers might suggest. Although made illegal, the IWW played a considerable part in the anti-conscription activities of the 1914–18 war, and during this time Childe came into close contact with them.

In September 1916 twelve leading Wobblies were arrested for treason, as a result of arson attempts in Sydney. 'The Twelve' were severely sentenced, mainly on the evidence of informers later shown to be perjurers receiving their instructions from the police. Various protests and enquiries about the trial took place over the next few years, and Childe himself addressed a memorandum to the Permanent Secretary of the Premier's Department on 17 November 1920. Compensation had been promised to The Twelve by the Labour Government if a Commission found they had been wrongly imprisoned. Childe suggested that Storey should bring the matter, now long overdue, before the Cabinet. But the refusal of the Labour Government to act in this matter provided an example of the corruption of Labour in office which he was later to criticize harshly in *How Labour Governs*.

Childe found many of his duties as private secretary irksome, and he also missed his more educated and cultured circle of friends in Britain. On 1 February 1921, following re-organization of the research and publicity posts in the Premier's department, he was appointed Research Officer at a salary of £439 p.a. At about the same time, Storey, who had been seriously ill, set off on a convalescent trip to England. He was also anxious to promote a favourable picture abroad of the Labour government in New South Wales, and to this end explored the possibility of sending Childe to London to take up the post of Research and Publicity Officer in the office of the Agent-General, Sir Timothy Coghlan. It was felt that such an officer was needed on the spot in London to correct false reports and supply authoritative information about the resources of New South Wales.

At the same time, he could perform a valuable service by keeping the state in touch with recent developments in legislation and scientific research in Britain, Continental Europe and the United States. Mr Storey decided that Gordon Childe was the man for the job, and cabled on 14 April 1921, to his deputy, James Dooley, to arrange his appointment for a few months' time. Meanwhile Childe familiarized himself with the state and its potential by touring the country districts, as well as liaising closely with other departments to ascertain their requirements in the way of information he could supply from London. He was in agreement with Storey that the Australian Labour Movement should be kept in closer touch with Socialist movements and social developments in Europe. He wrote to his Oxford friend David Blelloch, now on the staff of the International Labour Office at Geneva, explaining his new duties:

I shall have to deal largely with industrial and social questions, and therefore will probably draw to an extent upon your services. Most likely I will have to go over to Geneva to get into touch with things. Our Department has already written to secure the 'International Labour Review' published by your office.[12]

It was planned that Childe should be given every assistance to facilitate his research, and that one of his duties would be to prepare paragraphs on New South Wales affairs to be published in London newspapers such as the *Daily Mail*, *Morning Post* and *Daily Telegraph*. The Premier's Department was particularly concerned that the only references to Australia in British newspapers tended to deal with material of a 'discreditable' nature—droughts, floods and crimes. One of the qualifications which Storey suggested especially equipped Childe for the London post was his ability in modern languages. He therefore had to pass reading tests in French, German, Modern Greek and Italian, and it was noted that he also had a knowledge of Spanish; talents which were duly appreciated by the Public Service Board.

John Storey returned to Australia in July, and preparations proceeded apace for Childe's transfer. It was arranged that he should first travel to Wellington, New Zealand, breaking his long journey there for a few days as a guest of the New Zealand government. The Shaw, Savill and Albion liner, the 'Corinthic', which was due to sail from Wellington on 15 October would then take him on to England via Cape Horn and the Argentine. This slightly longer route was arranged as he already had some knowledge of the countries visited on the more usual voyage via the Cape of Good Hope. At the end of September 1921 Gordon Childe duly sailed from Sydney for Wellington on the first leg of his journey. He was looking forward to taking up his new duties as Research Officer at an increased salary of £525 p.a., and to being closer to the museums and libraries of Europe. But his departure was not an entirely joyful one, for hardly had he left Australia when news reached him that on 5 October his employer, 'Honest' John Storey, had died, his health undermined by overwork; James Dooley was elected Acting Premier in his place.

4. Turning-point

Childe began his new duties in London on 7 December 1921; but his employment was to be short-lived. In the New South Wales elections of 20 December, Dooley's Labour government was defeated and the Conservatives, under their Premier Sir George Fuller, gained power. One of the first actions of the new treasurer, Sir Arthur Cocks, was to request the annulment of Childe's appointment as Research Officer on the grounds that it was political, and also that his work was largely unnecessary duplication. To others it seemed obvious that Childe was merely a public servant in a minor post for which he had outstanding qualifications. In Australia McKell defended his friend; his biographer recorded that '. . . he regarded Cocks' action as paltry and despicable, and attacked it hotly in parliament. He said, "This man is a brilliant scholar. His qualifications are unassailable. He was appointed to the London position after being found suitable for it by the Public Service Board. No one inside or outside the Public Service can point to anything but honourable and straightforward conduct on the part of this man from the time he was a boy." '[1]

However McKell's anger did not influence Sir Arthur Cocks, who had no intention of retaining an extreme Left-winger on his staff, and the annulment remained. McKell had also written to the Premier, Sir George Fuller, describing his friend as 'harmless'; but this too had little effect. The Agent-General in London gave Childe a month's notice on 20 April 1922, although he obviously had no personal objection to him, and indeed asked whether he could continue to employ him in a minor capacity to answer enquiries on New South Wales. He described the young man as 'very well informed and apparently harmless': not perhaps how the 'Radical Laborite' thought he would be seen by the Conservative government! His dismissal was reported prematurely in the New South Wales press, and provoked the following letter from his father, the Reverend Stephen Childe, at 'Coronel' in Wentworth Falls. Addressed to Sir George Fuller, the new Premier, it read:

Will you if you please do me the kindness of telling me what are the terms of my son Gordon's dismissal; I mean whether he receives a month's or longer notice, and his return fare to Australia, or its equivalent. Of course I am not surprised at your cabinet's action; for all my sympathies are with you and your party; but Gordon has always been a good son and a generous helper of his invalid sister, making her a handsome monthly allowance from his salary. It is mainly on her account that I am seeking information as to how soon this will terminate since my daughter has been largely dependant upon it.

With hearty congratulations on your return to office, and with every good wish for a successful tenure,

Believe me, faithfully yours, (Revd.) S. H. Childe.[2]

Fuller's reply was to the effect that Gordon had been despatched to London at his own request and it had been understood at the time that in the event of the defeat of the Labour government he would be better placed remaining in London to look for a suitable job. The Conservative government therefore felt no obligation to provide a return fare, as the Rev. S. Childe had suggested; in fact his son was later offered the fare, but declined to take advantage of the offer. There was some talk of continuing to employ him at a much reduced salary in a temporary position in Sir Timothy Coghlan's office, but the suggestion was vetoed by the New South Wales Public Service Board. So Childe's employment was terminated on 4 June 1922, and, feeling particularly disillusioned with Australian politics, he resolved to stay in London. He had very little money in hand, especially if, as seems likely, he continued to send an allowance to his sister, and was soon badly in need of a job.

As soon as he had heard of his new posting Childe had written from Australia to his fellow-Queensman, Robert Chorley, who was at that time in London studying for the bar. Chorley was living in a cheap residential club in Cartwright Gardens called the Bloomsbury House Club, and he secured his friend a room there too. Childe lived at the club for the next five years, and spent much of his time working either at the British Museum or in the library of the Royal Anthropological Institute. Also living in Cartwright Gardens and working in the libraries was C. Daryll Forde, the anthropologist, who became a good friend of Childe's and later accompanied him on a journey through Europe.

Childe was still hoping to continue his career in politics, though the study of past societies continued to fascinate him and occupy much of his time. He soon made contact again with his Marxist friends at the Labour Research Department, where he was now regarded as a great authority on Australian politics, but they could provide him with no paid employment. He saw less now of Raji Palme Dutt and Raymond Postgate, for they were members of the Communist Party of Great Britain, formed in 1920, and he was not. Robin Page Arnot was also an early CP member, and was at this time running the Labour Research Department, which eventually became an unofficial subsidiary of the Party. Palme Dutt and Page Arnot remained CP members, but within a few years several of the 'young intellectuals' who had joined in the first flush of enthusiasm after the Bolshevik Revolution, had left. It is not clear what were Childe's reasons for not joining the Communist Party; certainly he was broadly in sympathy with their views and always said that communism was the only answer for mankind in the long run. His Communist friends always considered him as one of themselves, and he was undoubtedly regarded as a Communist by many people throughout his life. In 1942 he was writing to a friend that he had 'come round a long way towards orthodox Marxism', which suggests his earlier views differed from the CP line. Another possibility is that his objections were more to the *British* Communist Party, which has never been strong compared to those in most European countries; in 1931 he wrote to Mary Alice Evatt that he thought it was 'quite hopeless'.

Another place where Childe met a number of Left-wing friends was the 1917 Club in Gerrard Street. He and Chorley were both early members of the club, where Childe often enjoyed a game or two of bridge. The club was frequented by many famous figures, or those who later became famous, including Ramsay MacDonald, H. N. Brailsford, Sir Charles Trevelyan, H. G. Wells, Aldous Huxley, Rose Macaulay, Dr C. E. M. Joad, Sir Osbert Sitwell, E. D. Morel, and Elsa Lanchester. Douglas Goldring later described the scene:

The premises of the 1917 Club, at 4 Gerrard Street, Soho, had all the squalor and dinginess associated in the popular imagination with a conspiratorial den of Bolsheviks and thieves. The house, though some two centuries old, was without dignity and emphasized the fact that jerry-building had not been invented by the Victorians. The dining-room was, at first, situated in the basement. From the ground floor a narrow staircase, smelling strongly of invasions by the neighbouring tom-cats, led up to drafty, untidy, badly-furnished sitting-rooms and lounges. The street, one of the most unprepossessing in Soho, was frequented by tarts and souteneurs, contained several second-rate foreign restaurants, but was principally known to the outside world from the presence in it of the first of Mrs. Meyrick's famous night-clubs, 'Number 43'. This establishment was almost opposite the 1917 Club, and some of the less high-minded of our members used occasionally to pop across the road for a final illicit drink. Generally speaking, however, the club, though tolerant of all forms of revolutionary exuberance, was a home of political idealism, democratic fervour and serious progressive thinking.[3]

Here Childe first met J. G. Crowther, later a well-known popularizer of the history of science, who in 1924 became the technical representative of the Oxford University Press. Crowther was very impressed by his original views on prehistory and later relied on his interpretations when compiling *The Social Relations of Science*, published in 1941. In his autobiography he wrote that 'Childe had an understanding of technological and scientific factors in the evolution of man which made his view of prehistoric archaeology exceptionally interesting from the scientific point of view. I once asked him what was the social significance of his subject. He said that, for example, it showed that mankind had extraordinary powers of survival. There were moments in the hunting stage of mankind when a single comparatively small incident might have exterminated the human race. The dangers that man had survived were repeated and very great. Frightful though modern dangers might appear, there had probably been many even worse in the prehistoric past, which man had survived. This was a reason why mankind could face the future with optimism and confidence. The modernity and quality of his mind and conceptions were very striking; I was much influenced by them.'[4]

Childe asked Crowther whether he knew of any jobs available in the publishing world, for throughout the period 1922–24 he was seeking a job of some kind, whilst finishing off *How Labour Governs* and continuing his archaeological research. Not long after his arrival in London he had written to his old Oxford friend David Blelloch in Geneva, explaining his situation:

The ultra reactionary Government which has succeeded the Dooley Labor

Ministry in NSW will not want any advice on State Insurance Banks or Family Wage schemes such as I've been dishing up for the Laborites—nor will they want such a prominent Laborite as myself—in fact they have already indicated this by cable with indecent haste. So it behoves me to look for a job as I don't particularly want to go back to Australia—which is rather a bloody place per se and at the moment is particularly hopeless.

Don't you think Geneva wants someone badly to put them au fait with the Australian experiments in social legislation etc.?[5]

Blelloch, however, could not help his friend obtain employment with the International Labour Office; and meanwhile Childe set off at the end of August 1922 to attend a summer school organized by the Labour Research Department at Cloughton, near Scarborough. Here he spent two pleasant weeks playing tennis or walking during the day, with lectures in the evenings. Rajani Palme Dutt and his brother Clemens were there, together with other friends like Raymond Postgate, G. D. H. and Margaret Cole, H. P. Rathbone, Maurice Dobb and J. G. Crowther. George Bernard Shaw, H. N. Brailsford and Charles Trevelyan were among the speakers, and Childe himself lectured on the One Big Union, the idea favoured by the Industrial Workers of the World. J. G. Crowther later wrote of the occasion: 'The discussions at the Labour Research Department summer schools were very lively, but the entertainments were even more interesting. They were quite elaborate. Shaw read his play *O'Flaherty, V.C.*, giving superb expression to Irish accents and modes of thought, and the attitudes of the Irish and English towards each other. The Coles put in nights of work on the composition of revues, containing references to the foibles of members of the schools.'[6]

Not long after his return from Yorkshire, Childe was invited to travel to Vienna, to examine and sort out some unpublished material in the Prehistoric Department of the Natural History Museum there. This was one of a number of trips he was to make during the next few years, gathering material for future publications. He was already widely regarded as a prehistorian of exceptional promise, although so far this had not earned him employment. On 22 September, the day before he left for Vienna, he wrote to Blelloch: 'I have been busily—and fruitlessly—hunting jobs and—with more success though without financial result—prehistoric jerries.'

At Vienna Childe lived at the house of the Assistant Director of the Museum, Dr Mahr, conveniently saving himself the expense of a hotel. He had been invited to examine the material from the site of Schipenitz in Bukowina, whose Neolithic painted pottery was supposed to have links with the Aegean. Never one to delay in publishing results or hypotheses, his account of the Schipenitz material was available in the 1923 *Journal of the Royal Anthropological Institute*, complete with a series of awful drawings; on his own admission, his appreciation of the visual arts was always lacking. Whilst in Central Europe he took the opportunity to visit other museums too, especially in Czechoslovakia and Hungary. He realized that his European colleagues were labouring under immense difficulties, particularly the depreciation of their currencies after the war. He brought their plight, and the heroic efforts nevertheless being made, to the attention of British archaeologists in an article published in *Man* in August 1922.

'The position of the Vienna Museums,' he wrote,

is . . . very precarious. The Natural History Museum there undoubtedly contains the most representative collection of prehistoric objects to be found in Central Europe. But the bankruptcy of the State now paralyses the activity of the Museum. The Government grant in the present currency is exhausted in a couple of weeks. Wages are so high relatively that regular excavations are out of the question and most archaeological journals have had to suspend publication. . . . The Museum itself is virtually driven to subsist on the sale of photographs and reproductions. The models made of vases from Schipenitz or Laibach Moor, for instance, are truly admirable, such that one might well mistake the copy for the original. . . . And in spite of all, the Museum still opens its doors gratuitously to the public three days a week and is constantly thronged with visitors.[7]

He also drew the attention of British archaeologists to the deaths of two of their Central European colleagues, Professor Hoernes and Dr Palliardi. Jaroslav Palliardi had been a particularly important figure to Childe. A notary by profession, he had spent 30 years investigating the prehistory of his native land, Moravia, although his results were only partly published and mostly in Czech. He had conducted numerous excavations at Neolithic and Chalcolithic sites, and had assisted Vassits at the famous Danubian site of Vinča. His loss was especially great as he had in his private possession a famous collection of Moravian antiquities, including the painted pottery from Znojmo, and his personal knowledge of the collection was unparalleled. In the following year Childe himself was to view the collection, then housed temporarily in three rooms behind the old notarial office at Moravska Budejowice, under the care of Palliardi's friend and collaborator, Vildomec. The stratigraphically established sequence of pottery types which Palliardi had built up for southern Moravia were to provide the basis for Childe's four Danubian periods expounded in 'When Did the Beaker Folk Arrive?' and *The Dawn of European Civilization* in 1925.

Childe's financial position was slightly alleviated towards the end of the year. The general election of November 1922 had placed John Hope-Simpson, a friend of Robert Chorley's, as Liberal MP for Taunton. Hope-Simpson was anxious to have a part-time private secretary to help him with his new duties. Chorley was unable to undertake the work himself, but recommended Childe, whose previous experience made him an excellent candidate for the job. So he became part-time private secretary not only to Hope-Simpson, but also to two other MP's; this work brought him in a small salary until the general election of October 1924.

One of the other MP's was the unconventional lawyer, Frank Gray, Liberal MP for Oxford City from November 1922 until he was unseated on petition over irregularities in his election expenses in 1924. Frank Gray was quite a character, and very unlike his father Walter, a self-made man who became a bastion of the Oxford Tory Party. Frank liked to think of himself as not wholly committed to respectable society and later masqueraded, successfully, as a tramp and as an out-of-work Warwickshire miner to gain first hand experience of their living conditions. He and W. R. Morris (later Lord Nuffield) were instrumental in bringing buses to replace the horse-drawn trams of Oxford; and it was said of him, with truth, that he knew everyone in the city by sight. Gray and Childe had much in common. Gray's war service (he had refused to accept a Commission) had changed his outlook and he was now an enemy of class privilege. He also adhered to the view, so popular with Childe's anti-war friends, that Germany was not the only villain of the war, and in 1918 he stood as Liberal candidate at Watford firmly against the slogan 'Hang the Kaiser'. There was no Labour candidate for Oxford in the 1922 election, but Frank Gray proclaimed himself the Friend of Labour and won the seat from the Tories with a huge swing in his favour.

Gordon Childe's knowledge of languages once again stood him in good stead during these lean years, for he gained some extra income working as a translator for the publishers Kegan Paul, Trench, Trubner and Co., who were later to publish a number of his own major works. He also did some independent translations from French, Italian and German: *From Tribe to Empire*, by A. Moret and G. Davy, was published in his translation in 1926, *Primitive Italy* by Léon Homo in 1927, and *Scythian Art* by G. Borovka, Keeper of Scythian Antiquities at the Hermitage Museum at Leningrad, in 1928. As a further supplement to his income, he undertook some temporary lecturing for the London School of Economics in the mid 1920s. By that time he was employed as librarian at the Royal Anthropological Institute, whose President from 1923–25 was C. G. Seligman, a distinguished physician and pioneer ethnologist. Seligman, Professor of Ethnology at the University of London's School of Economics, was then in poor health and Childe was asked to replace him on a part-time basis for the Michaelmas term of 1926. He gave a course of lectures on 'Prehistoric and Early Man'; teaching practice which stood him in good stead as he was already being considered as a candidate for the Abercromby Chair at Edinburgh. The lectures proved so popular with the students that he was invited to give a further four lectures in the Lent term of 1927 on the 'Neolithic and Metal Ages', and covered the Aegean culture, the amber trade, the Continental Bronze Age, the introduction of Iron, and special problems of the British Isles.

He also received a certain amount of money from the sales of his first book, *How Labour Governs*, which was published in 1923. Childe had arrived back in England at the end of 1921 to find a political situation somewhat different from the one he had just left in Australia. Lloyd George's second coalition government, formed in 1918, had been expected to consolidate peace in the aftermath of the war. Lloyd George himself had great plans for post-war reconstruction and social legislation, to make Britain a 'land fit for heroes to live in'. But the Liberals and Tories who formed the coalition were becoming increasingly uneasy about the possibility of Labour coming to power. In 1920 Winston Churchill had made the now famous remark, 'Labour is not fit to govern'. However, after the break-up of the coalition government a new parliament met under Bonar Law in November 1922, and Labour was found to have almost doubled its poll and increased its representation in the House of Commons by 67.

It is against this background that the significance of *How Labour Governs* can be seen. The book was published in London by the Labour

Publishing Company, an offshoot of the Labour Research Department formed in 1920 to take over the increasingly time-consuming job of publishing LRD and related books. The first Board of Directors, headed by B. N. Langdon Davies, was nominated by, and partly consisted of, the executive of the LRD, which therefore had virtual control of the choice of publications. Gordon Childe's book was published by the company despite opposition by some members of the Labour Party, who felt it would do little to further their cause. It is probable that Childe would have been unable to find a publisher in Australia, for the book contained some very bitter criticism of the structure and personalities of the Labour movement in Eastern Australia. Indeed the emphasis on these aspects makes Childe's title something of a misnomer, for general party policy is not discussed very fully in the book.

Instead he concentrated on the struggle for power within the Labour Movement between parliamentarians and industrial activists, on the corruption of the leaders of the party, and on the high incidence of 'ratting'. He was unfortunate in experiencing Labour politics in Australia in one of its worst periods, and his disillusionment is reflected in the book. The failure of Labour in office he attributed to the fact that the working class man was trying to participate in a parliamentary system created by the upper classes and tailored to their needs. He criticized particularly the tendency of Labour ministers to become engrossed in the trappings of wealth and position, and divorced from the needs of their electorate and their party. This was a tendency which he had come to believe was inevitable, and had several times disagreed on this point with H. V. Evatt in Australia, who adhered to the view that true socialism was possible. Childe's personal experience of such events, and many others covered in *How Labour Governs*, adds greatly to the force of the narrative. His disillusionment is most marked in the final paragraph of the book, when he ends an account of the futile attempts to form One Big Union in Australia with the following words:

As the Labour Party, starting with a band of inspired Socialists, degenerated into a vast machine for capturing political power, but did not know how to use that power except for the profit of individuals; so the O.B.U. will, in all likelihood, become just a gigantic apparatus for the glorification of a few bosses. Such is the history of all Labour organizations in Australia, and that is not because they are Australian, but because they are Labour.[8]

It is interesting that *How Labour Governs*, for all its bitter criticism, is the book for which Gordon Childe is generally best remembered in Australia. In the '50's he discussed the book with an Australian historian, laughing off his good opinion with the remark that he 'had learned a good deal about history and about the application of Marxist notions since he wrote it'.[9] Even though Childe himself later regarded his first book as a work of juvenilia, it remains a remarkably perceptive account of Australian Left-wing movements in the years 1900 to 1920, and has not yet been superseded in the literature of labour history.

In spite of his shortage of money Childe managed to continue his travels to the museums of Central and Eastern Europe whenever the opportunity arose: a traveller with English currency in his pocket in the post-war years found that a few pounds went a long way. In May 1923 he took advantage of Parliament's Easter recess to visit Lausanne, Berne and Zürich, making sketches of artefacts in the museums there and becoming acquainted with the prehistory of the region. By now he was concentrating on writing a work of synthesis based on his wide reading and personal observations. Robert Chorley recalled how the two friends used to sit long hours in the study room of the Bloomsbury House Club; Chorley working for his law examinations, and Childe, eyes protected from the light by a huge green eye-shade, writing *The Dawn of European Civilization.*

Childe kept up both his political and archaeological contacts, but as time went on he became more and more engrossed in the study of the past. He joined the Royal Anthropological Institute in 1923, and lectured to the Society of Antiquaries on British Beakers in 1924. The two interests, politics and archaeology, were in fact complementary, based on his fascination with the forces at work in history and shaping society in his own time. As Jack Lindsay had observed in Brisbane, Childe was capable of feeling deeply about issues on one level and yet remaining detached from them on another. The study of ancient societies gave him scope to employ his intellectual powers to the full, and in revealing the prehistoric past he felt he was revealing the basic forces and activities which shaped humanity; yet in the distant past the story of man was impersonal, and so he could maintain his detached tone in a way he could not have done with later periods, including the politics of his own day.

That he was still pessimistic about the performance of Labour in office is clear from an article he contributed in 1924 to the new periodical, *Labour Monthly*, edited by R. Palme Dutt. Entitled 'A Labour Premier Meets his Masters', it dealt with the progress of the Labour government of Queensland, where Childe had been employed for a short time as a minor official. Problems had arisen when Theodore's government needed a loan and to obtain one from the capitalists had been forced to back down over their promises to the working class electorate. Theodore, claimed Childe, had reduced 'his cabinet and himself to the position of a subservient managing committee for the bourgeoisie'.[10]

In 1925 Childe was fortunate enough to be offered one of the very few archaeological jobs available in Britain, as Librarian to the Royal Anthropological Institute. He was no doubt recommended for this post by his Oxford supervisor, J. L. Myres, who was a very active member of the Institute. His appointment was the outcome of a Carnegie United Kingdom Trust grant which was associated with the library's adherence to the scheme for central lending then instituted through the Central Library for Students. He was in charge of bibliographical work, and his personal contacts with prehistorians in other European countries resulted in a lasting relationship between their libraries and that of the RAI. He began an outstanding collection of journals on prehistoric archaeology during his two years at the Institute, and maintained a close interest in the library throughout his life, serving on its Council and Executive Committee.

During his period as librarian at the RAI Childe became widely known amongst the British archaeologists of the time, though these were by no means so numerous as today. In 1925 he first met a man who was to become one of his closest friends—O. G. S. Crawford. Crawford, who was Childe's senior by some five or six years, was then an Archaeological Officer to the Ordnance Survey, a post he held until 1946. During the first world war he had had considerable experience of air photography as observer and photographic interpreter, and in later years was largely responsible for the development of aerial photography as an archaeological technique. *Wessex from the Air*, the famous book published in 1928, was based on 300 photographs of archaeological sites taken in two months in 1924 by Crawford and Alexander Keiller. Crawford was also the first clear exponent of the mapping of the distribution of prehistoric sites. As well as their mutual and complementary interest in prehistoric archaeology (Crawford had trained as a geographer, Childe as a classicist), the two men also shared a common belief in Marxist philosophy. It seems that O. G. S. Crawford was one of the very few people to whom Childe felt able to express his ideas freely; his letters to Crawford over a number of years certainly seem less guarded and more personal than much of his correspondence. Both men believed in stating their opinions regardless of the personal consequences, and both were early wearers of shorts and other unconventional attire.

Also in London at this time, as Keeper and Secretary at the London Museum, was R. E. Mortimer Wheeler (or Rik, as he was known to his friends), the great field archaeologist. His dream, and that of his wife Tessa, was to found an Institute of Archaeology, and he had come to London from Wales where he had been Director of the National Museum, to prepare the ground for such a venture. When his schemes eventually bore fruit they were to affect Gordon Childe's career, for after the second world war he spent ten years as Director of the London University's Institute of Archaeology. However, in the mid-'20s archaeological techniques and teaching were still in a primitive state and much work needed to be done before a research institution could be founded. Writing his auto-biography, *Still Digging*, some 30 years later Wheeler recalled: 'Those were the days when a vice-president of the Society of Antiquaries could display enlightenment with the remark that he "agreed with Dr Wheeler's advice to pay great attention to stratification. Whatever material was being dealt with, stratification formed a very useful principle to follow." The ingenuous undertone of that observation is sufficiently self-evident.'[11]

Childe had already become acquainted, through his work at the British Museum, with Thomas Kendrick, whose book *The Axe Age* (1925), like Childe's *The Dawn of European Civilization*, introduced the so-called 'short' chronology for the prehistory of Europe. In 1925 Childe had just landed a job and Kendrick later recalled his friend's pride in getting £750 a year, and how he was wondering what he would do with such riches. His post at the Royal Anthropological Institute was well deserved, and the remuneration contrasted with his near-poverty of the preceding few years. It is not clear what happened to the money left to Childe by his mother; presumably he had either used it to further his political ideals in Australia, or had gone through it during his trips abroad. Spending the money for either scholarly or political ends might square Childe's socialist conscience. He certainly lived in a near penurious state in the early '20s at the Bloomsbury House Club, for Robert Chorley sometimes feared the abstemious scholar might die of semi-starvation before completing his great work on European prehistory!

Luckily this was not the case, and in 1925 the remarkable work of synthesis which Childe had been writing at Cartwright Gardens was published, and established his reputation overnight. Both this book and its successor, *The Aryans*, were published by Kegan Paul, Trench, Trubner and Co. as volumes in the History of Civilization series. This ambitious series, with contributions by notable British, American and French scholars, was designed to form a complete library of social evolution and was edited by C. K. Ogden, the originator of Basic English and Childe's friend for many years. *The Dawn of European Civilization* reviewed the evidence for regional cultures for the whole of Europe, bringing together material from museums and sites scattered through many different countries, so that for the first time the prehistory of Europe could be viewed as a whole. In his autobiographical 'Retrospect' Childe wrote that '*The Dawn* aimed at distilling from archaeological remains a preliterate substitute for the conventional politico-military history with cultures, instead of statesmen, as actors, and migrations in place of battles.'[12]

In order to appreciate the outstanding importance of Gordon Childe's first archaeological book it is necessary to realize that in 1925 archaeology was still widely regarded as an amateur pastime. There was only one Chair of Archaeology in Britain, at Cambridge, and correspondingly few people trained in the methods and literature of archaeology. Nor were museums, other than the British Museum in London, concerned with wider themes than their own localities. The only notable attempt to summarize archaeological research in Europe which pre-dates Childe's was Déchelette's *Manuel d'Archéologie*, the prehistoric part of which was published in 1908.

The Dawn is the more remarkable when it is remembered that Childe, like so many of his generation, was virtually self-taught as an archaeologist. He was by training a classicist, with an interest in philosophy and philology. He had of course been fortunate at

Oxford to come under the influence of Myres and Evans, both of whom had tried to see the prehistory of Britain in a wider perspective. But mainly it was his own wide reading and his personal visits to Continental museums which enabled him to regard Europe, not just as a set of arbitrarily divided regions, but as a whole whose prehistory could only be understood by studying the interrelationships of the various cultures. The fact that he was an Australian helped him to see Europe as a geographical whole, paying attention to its natural features and disregarding contemporary political boundaries.

The importance of *The Dawn* as a work of reference was immediately recognized; nowhere else in English was the mass of data he had so painstakingly accumulated available to prehistorians. However, it was more than a mere reference book: Childe was one of the first prehistorians to produce a *model* to make sense of all the archaeological evidence. He was also responsible for the acceptance, by the main body of British prehistorians, of a number of concepts derived from foreign literature, such as that of an archaeological 'culture'.

The Dawn of European Civilization contained a number of themes which were to occupy Childe for most of his life. He stated in the preface to the 1925 edition:

My theme is the foundation of European Civilization as a peculiar and individual manifestation of the human spirit.[13]

He saw that the Europeans had contributed something of their own to the legacy from the East; and in *The Aryans* attempted to show how this had happened; but he was not to find an explanation which satisfied him till the end of his life. His thesis was that civilization had spread from the Near East to barbarian Europe, and this was a traditional viewpoint of British prehistorians; depending on a belief in diffusion.

Towards the end of the nineteenth century, as more civilizations and cultures were being discovered, prehistorians and historians began to pay closer attention to the mechanisms of culture change— the means which brought about change in a society. Diffusion, or the spread of a cultural trait from its point of origin (whether by movement of peoples, trade or imitation), was believed to have played a major part in the development of human societies by enabling the rapid spread of ideas or techniques. However some scholars, notably the Australian anatomist, Sir Grafton Elliot Smith, refused to believe that any major inventions had occurred more than once and adhered to the theory that all occurrences therefore derived from a single source, namely Egypt, whence they were spread by the 'Children of the Sun'. This hyper-diffusionist school, as it became known, held blindly to the theory of *ex Oriente lux* and did much to discredit the moderate diffusionism of Childe and others who were prepared to accept independent invention if the evidence suggested it.

Around 1925 high passions were aroused between 'Orientalists' and 'Occidentalists', the latter believing that the evolution of European prehistory was a self-sufficient process. Evolution and diffusion were widely considered mutually exclusive, though Childe was at pains to point out that this dichotomy was a false one. The main exponent of the Occidental school, Gustav Kossinna, was also a firm diffusionist, though he attributed the progressive elements in the cultures of prehistoric Europe, not to the Children of the Sun, but rather to the Indo-Europeans or Aryans. Childe's *The Dawn* of 1925 effected a compromise between the Orientalist diffusionism and the independent evolution of European cultures. He emphasized the contribution made by the battle-axe invaders of South Russia, who he believed had prevented the cultural stagnation of Central Europe. He considered two major channels for diffusion from the East—one along the Mediterranean and Atlantic coasts, and the other the Danube valley. A third channel, whose role he discussed more fully in 1956 in *The Prehistory of European Society*, was via the amber routes over the Alps. In *The Dawn* of 1925, emphasizing the sea coast route, he attributed the rise of the Iberian civilization to colonization from the East, but by the 1927 edition he had relegated these voyagers to a secondary role and acknowledged the supremacy of the Danube thoroughfare.

The Aryans: a Study of Indo-European Origins was published in 1926, a year after *The Dawn*, and the two books were meant to be studied together. *The Dawn* dealt with the material culture which spread from the Orient to Europe, and in *The Aryans* Childe showed how the Indo-European speaking peoples took advantage of it to develop a distinctive European civilization. These themes can also be traced in Harold Peake's *The Bronze Age and the Celtic World*, a book which probably had some influence on Childe.

Looking back in 'Retrospect' he wrote that 'like Gustav Kossinna I came to prehistory from comparative philology; I began the study of European archaeology in the hope of finding the cradle of the Indo-Europeans and of identifying their primitive culture.'[14] He had already explored the available literature for his B.Litt. thesis at Oxford, but now he incorporated in *The Aryans* the new discoveries of the Ancient East and Europe, and especially of Greece. Comparative philology had long been a recognized tool in the study of origins, at least to provide hypotheses for archaeology to test. *The Aryans* was a discussion of the various Indo-European theories which philology had suggested, reviewed in the light of the available archaeological evidence.

Childe also made an attempt to explain the uniqueness of European civilization: 'Favourable climatic conditions, peculiar natural resources, a happy conjuncture of trade routes do not suffice to explain this phenomenon; behind it lurks the true historic fact of personal initiative. That archaeology cannot grasp . . .'[15] This explanation owes nothing to Marxist doctrines and indeed suggests the 'Great Man' theory of history which Childe was later to reject so explicitly in *History* in 1947. It is clear that he had in mind not so much a 'Great Man' as a 'Great People': '. . . the Aryans do appear everywhere as promoters of true progress and in Europe their expansion marks the moment when the prehistory of our continent begins to diverge from that of Africa or the Pacific.'[16] He equated these original Indo-European speakers with a vast complex of battle-axe cultures which spread across Europe from Jutland to south-west Russia. Unlike Kossinna, he located their (admittedly hypothetical) homeland somewhere in the latter region.

In *The Aryans* Gordon Childe attributed a remarkable importance to language:

Words are the very stuff of thought. It follows then that a common language does imply a common mental outlook in its speakers; it not only reflects but also conditions ways of thinking peculiar to the users of the tongue in question. Moreover, intellectual progress may to a large extent be measured by the refinement of language. Hence to inherit an exceptionally delicate linguistic structure gives a people a vantage point on the path of progress.[17]

So in fact he, like Gustav Kossinna, was convinced of the superiority of the Aryans; they passed on to the peoples they conquered 'a more excellent language and the mentality it generated'.[18]

In later years Childe disowned the Indo-European linguistics he had used in *The Aryans*, for the Nazis adopted and exaggerated the linguistic teachings of the German nationalist prehistorian, Kossinna. Childe's friends soon learnt to avoid any mention of *The Aryans*, and after about 1930 he tended to concentrate purely on materialist diffusion. This reaction against the political connotations of his Indo-European thesis had a profound effect on the development of his theories from this time right up to the mid-1950s, when he once again attempted to balance Oriental diffusion against Occidental evolution. It caused him, in 1956, either to forget or to deny that he had recognized the uniqueness of European prehistory in the '20s.

Gordon Childe continued to travel widely in Central and Eastern Europe during his years at the Royal Anthropological Institute, collecting material for later works. Finance for some of these early travels came personally from Louis Clarke, Curator of the Cambridge University Museum of Archaeology and Ethnology from 1922 to 1937. Childe's companion on a trip to Yugoslavia, Rumania and Hungary in 1926 was Daryll Forde, his friend from Cartwright Gardens who later became professor of anthropology at the Universities of Wales and London. On a radio programme broadcast the year after Childe's death Forde described his friend's inveterate love of travelling:

He could settle down and make himself at home because he had no very high demands for comfort, in any small hotel anywhere. He did tend to get fussed about catching trains and wonder if one would be able to get from one place to another, but that was really very secondary to his delight in seeing new places. In 1926 Childe was planning a very extensive journey in S.E. Europe to visit museums and sites which were practically unknown to most people in Britain except from the literature. He was good enough to invite me along and I went for a month to six weeks with him to Yugoslavia, Rumania and Hungary. It was a very exciting trip. Belgrade at the time had hardly recovered from the First World War, the paved streets ended a quarter of a mile outside of what was a rather small city and we travelled by car to various sites. Our driver was a shaven headed White Russian general who now had a job as a chauffeur—drove us in a large and rather over-sprung American car over appalling roads to sites like the famous neolithic site of Vinča which is a type site for the Danubian civilisation. The stratification could be seen in a quarry at the edge of the Danube and I can remember Childe clambering on rocks digging away with a penknife getting out specimens from the various layers to check the stratification as described in Vassits' paper.[19]

The great settlement of Vinča overlooking the Danube near Belgrade was recognized as a key site in the study of European prehistory. Childe had evidently already read the 1908 paper by Miloje Vassits entitled 'South-eastern elements in the prehistoric civilization of Serbia', which initiated many years of research by Balkan scholars. For Gordon Childe the site's importance lay in its role as a link between the prehistory of the Aegean and of Central Europe, and he believed that the material at Vinča showed Aegean influences, including metallic ore beads and pottery with incised signs. For many years, before the acceptance of radiocarbon dating, there was little disagreement that there was some connection between the early Bronze Age of the Aegean, especially Troy, and the Balkan Copper Age. These links were the first step in building up a chronological scheme for the whole of prehistoric Europe.

One story which Daryll Forde did not reveal on the broadcast for the BBC was that in those days in the remote villages of South Eastern Europe the single hotel offering rest to the weary traveller was as often as not also the local brothel. Great was Childe's embarrassment when the two friends knocked at the door of such hostelries and had to explain that they required only shelter, and not any further services.

In 1927 Childe was offered the post of first Abercromby Professor of Archaeology at Edinburgh University. The post had previously been offered to Miles Burkitt of Cambridge, and (according to his autobiography, *Still Digging*) to Mortimer Wheeler; both of whom had other projects afoot, and declined the position. However when the post was advertised, a special letter was sent to Childe drawing his attention to the advertisement. The terms of the Abercromby Chair of Archaeology, established by a deed of bequest, dated 1916, of the distinguished Scottish prehistorian, Lord Abercromby, had a precise formulation; although it is a little-known fact that a codicil to his will, dated 1923 (the year before his death), freed the University Court 'in view of the changing conditions of the times' from the express conditions of the Trust Disposition. Nevertheless the stipulations are interesting in that they embody Lord Abercromby's views regarding the incumbency of the Chair; and also because it is possible to see how, during his career at Edinburgh, Gordon Childe tried to carry them out:

(First) I limit the subject for which the proposed Chair is to be founded to that department of the science of Archaeology which treats of the antiquities and civilisation of the Countries of Europe and the near East from the earliest times to the period at which the written history of each Country may be said to begin: (Second) It shall be a *sine qua non* that the Incumbent of the Chair shall be proficient in the French and German languages and shall have at least a working knowledge of the Italian language: (Third) The Incumbent of the Chair shall keep himself at all times as far as possible abreast of the whole literature of the subject that is published in Europe; and it is my desire that he shall impart his acquired knowledge not only to his classes, but to a wider audience through the medium of the Press and otherwise; (Fourth) I desire that the Incumbent of the Chair shall not content himself with the passive role of merely disseminating the facts and theories of other Writers, but that he shall also apply himself to the investigation and solution of some of the many problems and difficulties that encompass the study of Archaeology, and to achieve this end and to insure the success of the project from its initiation, the first Incumbent of the Chair ought not only to be a specialist in Archaeology but also a vigorous man in the prime of life.[20]

The terms of the bequest were in fact largely the result of Abercromby's disapproval of several old members of the Society of Antiquaries of Scotland, whom he found provincial in outlook and insular in scope. Not long before writing his will he had quarrelled with members of the Society and been displeased at the way they carried out an excavation he had financed. He was determined that archaeology in Scotland should be set on a new footing, and the terms of the bequest, whilst excluding any potential applicants from among the ageing members of the Society of Antiquaries of Scotland, might have been framed for Gordon Childe. He accepted the position and left for Edinburgh in September 1927; though not without misgivings, for it meant being largely isolated from old and valued friends in London. The decision was to set him irrevocably on a career as an academic prehistorian. His Communist friend R. Palme Dutt later explained Childe's choice:

. . . he wrote to me that he would have chosen revolutionary politics but he found the price too high, and that he preferred what he termed the *bios apolausticos* (fleshpots) of professional status.[21]

5. Abercromby Professor

With his appointment to the Edinburgh Chair Childe became, at the age of 35, the only academic prehistorian in a teaching post in Scotland. The position was one of immense possibilities, and an unequalled opportunity for the new professor to exert his influence on the study of prehistoric archaeology in Britain. During the next 20 years Childe rose to a highly respected position in the field of prehistory, not only in Britain, but throughout the world. This he achieved through publications based on an incredible grasp of the European and Near Eastern material, gained not just from his wide reading but by personal observation.

Great advances were being made in archaeology in the years between the wars. During the '20s and '30s numerous excavations, both in Europe and the Near East, took place, and they utilized increasingly scientific methods of detection, retrieval and conservation. The usefulness of air photography to archaeologists had been demonstrated during the first world war, and many hitherto unknown sites were discovered by this means. Excavation of British sites greatly increased, and with it came an awareness of the value of the study of geography to archaeology. O. G. S. Crawford and Lord Abercromby both realized the importance of distributional maps of prehistoric sites; and Crawford stressed too in *Man and His Past* (1921) the reconstruction of prehistoric environments. Sir Cyril Fox's famous book *The Personality of Britain*, published in 1932, studied prehistoric distributions against a background of local ecologies, and provided a new approach to both geographical and prehistoric studies.

However what still captured the imagination of the public were spectacular finds in distant lands; and there were plenty of these in the years between the wars. In 1923 a world-wide sensation was caused by the discovery of the splendid treasures in the tomb of Tutankhamen by Howard Carter and Lord Carnarvon. 1926 saw the excavation by Sir Leonard Woolley of the great prehistoric cemetery at Ur, with its 'Royal Tombs' containing treasures of gold and lapis lazuli. Woolley's full and popular publications, such as *Ur of the Chaldees* (1929) brought the Sumerian civilization of Mesopotamia to the public's notice. Nearer home, the discovery of the well-preserved Sutton Hoo ship burial near Ipswich in 1939 brought alive the legends of the pagan Anglo-Saxons.

Gordon Childe began his life at Edinburgh as Abercromby Professor under a cloud of dislike and disapproval from the Scottish archaeological Establishment. Older members of the Society of Antiquaries of Scotland especially resented an 'outsider'—and not just an Englishman, which would have been bad enough, but an Australian—holding the Edinburgh Chair. In spite of, or perhaps because of, his undoubted abilities, not for very many years did they even ask Childe to be on the Council of the Society. It seems many Scottish archaeologists resented the newcomer's width of approach, contrasting so strongly with their own provincial attitudes. He stood head and shoulders above most of them in erudition and ability, and introduced a wind of change into prehistoric studies in Scotland not acceptable to many antiquarians entrenched in their own smugness. This was not of course the case with all the archaeologists with whom he came into contact; Sir W. Lindsay Scott, Alexander Curle, J. G. Callender and Walter Grant, for example, became respected friends of Childe's.

Other factors which hindered his acceptance in Edinburgh were his own character and beliefs. His reticence made him a difficult man to know, and his occasional abruptness of manner belied his kindly and gentle nature. Those who took the trouble to try to get more in step with him found him a delightful companion, with never an ill word for anyone. But many saw no further than the colonial with unorthodox political and religious views. Even a less sensitive man than Childe could not fail to be affected by the fairly wide-spread hostility he encountered; on one occasion (it must have been after a particularly bad day) he wrote to a friend: 'I live here in an atmosphere of hatred and envy'.

Nevertheless on his more cheerful days he must have acknow-ledged that his post at Edinburgh resulted in several lasting friendships. It was here, not long after his arrival, that he met the Tait Professor of Natural Philosophy, Charles G. Darwin, grandson of the Charles Darwin who wrote *The Origin of Species*, and his wife Katherine. He felt immediately at home with the rationalist and liberal attitudes of the famous scientific family, and often stayed with them on family holidays, the two professors greatly enjoying long walks on the mountains of Scotland. Childe was very fond of the five Darwin children, perhaps catching a glimpse of the family life which he was never to enjoy, and he acted as godfather to the youngest son, Edward.

He was also on friendly terms with the Principal of Edinburgh University, Sir Alfred Ewing, and with the Dover Wilsons. John Dover Wilson, the Shakespearean expert, was Regius Professor of English Literature at the University from 1935 to 1945, although he did not in fact arrive in Edinburgh until Easter 1936. Honours students did not have to choose their specialization until after the first year courses, and Childe and Dover Wilson no doubt had a number of students in common. However on one subject the two friends did not see eye to eye. Dover Wilson and some of his colleagues were concerned at the ignorance of the Bible amongst their students and a motion was brought before the Senatus for the appointment of a lecturer in Biblical History. Attendance was to be voluntary, and the lecturer, of course, a member of the Church of Scotland. The motion was carried with only two dissentients—the atheist Gordon Childe, and Professor Whittaker, a well-known mathematician and ardent Roman Catholic.

Also in the Faculty of Arts was the Professor of History and great personality Vivian H. Galbraith. His years at Edinburgh were 1937–44, and he then overlapped with Childe for a while at London University, as Director of the Institute of Historical Research between 1944 and 1948. *The Times* obituary of him in 1976 described his 'robust opinions and colourful expression of them'. His studies of the Domesday book began at Edinburgh; perhaps Childe had him in mind when he wrote in 1957: 'Even Domesday Book can profitably be supplemented, not just illustrated, by excavation of village sites.'[1] Gordon Childe had much in common too with Arthur Berriedale Keith, Regius Professor of Sanskrit and Comparative Philology at Edinburgh. Childe himself had studied Sanskrit at university, and mastered it sufficiently to have a passable reading ability at one time; in fact the story goes that it was because he spent too much time studying Sanskrit that he did not do as well as expected in some university examinations!

Whilst at Edinburgh Childe was not completely out of touch with many old friends, and in his capacity as Abercromby Professor he soon became acquainted with most of the leading figures in his field. One meeting place with much high-powered archaeological discussion was at Youlbury, the home of Sir Arthur Evans at Boar's Hill near Oxford. Also present at some of the weekend house parties at Youlbury was the young wife of archaeologist Humfrey Payne, later to become well-known under the name Dilys Powell. She recalled: 'I would make a timid entry into a drawing-room which seemed to me full of revered names: the prehistorian Gordon Childe, H. R. Hall, author of a standard *Ancient History of the Near East*, Leonard Woolley, excavator of Ur of the Chaldees—all amiable characters, I am sure, but not men to indulge in small talk.'[2]

One thing which Childe failed to do as Abercromby Professor was to found a strong school of archaeology in Scotland. He already had some experience of teaching from Australia and London, but his primary interest at Edinburgh was his own research and he was never on very close terms with his students. Though they usually recognized his underlying kindness, Childe could be rather terrifying to a young undergraduate; his behaviour at oral examinations was obviously particularly frightening. In his first years at Edinburgh he often asked Miles Burkitt of Cambridge, a palaeolithic archaeologist whom he had met in the early 1920s, to act as external examiner. The procedure was carried out with great formality, Childe insisting that the two examiners wore academic gowns for the occasion. They sat down at a long table, and a uniformed janitor ushered the first examinee into the presence. If the candidate was a girl, the two half-rose out of their seats in a formal bow, and the nervous candidate was soon reduced to tears. After one such harrowing episode, Burkitt turned to Childe and said: 'Well, Gordon, I had to lend that girl my handkerchief today; tomorrow you'll have to bring a towel'.

The departmental facilities at Edinburgh left much to be desired; housed in cramped rooms in the old Mathematics Building in Chambers Street, it consisted of Childe's study with his vast personal library, and one lecture room, with Childe the sole lecturer.

A student of those days recalled one lecture on the post-glacial period 'delivered from beneath an umbrella, while a leaking ceiling, reprehensibly ignored by a deaf and indifferent Senate, dripped steadily upon it'.[3] He rarely had more than a handful of students attending courses, and only one read honours archaeology during the 19 years of his professorship. The blame for this can to some extent be laid at Childe's door, for he did not by any means devote his energies to building up a vigorous school; once he actively discouraged a history student to whom he had been appointed advisor from changing to an archaeology degree. Amongst those who did spend at least part of their years at Edinburgh University studying under Childe were Stewart Cruden, Basil Skinner, J. H. Burns, Margaret E. Crichton Mitchell and R. B. K. Stevenson.

The curriculum he composed at Edinburgh was for a BSc degree, conforming to Lord Abercromby's and his own belief in archaeology as a scientific discipline; there was a bias on geology, with anatomy for honours students. The pattern of the course must have been extraordinarily confusing for undergraduate students. He began with the Scottish Iron Age so that he could take parties out to see nearby hill-forts, and progressed backwards, but rarely actually reached the palaeolithic by the end of the course. He was a difficult lecturer for undergraduates in other ways too: he articulated badly (a defect possibly inherited from his father) and had an individual accent and slightly metallic or reedy tones. Apart from the resulting lack of clarity which some found in his speech, Childe's immense knowledge and intelligence made him difficult to follow. Margaret Crichton Mitchell recalled how 'he completely ignored what he regarded as the unnecessary stages of an argument. One's mind was always leapfrogging to keep up with him and most of his class were hopelessly lost. And yet he had a strange quality of magnetism which made it imperative to listen even though one hadn't understood.' However, the confusion created by a welter of foreign place-names and intellectual leaps did not entirely obscure the general effect of Childe's width of view. He scorned parochialism, and he may have been lecturing on Scottish prehistory, but it was Scottish prehistory set against a vivid background of European archaeology.

Childe always had immense enthusiasm for practical demonstrations in archaeology. His students spent sessions with the professor chipping flint instruments, and incidentally acquiring respect for the superior artefacts of palaeolithic man. He liked to use the scientific method of trial and observation, and his experiments on the production of the phenomena distinctive of vitrified forts at Plean and Rahoy in 1937 were characteristic of this. Vitrified forts, of which there are over 30 Scottish examples (and which Childe listed in a special final chapter in *Scotland Before the Scots*) had puzzled archaeologists for years. 'Vitrified' is the description applied to those forts which had within their ramparts broken stones fused together to form a solid mass. The extent of vitrifaction varies enormously from site to site, some having only a few stones fused, whilst in others it appears that a substantial wall of vitrified material runs almost continuously around the whole perimeter of the enclosure. The rocks known to have been vitrified vary too, though all contain a relatively high proportion of minerals other than quartz.

Gordon Childe, together with another Fellow of the Society of Antiquaries of Scotland, Wallace Thorneycroft, had been fascinated by vitrified forts for years and had excavated examples at Finavon, Angus in 1933–4 and at Rahoy, Argyllshire in 1936–7. At both these sites they noted evidence for a fierce conflagration within the forts, and also casts of pieces of timbers enclosed in the vitrified masses, exactly as had been reported at similar forts in France. Childe recorded in the Proceedings of the Society of Antiquaries of Scotland the satisfactory nature of the evidence for dating at Rahoy: 'The fort's occupants had used no pottery, and relics were very scarce. Six weeks' trowel and brush-work yielded one flint scraper, two saddle querns, an iron spear-butt, an iron axe, and a broken bronze fibula. But had we salted the site, these were precisely the objects I should have inserted; they do establish the pre-Roman date of the occupation.'[4]

Many theories had been put forward, from the eighteenth century onward, to account for vitrifaction, but Childe and Thorneycroft's experiments at Plean and Rahoy in 1937 were designed to test a hypothesis put forward by Schuchhardt, accepted by Déchelette, and later supported by the excavations of Gerhard Bersu. These archaeologists maintained that vitrifaction was the result of the combustion of the wood in a wall composed of stone and timber built in the manner of Caesar's *murus gallicus*. Childe and Thorneycroft constructed a model *murus gallicus* at Thorneycroft's Plean Colliery, Stirlingshire, in March, and a smaller one at Rahoy, built from stones actually used in the ancient fort, in June. The two men had great fun setting the walls alight and watching their progress, especially at Plean, where the March wind whipped the fire up to a spectacular blaze. Great was their delight when the result was vitrifaction and they were able to conclude that the puzzling phenomenon was indeed the by-product of the destruction by fire of a *murus gallicus*.

Childe's interest in vitrified forts adds some weight to the idea that he was the prototype for a Professor Porlock in the novel *And Then You Came*, by Ann Bridge, published in 1949. The authoress was in fact Lady O'Malley, who had met Childe through her relative, Angus Graham, his colleague from the Royal Commission on Historical Monuments (Scotland), and the book contains a dedication to him. Professor Porlock was also fascinated by vitrified forts, and many of Childe's friends at the time were certain he was the basis for the character. The authoress also endowed him with a knowledge of Australia which would have fitted Childe equally well: 'Professor Porlock, having the precious gift of the historic imagination, was wont to dwell with rapture on the occasional disruption of telegraphic communications in Australia because the black aborigines would climb the telegraph poles and remove the white china insulators, in order to chip them, with millennial skill, into spearheads!'[5]

Gordon Childe was not in many ways a practical person, but his position as the only university teacher of archaeology in Scotland obliged him to excavate, and he carried out his duties conscientiously. When pressed by Mary Alice Evatt, wife of Australian Labour leader H. V. Evatt, to visit his native land in 1931, he wrote: 'I'd love to come to Australia again to see you and Bert and Billy McKell and Jack Lang too not to speak of Sir Alexander [Gordon] the Sydney Bridge and Canberra. And really I could afford it if only I felt I'd earned a holiday by getting Scottish prehistory back on its legs. At the moment it's very backward and I have to dig which I loathe a good part of the summer (so called) while in winter I must lecture for two terms.'

He conducted his own excavations almost every year, and visited many other sites in Scotland and elsewhere; but he did not enjoy excavation, and felt that he did it badly. There is some difference of opinion over his skills in this direction among those who worked with him in the field. Stuart Piggott has pointed out the possibility that 'his inability to appreciate the nature of archaeological evidence in the field, and the processes involved in its recovery, recognition, and interpretation, led in turn to a tendency to ignore the potential inequality in the reliability of the evidence he employed in his works of synthesis.'[6] Certainly Childe did not excel as an excavator, being more interested in interpretation than the neatness of the site, but he *was* aware of some of the problems of excavation and how these could affect interpretation. In 1942 he wrote to his colleague and former tutor, J. L. Myres:

. . . in a cave the main relic beds are generally separated by sterile layers of stalagmite or fallen roof-blocks; a *tell* is liable to offer quite other problems, being usually continuously occupied. Two methods of dissection have been adopted and really give your two different kinds of results though excavators often and their interpreters normally fail to distinguish between them. (1) you may dig trenches or sink shafts . . . recording merely the levels of the relics found. In this case provided you have a great abundance of relics of the same class—potsherds or flints—, you get a sequence that is statistically reliable. But not much chronological significance attaches to the position of isolated objects found and recorded on this principle. Alternatively (2) you follow the floors of the successive settlement, recording together objects found on each successive floor and not worrying much about numerical levels; for floors are seldom horizontal and are liable to be interrupted by bothroi. In this case all objects on a given floor are archaeologically contemporary. This is the method Schliemann I suppose wanted to follow in his excavation, but in his recording, (if any, some say he wrote the depths out of his head after dinner!) he adopted method (1). . . . Owing to the confusion of these two methods and what they can tell, Vassits' Vinča dig is a classical example of how not to dissect a tell. The first reliable dissection in Continental Europe was I suspect poor old Marton's at Tószeg, but he only published the barest summary in an obscure Hungarian journal—in 1907—so really lost the credit; unless I rescued it for him after seeing his work. But then I did not myself grasp the difference. I still believed that absolute levels were significant for individual objects when I started digging Skara Brae and only fully grasped its limitations when I did Larriban in Antrim. . . . Finally of course there are sites that, though inhabited repeatedly are quite unstratified; Bersu was I think the first to show how to extort the sequence from these but as he did not publish Goldberg, Buttler snaffled the credit with Köln-Lindenthal.

One of Childe's Edinburgh students, R. B. K. Stevenson, who visited several of his sites in southern Scotland as well as working with him at Larriban in 1935, recalled that 'the scale of the operations was always very small, a couple of labourers and several students, to one labourer and no volunteers. I think that the standard of observation and recording was quite as good as most at that time. Decent areas were opened, unlike the narrow trenching usual on Roman sites in Scotland then.' One of Childe's earliest students, Margaret Crichton Mitchell, who also excavated with him on a number of sites, recalled that he did not appear to be interested in excavation techniques. 'He knew virtually nothing about surveying. His photography was deplorable; his methods non-existent. And yet—he had a genius for interpreting evidence which was uncanny.'

He was particularly interested in the excavation and classification of various types of megaliths—chambered cairns, barrows, cists, stone circles, etc.—and he made an important contribution to Scottish prehistory with his re-assessment of the chambered tombs against a European background. He was primarily a thinker rather than an excavator, and indeed on at least one occasion successfully used theory to discover where sites might lie. His interest in geology, which he had studied since his first year at Sydney University, came into play when T. H. Bryce, describing the segmented cists of Arran, had mentioned the likelihood of finding similar structures along the shores of Loch Fyne. Balnabraid and Auchoish were cists on the loch's western shore, but the eastern shore remained a blank until Childe studied his geological map of the region:

Only in the vicinity of Kilfinan does the geological map show a considerable stretch of the well-drained soil that the builders of long cairns seem to have selected for settlement. The presence of copper lodes, recently worked, as near Kilmartin, provided an additional pointer to the district. Accordingly, seeing several cairns marked on the Ordnance Map, I visited the district with Mr Kilbride Jones, one of my students, at the end of March 1932, and found that two of the cairns indicated were indubitably of the chambered variety.[7]

Generally the professor, following the common procedure of those days, employed mainly professional labour to excavate his sites, though often he also had the assistance of colleagues and friends. Sean O'Riordain, of the Irish Museum, turned up in May 1932 near the end of Childe's excavations at Castlelaw Fort, which is one of a chain of hillforts along the south-east slopes of the Pentlands. Also in 1932 he collaborated with the anthropologist C. Daryll Forde, now at Aberystwyth University, over the excavation of two Iron Age hillforts at Earn's Heugh on the Berwickshire coast. Here differences in construction between the forts, such as the relative position of the ditches and arrangements of the gates, suggested different ages. After their excavations, however, the two friends drew the conclusion that their results were ambiguous, although on the whole they favoured an earlier date for the West Fort.

Whilst at Edinburgh, Gordon Childe founded an archaeological society which he called the Edinburgh League of Prehistorians, with an intentional similarity to the title 'Young Communists' League'. Many of his keener students were members, and as well as attending lectures from visiting archaeologists, they spent many weekends and vacations excavating with their professor. Unlike all too many excavators, he was always scrupulous in acknowledging help from his students and other diggers, and also in writing up his almost annual reports for the *Proceedings of the Society of Antiquaries of Scotland*.

Childe's 1930 excavations at the chambered long cairn at Kindrochat had special relevance to his 1929/30 Munro Lectures and the work was carried out by several members of the Edinburgh League of Prehistorians with a grant from the university. The significance of the Kindrochat cairn as an isolated outlier of the Clyde group of chambered cairns defined by Bryce had first been noted by the famous French archaeologist, the Abbé H. Breuil, on a visit to Scotland the year before. The fact that Edinburgh now boasted a Professorship of Archaeology, with such an eminent European prehistorian as Gordon Childe in the Chair, meant that distinguished archaeologists from other countries, as well as from other British universities and museums, made more frequent visits to Scotland; and its archaeological evidence was undoubtedly less neglected than had previously been the case.

Childe's skill as an excavator may have been indifferent, but this does not seem to have prevented his Irish colleagues from issuing him with several invitations to excavate in Northern Ireland. Once his Belfast friend Miss M. Gaffikin had occasion to regret his help when she received a letter from an irate farmer after Childe had virtually abandoned a site in bad weather without even filling in. The missive read: 'You and that Mr Childe has left the Doonan in a bloody mess.' He was on very good terms with many Irish archaeologists of those and later years, including Paddy Hartnett, Jo

Rafferty, E. Estyn Evans, Michael 'Brian' O'Kelly and his wife Claire, and, especially, Sean O'Riordain. One of his best-known Irish excavations was of a promontory fort at Larriban in June 1935. Larriban (Leath Rath Ban or Half White Fort) was the name given to a limestone promontory rising sheer for some 150 ft above the sea near Knocksoghey. A hundred feet of the neck of the promontory was cut off by a rampart and ditch, but during the first world war over half of the enclosed area had been quarried away. One lucky result of the quarrying was that a clear section through the rampart had been left, and here a Mr Blake Whelan had discovered pieces of pottery in what appeared to be a kiln. At the suggestion of Mr Whelan and the invitation of the Prehistoric Research Council for Northern Ireland, Childe undertook trial excavations at the site in 1935, clearing strips 12 ft wide to discover that the rampart was 17 ft wide at its central point.

He employed mainly labourers as usual, though this time he noted with approval that 60 per cent of the wages were paid by the government of Northern Ireland under 'an enlightened scheme for the relief of unemployment'. The pottery sherds at Larriban turned out to represent a very characteristic Northern Irish fabric also found at Donegore, Kilbride and Malone, with no comparable material in the rest of Britain or even Eire. Dating, as always on a prehistoric site, but particularly in the pre-radiocarbon days, was a problem, and Childe was delighted to find a fragment of a glass armlet, almost certainly imported, which allowed him to date the lower levels to around A.D. 800. The date was of course a tentative one, based on relative dating techniques, and he was careful to emphasize, in his report on Larriban read to the Society of Antiquaries on 21 November, that caution was needed when attempting to date forts and pottery on purely technical and architectural criteria. At Larriban, he pointed out, it had been revealed that communities in Antrim were in existence at the end of the Dark Ages whose defensive architecture, industries and economy resembled the pre-Roman or Roman Iron Age of other parts of Britain.

One excavation which Childe did enjoy was that for which he is most famous, at Skara Brae on Orkney, a Neolithic village where not only the buildings, but also the tables, beds and cupboards were built of stone because of the lack of trees on the island. His excavations here have become well-known, and were visited by several eminent archaeologists from all over the world, as well as his friend from Oxford days, Raymond Postgate, with his father-in-law, the MP George Lansbury. Another visitor was the Scottish historian, Alan O. Anderson, who first met Childe in July 1929 during the third year of excavations. Anderson was particularly interested in the stone slab with markings found on the site, which it was then thought might be an example of early writing. Much to his amusement Childe, wary of allowing a stranger to inspect it, sat on the slab the whole time they were talking!

Childe spent many seasons working on the western and northern islands, which he grew to love, and in their turn the local inhabitants grew to love him. Shortly after his death his former student Stewart Cruden wrote:

In the far north he is remembered with high regard and vivid reminiscence for it was characteristic of the man to win affection among those with whom he worked and lived, albeit their reactions to his personality are not innocent of wonder and humour. To them he was every inch the professor. The Stromness landlady who looked after him during the epic days of Skara Brae commiserated with genuine solicitude on how the poor man never ate, too upset when he didn't find anything, too excited when he did.[8]

Skara Brae is situated on the southern corner of the Bay of Skaill on the mainland of Orkney, and the ruins of the village were first discovered when a fierce storm in 1850 revealed portions of the buildings peeping out from beneath the sand. By 1868 William Watt, the laird of Skaill, had dug out four huts and carried off many relics to Skaill House. Apart from casual digging in 1913 by members of a houseparty which included Professor Boyd Dawkins, the site was then left undisturbed until in December 1924 a second great storm brought waves over the site. Earlier that year the ruins had been placed under the guardianship of HM Commissioners of Works and to prevent further damage they began to build up the sea wall and consolidate the buildings. It soon became clear that an organized re-excavation was required, and Gordon Childe was asked to supervise extended digging from 1927–30.

The excavation of Skara Brae presented unusual conditions and problems, for the buildings and other remains were of stone, and therefore much better preserved than on other contemporary sites, especially as they had been hidden underneath layers of sand for generations. At the same time, Childe had to take into account the previous somewhat haphazard excavations on the site. Both Skara Brae and another village at Rinyo, on the island of Rousay in the Orkneys, discovered later and excavated mainly by Walter Grant of Kirkwall, revealed several structural periods; but both were recognized as classical illustrations of self-sufficient Neolithic communities. J. G. Callender was one archaeologist who deviated from this view when in 1931 he opined that Skara Brae approximated more closely to an Iron Age culture. However the site assumed further importance in Childe's eyes in 1936 when Stuart Piggott noticed similarities between the earlier Skara Brae pottery and the Grooved Ware of East Anglia. The Rinyo excavations of 1937 confirmed his thesis by producing further parallels to East Anglian shapes and motifs.

The inhabitants of Skara Brae were essentially stockbreeders, and enormous quantities of the bones of sheep and cattle were discovered throughout the deposits. However no evidence at all was discovered for agriculture—no preserved grains, no querns, and no sickle gloss on the many flints. Surprisingly few fish bones or fishing equipment turned up (though with the methods of 1930 it is possible some were overlooked), but limpets obviously formed a large part of the diet.

The stone huts and furniture made Skara Brae an exciting and unique excavation. The site had apparently been hastily abandoned by the inhabitants, and each single-roomed hut was just as the occupants had left it—a Pompeii of the Orkneys. The furniture consisted of stone beds once containing heather mattresses, shelves, dressers and water-tight small stone boxes or cists let into the floors. Fine necklaces and the bones of choice joints of meat were found in the sleeping places, where presumably such valuable belongings had been hidden by their owners underneath the heather. Another very human touch was provided by a string of beads leading from the narrow doorway of a hut along a passageway; Childe suggested that a woman had broken her necklace in her haste to flee, leaving her treasured beads behind her as they fell. The linking passageways between the huts were paved and roofed, and the whole village had a common drainage system—evidence which provided fuel, in his explicitly Marxist *Scotland Before the Scots* of 1946, for Childe's theory that the inhabitants of Skara Brae considered themselves to be related members of a single great family or clan: 'With such a sociological structure there are neither ruling nor exploited classes and the land at least is communally owned. As long as the principal means of production—in this instance flocks and herds—are likewise held in common, we have 'primitive communism' in the Marxian sense; this does not preclude private property in articles individually made and used, such as tools and ornaments.'[9] However in its final stages Skara Brae did exhibit one 'industrial' hut, which lacked the usual furniture but was provided with a kiln and had been used as a workshop by a flint knapper. So although Childe did not like to admit it, it may be that specialization had begun to creep in to this 'primitive communist' Utopia!

Curiously few items which held a clue to the ideology of the Skara Brae dwellers were recovered. No regular burials were found, though two old women had been buried under the wall of one hut, possibly implying a belief in the widespread superstition that a ghost was needed to hold up a wall. Nothing suggestive of a shrine or temple was revealed, and Childe was happy to conclude in *Scotland Before the Scots* that 'Magic powers and ghosts would have been recognized, but gods no more than chiefs'.[10]

Childe published the results of his seasons' work on Orkney in 1931 in *Skara Brae*, illustrated with numerous photographs taken by him. Before this date he had also produced three major books, *The Most Ancient East*, *The Danube in Prehistory* and *The Bronze Age*, which completed the enormous piece of research he had begun with *The Dawn of European Civilization*. Although he concentrated mainly on his own research and did not devote much time to building up the Edinburgh department, Childe had a strong influence on a number of his students, inspiring many of them to undertake further study and research in prehistory. His intellectual power and width of knowledge created a barrier his young students often found it difficult to overcome; but one of them recalled:

. . . a professor who invited one to his residence, spoke apparently most European languages and read them all, understood the chemistry of the Bronze Age, discoursed on Handel's Variations with records, read the classics with ease and enjoyment and taught one how to do long division in Latin numerals made an inspiring impact on the mind.[11]

Childe's own dedication to prehistory was so complete that he looked for nothing less from his students: an inspiring if somewhat daunting ambience in which to work. He was immensely kind to his

71

students, and was more than just an academic adviser, for he felt that he should communicate with his students on a social level too. He frequently invited students for a meal at his rooms, and was most willing for them to accompany him on his long tramps over the hills and moors of Scotland. He would give a brilliant analysis and assessment of a site for the sheer pleasure of instructing those who were with him.

During one year of the second world war Childe had only three students: Mrs Hester Scott, J. H. Burns and a Mr Nicolson. He invited them out to lunch time and again until eventually they decided to reciprocate, and planned a specially prepared meal at a Chinese restaurant. The gathering was brought to an end in an unusual way, as Mrs Scott recalled: 'In due course we all four assembled and everything went well with the luncheon party until we had been talking together for quite a long time after we had finished eating. Gradually it dawned on me that one of us three should make the first move to leave the table. . . . So I tried to kick Jimmy [Burns] under the table. Judging by the way Professor Childe shot up like a jack-in-the-box, I obviously kicked him instead and so ended our luncheon party.' In later years, however, Gordon Childe was to remark sadly to a postgraduate student at the Institute that during the whole of his 19 years at Edinburgh, not once had he been invited by a student to cross his threshold. Margaret Crichton Mitchell later explained:

It was the intellectual power and the breadth of his knowledge that created a barrier none of his students (whom I knew) ever really overcame. I don't think he himself was conscious of what kept him apart and I think there were occasions when he rather clumsily and pathetically tried to communicate on our level—but never with much success.

Childe's first lodgings at Edinburgh, at Liberton, were admirably situated near the Braid Hills for the walks he so enjoyed; and perhaps their distance from his department in Chambers Street was a good excuse for him to buy his first car, an Austin 7. He wrote to Mary Alice Evatt in 1931: 'I love driving (when I'm the chauffeur) passionately; one has such a feeling of power.' The story is that it was after overturning this car that he procured a large and powerful American tourer, which he drove equally badly, though he seems to have had a charmed life. He was enormously proud of his cars and would happily give lifts to colleagues and students foolhardy enough to accept the offer. Quite a bit of ingenuity was exercised persuading Childe to let someone else do the driving on such occasions. One of his own favourite stories, joyfully told, was about the time he drove down Piccadilly at high speed at three o'clock in the morning in his vast car, all by himself and just for the fun of it; and on at least one occasion, when a policeman approached to tackle the erring driver of his speeding car near Regent's Park, Childe relied on the charm of his female passenger to extricate him from the situation.

Apart from his walks on the hills, his visits to classical concerts and his bridge-playing, Childe spent most of his spare time at Edinburgh at work in his rooms. He lived for many years in the appropriately-named Hotel de Vere in Eglinton Crescent, a comfortable semi-residential hotel. His rooms were rather functional, for he had not the gift of creating a home, and in any case his large and spacious New Town drawing room had a complete mixture of furniture and looked well-suited to a bachelor academic. Although he was brought up in a family where his sister Alice at least was extremely fond of literature, Gordon Childe was not a great novel-reader. He did very much enjoy D. H. Lawrence's *Kangaroo*, first published in 1923, which reflected his own feelings about Australia and Australian Labour politics in the early '20s: 'the profound Australian indifference, which still is not really apathy'.[12] Of Koestler's *Darkness at Noon* he wrote: 'though definitely anti-Soviet propaganda [it] does give a psychologically intelligible account of how the confession might have been obtained and what the outlook of a convinced totalitarian Party member may be . . .'.[13] He was very fond of poetry, and Wheeler paid tribute after his death to a scholar who could declaim a Pinder ode in the original language. Childe liked the poetry of Keats particularly, though he said that his two favourite poems were Wordsworth's 'Ode to Duty' and Browning's 'A Grammarian's Funeral'. Stuart Piggott has pointed out that Childe was as 'soul-hydroptic' or as dedicated to archaeology as the Grammarian was to his branch of learning.

During Childe's tenureship of the Abercromby Chair he was only obliged to lecture in the first two terms, and could spend almost six months of the year (apart from his weeks of excavation) elsewhere. Often he was abroad, but he also spent a great deal of time in London, using the libraries and keeping in touch with old friends.

73

Sometimes he stayed in a flat in Moscow Mansions (again, chosen for its name); but frequently he would sub-let the flat of a friend abroad—Daryll Forde, or, on one occasion, the zoologist, Solly Zuckerman, to whom he had been introduced by the anatomist Elliott Smith. Zuckerman later wrote that when he returned to his flat in Ormonde Terrace in 1934 after a trip to the USA, he 'was amazed to discover from the empty bottles that Gordon Childe seemed to drink only Madeira wine—or was it Marsala? He appeared to have done all his reading and writing in an armchair, and I never did understand how he assembled the vast store of information for the books which he wrote.'[14]

Other friends Childe enjoyed meeting in London were Stuart Piggott and his archaeologist wife, now Margaret Guido. Piggott, who later succeeded him to the Abercromby Chair, was almost 20 years Childe's junior but the two shared a great dedication to prehistoric archaeology and the friendship flourished until Childe's death in 1957. In 1929 Piggott was appointed to the Royal Commission on Ancient Monuments (Wales), and in 1934 Assistant Director of excavations at Avebury, Wiltshire; his work on the Neolithic of Britain earned him immediate recognition as an outstanding young archaeologist. Never an insular prehistorian, he took advantage of his leisure hours when posted to India in the second world war, studied the Chalcolithic or Copper Age material, and presented his analysis in *Prehistoric India* in 1950.

Another way in which Gordon Childe kept in contact with other intellectuals of the day was by becoming an early member of the informal dining club, known as the Tots and Quots, founded by Solly Zuckerman. In the years between the wars the members of the club included many up and coming young scientists who later achieved fame: Joseph Needham, J. B. S. Haldane, J. G. Crowther, J. D. Bernal and Hyman Levy, the mathematician and one of the founders of the Association of Scientific Workers. The group of young men were serious in intent and particularly concerned with the question of the role of science in society. Zuckerman later recalled the club's founding and atmosphere:

Our opening 'meet' took place in 1931 at a now defunct, but then well-known Victorian restaurant, Pagani's, in Great Portland Street. We then dined at more or less monthly intervals in a private room in whatever Soho restaurant I chose. As convenor, it was not only my responsibility to decide the menu, but also to agree the topic on which our after-dinner discussion would focus, and to arrange for the opening speaker. But the club did not run in the way that some had expected. Gip Wells resigned after our first dinner, saying that he had hoped the whole thing would be fun, whereas we were obviously going to become monastic and deadly serious. We may not have been monastic, but we certainly were serious.

The notes that survive from that first discussion merely say that the number of members was to be limited to twenty, that fourteen had already been nominated, that further elections had to be by unanimous vote, and the objects of the club would emerge from discussions to which people of different interests would contribute. The question of a name was raised, but not decided until the next dinner when, after a number of conflicting suggestions, Jack Haldane remarked, 'quot homines, tot sententiae'. Lancelot Hogben, who had recently returned from South Africa, then said 'the quottentots', a play on the word Hottentots, that tribe of primitive South Africans of whom he may just have encountered one or two survivors before all became extinct. And so we became, first, Quottentots, and then finally The Tots and Quots. . . .

The experience of the first year or two of the Tots and Quots showed all too well that the name by which the club had come to be known was more than appropriate. Every discussion provoked a clash of opinion, and the greater the measure of disagreement, the more stimulating the meeting. Our talks roamed over wider and wider issues, but more and more what we debated was the question of the general significance of science to society, and the conscious role science might play in social development.[15]

Gordon Childe was always deeply concerned with the international exchange of scholarship, and his own trips abroad were frequent during his Edinburgh days. He attended congresses all over Europe, and took advantage of his travels to establish contact with scholars in museums and universities. In the late '20s J. L. Myres and other prominent scholars of many countries were engaged in a project to found an international congress of prehistorians. Childe was much interested in and involved with this work, and joined Myres in Switzerland at a preliminary gathering to launch the scheme. The first International Congress of Prehistoric and Protohistoric Sciences was held in London in 1932, and the second in Oslo in 1936. Childe was a regular attender, and was very disappointed when the third congress, scheduled for Budapest in 1940, had to be postponed because of the war.

He soon became a well-known and well-loved figure at such meetings, remarkable equally for his eccentricities and his wide scholarship. His appearance was strange enough to excite comment wherever he went, for his clothes served to accentuate his already odd looks. He always wore a large black wide-brimmed hat, reminiscent of Australian sheep-farmers and commonly supposed to have been acquired in some outlandish East European country; though in fact it was purchased from a highly respectable Jermyn Street hatter. His shirt or tie was as often as not red, to emphasize his Left-wing views, and clashed violently with his bright pink nose and rather carrotty hair. In summer he frequently wore very short shorts, with socks, sock suspenders and great heavy boots. Extremely characteristic of the man was his shiny black mackintosh, carried over his arm or flung carelessly over his shoulders like a cape. Childe was undoubtedly well aware of the sensation his appearance could cause, and on occasions enjoyed the discomfiture of the Establishment at his inappropriate dress.

He was extremely proud of his knowledge of languages, and took every opportunity of showing off his supposed skills. The problem was that although his reading knowledge of several languages was adequate, his spoken renderings were usually unintelligible. He spoke them all in his own individual accent, with no concessions to the correct pronunciation, rather on the Churchill principle. At Oslo for the second International Congress in 1936 this caused some amusement to his companions. One hot day about a dozen of the delegates, including Childe, decided to miss the afternoon lectures and go and sample the local raspberries and cream which were then in season. The group seated themselves at a restaurant, and the waiter approached. 'I'm beginning to master Norwegian,' declared Childe. 'I know the word for raspberries.' The assembled prehistorians looked apprehensively at one another; Childe summoned the waiter: 'Bringebaer.' The waiter went off, and re-appeared with twelve glasses of lager. Obviously the Norwegian word bringebaer meaning 'raspberry' had been taken for the English 'bring a beer'. A lesser man might have realized that his Norwegian lacked fluency, but Childe, nothing daunted, repeated loudly, 'Bringebaer!' Now 24 glasses resided on the tables. Then one of the party turned to the waiter and said: 'What we want are raspberries.' 'Oh,' said the waiter in faultless English, 'I'm so sorry. I'll go and fetch some.'

In 1935 Childe paid his first visit to the USSR, and came back with a renewed interest in the future of communism and the role of archaeology in a communist society. He spent 12 days in Leningrad and Moscow attending a Persian Arts Congress, accompanying two

great friends, David Talbot-Rice, Professor of Fine Arts at Edinburgh, and his Russian-born wife, Tamara. Childe was the first to
admit that he had little appreciation of the visual arts; and his main
interest on this trip was to become acquainted with Russian archaeologists and visit their museums. He was very impressed by the
central organization of museums and excavations made possible in
the communist state. He often gave the impression of having a blind
spot for Soviet Russia. Undoubtedly he had a rosy view of communism in its early years, in common with many others; and he was
indignant if political prejudice blinded fellow-archaeologists to the
positive aspects of archaeology in the USSR. However he was not
unaware of the possible dangers of life in the Soviet Union, and
before leaving for a visit to the USSR in 1953 he left everything in
order on his desk in case, as he said, 'he should decide to remain in
the Soviet Paradise'. Knowing that praise of communism annoyed
some colleagues, he was never averse to playing up to his reputation
as the 'Red Professor', but in private his views could be more
critical. He was horrified at the Stalin–Hitler pact, and he was to
write in the early years of the second world war that he had become
definitely anti-totalitarian.

Many colleagues and students did not know quite how seriously to
take Childe's beliefs, for there were undoubtedly occasions when he
consciously exploited his Marxism to tease people. In 1933 the
communist *Daily Worker* was founded, and Childe made sure
everyone knew he read the paper. A typical story is told by Stuart
Piggott: 'Once, as I went into his room at the Institute of Archaeology with him, he said, looking at his disordered desk and grinning
delightedly, "My *Daily Worker* isn't conspicuous enough!" and then
rummaged among his papers until it was found, and prominently
displayed for the next visitor.'[16]

He certainly enjoyed the comforts of good living, and once
remarked disarmingly to an Edinburgh student that his politics
became bluer as his income rose. However his conscious emphasis
on the fact that he was a 'Red' acted as a form of protection for his
deeply-held beliefs. Conservative colleagues could accept him more
readily if they could laugh off his 'Communist' tendencies. It is
significant that while he made much of his red ties and *Daily Worker*,
he left his colleagues unaware of his actual contributions to Left-
wing periodicals and societies. As far as many were concerned, his

Marxism went no further than a love of Russia and the occasional mention of 'communist societies' in an archaeological lecture.

Childe was always keen that education should be available to anyone who wanted it; this lay behind his support for the Workers Educational Association, and his firm belief that the Iron Curtain should not be a barrier to the international exchange of knowledge. Part of his enthusiasm for Soviet-organized archaeology was that it encouraged the immediate publication and central indexing of excavation reports and new material. It is not surprising then that he was a staunch supporter of *Antiquity*, the periodical founded in 1927 by his Left-wing friend, O. G. S. Crawford. The periodical filled a need in the steadily expanding study of prehistory not catered for by the old-fashioned *Antiquaries Journal* and others. Childe told Crawford that as well as providing prehistorians with material and ideas on the latest archaeological data, *Antiquity* had great value in democratizing archaeology.

In January 1937 Gordon Childe's uncle, Canon Christopher Venn Childe, died at the age of 90. Gordon had visited his uncle occasionally since 1914 and whilst the two men no doubt held widely differing views on some subjects, Canon Childe admired his nephew's learning and used to say that his political views were not exactly red, but certainly a very dark shade of pink. His father, Stephen Childe, had died in Australia almost ten years before, and Gordon Childe's links with his upbringing and ancestry were finally broken. He had long been a rationalist and atheist, though not a polemical one, and this may well have contributed to his refusal to visit his Australian relations until near the end of his life. He had few good words to say about religion in his archaeological writings, and tended to regard it as a brake on man's progress in controlling his external environment. In *History* (1947) he compared magic with religion: 'Magic is a way of making people believe they are going to get what they want, whereas religion is a system for persuading them that they ought to want what they get.'[17]

But he was a man who needed a faith of some kind, and he sought it in the philosophies of Hegel and Marx. Although he is usually described as a 'Marxist', his beliefs were never dogmatic, always idiosyncratic, and were continually changing throughout his life. When assessing the influence of Marxism on his thought, it is important firstly to distinguish between Marxism as a system of thought, and Marxism as it is too often popularly understood, as solely the experiment in communism in the Soviet Union. Secondly, the label 'Marxist' tends to be misleading as there is no homogeneous doctrine to which every 'Marxist' adheres. Gordon Childe's Marxism frequently differed from contemporary 'orthodox' Marxism; partly because he had studied Hegel, Marx and Engels as far back as 1913 and still referred to the original texts rather than later interpretations, and partly because he was selective in his acceptance of their writings. It is doubtful too whether a strict Marxist would have agreed that Childe's spell as political secretaries in Australia and England and his later attendance at the meetings of politically motivated groups would really have satisfied Marx's demands for the unity of theory and practice.

Marxist views on a model of the past were largely accepted by Childe, offering as they do a structural analysis of culture in terms of economy, sociology and ideology, and a principle for cultural change through changes in economy. Unlike either extreme Marxists or extreme diffusionists, he was willing to allow that both internal development and external contact effected change. Only once, in 1949, did he set out an explicit statement of his views on the value of Marxism to the study of prehistory. This was in the form of a rejoinder to a paper by Glyn Daniel published in the short-lived *The Cambridge Journal*; Childe's article was published for the first time 30 years later, and is worth quoting in full.

In his masterly 'defence of prehistory' Dr. Daniel names me as an exponent of Marxist prehistory but does not explain what the latter is beyond indicating that the adjective is to be understood as a pejorative. But your readers might be interested to know. The Marxist view of history and prehistory is admittedly material determinist and materialist. But its determinism does not mean mechanism. The Marxist account is in fact termed 'dialectical materialism.' It is deterministic in as much as it assumes that the historical process is not a mere succession of inexplicable or miraculous happenings, but that all the constituent events are interrelated and form an intelligible pattern. But the relations are not conceived mechanistically. The process is not repetitive or predetermined as are the operations of a machine which however complicated grinds out just that which it was built to make and nothing else. It produces a pattern none the less and its uncompleted portions must harmonize with what is already there though there may be various combinations to complete the pattern.

It is the business of historical science to discover the pattern, to find out by observation of what has been done or happened, the general principles relating the events. For Marxists regard history as a science—at least potentially. Since scientific knowledge is practical knowledge—a view shared also by idealists such as Benedetto Croce—these principles must furnish rules for action. But note that 'action' includes the acquisition of fresh knowledge. To this extent Dr. Grahame Clark's excavations at Flixton last summer prove that prehistory can legitimately claim to be a science. Parts at least of the pattern of European prehistory are now sufficiently plain to allow of reasonable prediction as to what sort of relics should be found in what sort of place in certain periods. Clark's excavations justified such a prediction, but at the same time of course substantially enriched our knowledge of the pattern.

Marxist history is materialistic in that it takes a material, biological fact as the first clue to discovering the general pattern underlying an apparent chaos of superficially unrelated events. It starts from the obvious truth that men cannot live without eating. So a society cannot exist unless its members can secure enough food to keep alive and reproduce. If any society approved beliefs or institutions that cut off the food-supply altogether (if for instance all Egyptian peasants had felt obliged to work all the year round building a superpyramid) or stopped reproduction (as an universal and fanatical conviction of the virtue of celibacy might do), the society in question would soon come to an end. In this limiting case it is quite obvious that the food supply must exercise a final control in determining even beliefs and ideals. Presumably then methods of getting a living in the end exercise a similar control more concretely. The way people get their living should be expected in the long run to 'determine' their beliefs and institutions.

But the way people get their living in turn is determined on the one hand by the environment—natural resources, climate, and so on—on the other by science and technology—the knowledge that society can apply in the exploitation of that environment. But human exploitation of any environment necessarily involves co-operation. This is always organized. It is always stimulated by symbols and beliefs that reinforce or entirely replace the supposedly innate urges to feed one's self and rear a family. For after all even in very simple societies the relation between the work you must do today (for instance clearing your corn-plot) and the food you are going to eat is often quite remote. Marxists have been at pains to show that in any given environment with a given equipment of tools and knowledge one form of organization secures the smoothest and most efficient exploitation while any other is likely to impede production or may even paralyse it. And in general just one *kind* of ideology—institutions, beliefs and ideals—will keep that organization functioning most smoothly.

Dialectical materialism thus differs radically from environmentalism or geographical determinism such as that expounded by Buckle. It is not the individual human animal that has to be 'adjusted to his environment' in order to 'survive' as each rabbit or each rat must be. It is his society that must be adjusted, and the adjustment is precisely what anthropologists since Tylor have called culture. But the individual himself is determined by his society's culture; from his society he learns how to talk, how to get his food and what to eat, how to use—and, in simpler societies, to make—his tools, in a word how to live humanly. No doubt society is made up of individuals; if all its members perish, so will the society. It is just as true that there can be no human individual apart from society, and the culture society sustains. And in the long run this culture must satisfy society's needs—above all its members' needs for food—by exploitation of the environment.

Now in abstract theory the environment may have remained stable. Even then knowledge has been accumulated and the techniques of production have been improved. Of course, these have really changed the environment too. Archaeology shows that unambiguously even if old-fashioned politico-military-ecclesiastical history books ignore it. Social organization in turn must be adjusted to each advance, and the reorganization must be supported and sanctified by appropriate innovations in institutional behaviour and beliefs. In practice, of course matters are extremely complicated. The relations between productive equipment, the organization requisite for operating it and distributing the product (the economy), and the legal, religious and artistic institutions and ideals that inspire it are not one-sided, but dialectical like the relation between society and its members.

These complications are least obtrusive in the case of the simpler societies with the poorer technical equipment. It is precisely with the cultures of such societies that prehistoric archaeology deals. Naturally dialectical materialism with its emphasis on society rather than the individual, whom, as Daniel has remarked, archaeology alone can hardly reach, and on productive equipment, which bulks so largely in the archaeological record, is an instrument peculiarly fitted to convert assemblages of monuments and relics into historical data.

Now as early as the 18th century historians, having now to take account of preliterate peoples in the New World, envisaged an hierarchic classification of peoples as representing 'savagery', 'barbarism' and 'civilization' respectively. In the nineteenth century ethnographers applied these terms to successive stages in an hypothetical evolutionary process which they deduced from comparative studies much as Lamarck deduced an evolutionary series of zoological species from a comparative study of existing organisms. They lacked the evidence, that only archaeology could provide, to convert their logical series into temporal series, just as Lamarck lacked the palaeontological evidence required to justify his treatment of the hierarchic order of species as representing an historical process. Even the pioneer attempt of Engels to utilize archaeological data in support of Morgan's scheme admittedly needs modification and correction in the light of richer and more accurate evidence, both archaeological and ethnographic.

Today archaeology can show that the logical series—savagery, barbarism and civilization—corresponds to a temporal succession provided the criteria be made the ways in which the societies classified got a living. In fact at first, throughout the Old Stone Age, all societies lived entirely by collecting or catching the wild food nature offered. Then in the New Stone Age some societies began producing food by cultivating edible plants or breeding animals for food or combining both activities, but still without regular division of labour and without dependence on 'foreign' trade for any necessities of life. Finally a few farming communities began producing a surplus of food large enough to support full time specialists who engaged in secondary industry, in trade or in organizing social co-operation; such did not contribute directly to the food-supply, but their activities should indirectly augment it by providing primary producers with better equipment, more efficient techniques or perhaps merely more potent stimuli to labour.

Marxists frankly expect that existing simpler societies, classified on the same criteria, will illustrate, though only in a general way, the sort of institutions, beliefs and aesthetic ideals attributable to corresponding prehistoric groups. But now they have realized that the application of these principles is harder than it sounds. (Russian archaeologists, mostly recent converts to Marxism, tried in the early thirties to apply Engels' scheme bodily to local prehistory, but most had recognized by 1940 that that would not work.)

The foregoing definitions of barbarism, savagery and civilisation are very abstract. Closer scrutiny of the ethnographic and the archaeological records reveals that the blanket terms 'wild food economy', 'subsistence farming' cover a wide range of significant varieties in productive activities. It is indeed easy enough to classify an archaeological 'culture' or a contemporary tribe under one head or the other. It is not nearly so easy to decide from the surviving evidence, for example, to which contemporary hunting group any particular palaeolithic culture corresponds even economically. No Old Stone Age group in Europe had to contend with or profit by an environment like the Australians who had no larger beasts than marsupials to hunt or to escape. But these environmental differences would impose also differences in hunting weapons, in organization for the chase and so, *ex hypothesi*, in social structure and 'ideology'.

At present then prehistorians who use Marxist methods of interpretation are likely to be more cautious in drawing concrete conclusions from comparisons between our preliterate ancestors and modern savages or barbarians than non-Marxist writers who on the strength of similarities in equipment alone have been known to treat the Esquimaux as representatives of the Magdalenians. No doubt more detailed knowledge of the economy of prehistoric communities, combined with a full understanding of relevant societies today will yield more precise but yet reliable results. A Marxist prehistorian will aim at deducing from the assemblage he calls a culture a detailed picture of a working economic organization that can be compared point for point with existing preliterate societies.

Just as keenly will he scrutinize the record for the evanescent traces of magical or religious practices, of ear-chiefs or divine kings, if only to check any deductions he may be tempted to draw from a comparison between the fossilized fragments of an extinct culture and the living whole observable today in New Guinea or Patagonia. In so doing he will at least come nearer to writing prehistory than those who regard prehistory as a record of migrations to be traced by similarities in the forms of tombs, flint arrow-heads or clay stone vases.

The Russians have dubbed such 'relicologists' because they are generally so preoccupied with the forms of relics that they forget that the relics were made by men to satisfy some human need—like a certain Nazi who devoted many pages to the classification of 'axes' (Beile) by shape and section without ever asking himself what they were used for—half of them were actually adze-blades, that could never have served as axe-heads. At the same time no Marxist would deny the importance of diffusion, whether by migration or otherwise, as an agent of cultural change, and it is precisely change that Marxists wish to observe. So as arbitrary similarities in form may provide a reliable indication of intercourse, of opportunity for diffusion, there is no danger of formal differences being ignored. Moreover, even in the domain of 'material culture', diffusion always means the transmission of ideas; the transportation of millstones without the knowledge how to make and use them will not constitute the 'diffusion' of the rotary quern. So prehistory may after all in a Marxist sense be the history of thought that Collingwood said all history must be.[18]

Gordon Childe's philosophical views on the nature of reality and the historical process coincided closely with those of Marx. Firstly he denied that there was any source of reality outside the historical process, and so he, like Marx, adhered to the materialist philosophical tradition. Secondly he emphasized the changeable nature of reality, and this was an important factor which caused him to adopt the materialist or realist conception of history. However he deviated from Marxism in that he did not always employ dialectical laws to explain change and in that he gave little emphasis to the role of class in the historical process. In the USSR these were particularly significant issues; Soviet scholars raised the laws of the dialectic above the historical process, causing them to represent eternal laws immune to change. But an important tenet of Childe's philosophy was that there was no transcendence of *any* kind, religious or non-religious.

Peggy Burkitt, wife of the Cambridge prehistorian Miles Burkitt, once asked Childe in the early '30s what his philosophy was. He replied, 'I suppose I count myself a Gentile-Crocian.' Giovanni Gentile (1875–1944) and Benedetto Croce (1866–1952) were Italian philosophers, students of Hegel and Marx, who became the leading exponents of the twentieth century idealist movement in Italy. Croce was a minister of education, though under Mussolini he was in retirement; it was mainly through his writings that the works of the philosopher Vico were re-studied. Croce's own works are obscure. His system of philosophy he described as the science of the mind or spirit. He rejected all forms of transcendentalism and substituted pure immanentism, with no objective world to be a standard of truth or eternal moral principle to be a norm for the will. He opined that history absorbs philosophy to become the only genuine form of knowledge. Gentile was associated with Croce for a decade, though he rejected the latter's distinction between theory and practice and argued that the essence of mind is the activity of becoming self conscious. Gentile later became minister of education under Mussolini and was eventually assassinated by anti-Fascists.

Childe too was an anti-transcendentalist: an article which he contributed to *The Rationalist Annual* in 1945 is, together with *History* (1947) and *Society and Knowledge* (1956), an important statement of his own philosophical ideas. Entitled 'Rational Order in History', the article examined theories of order in history, and admitted that historical order had limitations: the historian can only define tendencies, not uniformities. Man, as an agent in the historical process, has difficulty in seeing order in the incomplete pattern of history. But Childe always firmly rejected any form of transcendentalism or external laws:

Hegel's grand conception has been purged of its quite unnecessary trappings of supernaturalism and transcendentalism—on the one hand by the dialectical materialists; on the other by idealists like Croce and Gentile.[19]

Although his views on religion and politics were unorthodox for his day, he found certain aspects of the way of life of the Establishment irresistibly appealing. In 1937 he was elected a member of the Athenaeum Club in London, and soon became a well-known if eccentric visitor. He loved company, and frequently played bridge at the club or dined there. He was very fond of a bottle of good wine with his meal, regarding himself as something of a connoisseur, and he enjoyed a considerable amount of whisky too. Rumours of his consumption of a bottle of whisky a day were rife, but these were undoubtedly exaggerations, and no one (after his student escapades at Oxford) saw him the worse for drink. His love of high living, which seemed to many to conflict with his Socialist ideals, did little to improve Childe's standing with some of his colleagues. However there is no evidence that he regarded asceticism as an essential part of Marxism; perhaps he felt that equality in life belonged to the proletarian state and not to imperialist Britain. In any case, he made the most of his professorial salary, always travelled first class and stayed everywhere in the best hotels.

The second decade of Childe's tenure of the Edinburgh Chair of Archaeology was overshadowed by the threat of Hitler and the second world war. Childe's Socialist convictions were still strong and the abhorrence felt by many people for the ideals of Fascism was intensified in him. But his philosophical views were continually changing and during the years of the war it is clear that his belief in communism, as the experiment in the Soviet Union developed, was not unshakeable. He had always followed keenly political events throughout the world, and as the threat of Hitler's power in Germany increased during the 1930s he made his feelings about Fascism plain. He wrote in May 1933 to Mary Alice Evatt, describing his impressions of his recent visit to Berlin: 'Externally Hitlerite Germany looked rather cheerful and prosperous. One saw no Jews getting beaten up nor Communists in chains. The restaurants and the forests were thronged. The new museums are superb. But it really is a bad business. What is one to say of a nation which rejects Einstein, Reinhart and Walter! And to justify it with travesties of anthropology and history is worse still!'

Childe felt very strongly about the prostitution of prehistory for political purposes. His introductory lecture for his course at Edinburgh in 1933–34 was published in *Antiquity* as an article entitled 'Is Prehistory Practical?'. The lecture dealt with the question of the usefulness of archaeology, a subject to which he was to return throughout his career, and he pointed out:

In 1933 it can hardly be alleged that Prehistory is a useless study, wholly remote from and irrelevant to practical life. In one great country at least, interpretation of supposed facts of Prehistory, imperfectly apprehended by an untrained mind of undoubted genius, have revolutionized the whole structure of society. No one who has read *Mein Kampf*, or even the extracts therefrom in *The Times*, can fail to appreciate the profound effect which theories of the racial superiority of 'Aryans' have exercised on contemporary Germany. In the name of these theories men are being exiled from public life and shut up in concentration camps, books are being burned and expression of opinions stifled just as, in the name of religious ideas, they were during fifteen long centuries of darkness.[20]

As always, Childe disapproved of the nationalist study of prehistory, preferring the wider approach emphasized in his own work: 'Objectively studied Prehistory will rather emphasize how much more precious and vital is the growth of the common tradition that leads up to civilization than the idiosyncrasies and divagations of any separate groups, however brilliant.'[21]

He was concerned too when, in May 1936, he read an article in the *Edinburgh Evening News* entitled 'Are you an Aryan?'. It reported a conference which had been held preparatory to the first general congress of a new International Association for Ethnology, due to take place in Edinburgh the following year. The new association was heavily funded by the German Research Institute, and Childe expressed his disapproval in *Nature*:

In view of the connexion between ethnology and the political philosophy of the Third Reich, one wonders whether this generosity is entirely inspired by a disinterested desire to further international science or an attempt to secure 'that recognition in kindred countries that the Nordic peoples must feel themselves a *Schicksalgemeinschaft*' desired by Reichsminister für Innern, Dr. Frick . . .[22]

During the summer session of 1939 Gordon Childe was Visiting Professor at the University of California. Although he had visited the USA a number of times before, and had represented prehistoric archaeology at the Harvard Tercentenary Conference of Arts and Sciences in 1936, he had never displayed much interest in New World archaeology. Indeed he can be criticized for largely ignoring evidence from the Americas in his books, and if questioned about it he would reply in an offhanded manner, 'Never got round to reading about it.' Why he ignored such evidence is not clear, but it is a serious omission and lowers his standing as an objective scholar, for it suggests that he did not want to consider evidence which might disprove his hypotheses. He did not admire the American way of life, and used to refer to Americans in his lectures at the Institute as 'loathsome fascist hyenas'; though many individual Americans were his good friends. But whatever his personal feelings, the truth remains that he did virtually ignore any archaeological evidence outside Europe and the Near East, even though much of it had a bearing on the problems of the birth of civilization with which he was so concerned. The Maya and Inca civilizations, for example, were accepted by most prehistorians as independent occurrences of civilization, quite unconnected with those of the Near East. It is clear from the first chapter of *What Happened in History* that Childe considered the prehistory of the Americas to be outside the 'main stream' of human progress, with which he was chiefly concerned. He explained to Robert Braidwood, an American colleague who had tackled him on the subject:

As to my 'revolutions' I have always been conscious that the Mayas did not fit in. But in the Old World urbanization was bound up with metal, the trade it required and the new transport facilities that it indirectly made possible.[23]

The 'revolutions' to which Childe was referring were his 'Neolithic' and 'Urban' revolutions, which he postulated as separating man's progress into stages. From 1928 onwards these ideas can be traced in his work, which will be discussed in the next chapter, and they were eventually detailed in *Man Makes Himself* in 1936.

Childe sailed from Boston on 16 August 1939 and landed in England amid the crisis surrounding the outbreak of the second world war. His view of the coming months was gloomy, and he wrote to the Scottish prehistorian, Sir Lindsay Scott: 'That I can be of any use in the forthcoming catastrophe I don't now feel convinced and a retreat into rather than across the Atlantic seems most reasonable.' He was convinced that in this second war it was right to oppose the threat of Hitler's Fascism with force. He was also sure he would be on the Nazi blacklist and in the event of a successful invasion, said he intended to drown himself in the canal. O. G. S. Crawford wrote after Childe's death that 'by temperament he was inclined to pessimism but his fundamental goodness saved him from cynicism.'[24] This pessimism was naturally to the fore during the early years of the war, and he several times wrote to Crawford about the advisability of committing suicide.

One escape from the horrors of war was to submerge oneself in the past; and Gordon Childe not only produced a large number of books and papers during the years 1939–45, but also took over the jobs of archaeologists who joined the forces. There were additional duties too: during the war the Royal Commission on Historical Monuments had a policy of photographic and quick superficial surveys of buildings and field monuments thought to be in danger from bombing or from troops in training. Childe, as a Commissioner for Scotland, was extremely active on the prehistoric side of this scheme and made many expeditions in all weathers. His companion on several of these trips was Angus Graham, who had come to Edinburgh in 1935 on his appointment to the Secretaryship of the Royal Commission on Historical Monuments (Scotland). He later recalled: 'I carried away the greatest admiration for his massive learning and also for his astonishing capacity for withstanding physical fatigue—the more remarkable in a man of rather poor physique.'

The privations of wartime were not so much in evidence in the remoter Scottish islands and in 1941 Childe was happy to inspect ancient monuments in the Orkneys for the Ministry of Works. He wrote to his half-sister, Alice, from the Standing Stones Hotel, Kirkwall, on 16 July: 'I've just been spending ten days in these islands which at first I hated but have come to love dearly. The climate really is not nice but this time has been exceptionally calm and mild. The birds and flowers are wonderful. I never saw such splendid foxgloves even in England and there are wild roses and yellow iris blooming too while the scent of the clover is intoxicating. The people are particularly charming and I am very popular for my excavations at Skara Brae and the advertisement I've given them have brought many visitors to the islands. Rousay where I've been staying is perfectly peaceful and I have feasted on unstinted butter cream cheese eggs home made scones and oatcakes homebrewed ale strawberries honey and other now rare delights.'

He was also a staunch supporter of refugees from Hitler's régime; he and O. G. S. Crawford were of considerable help, both financial and otherwise, to Gerhard and Maria Bersu, German archaeologists who escaped from their country just before the war and were interned on the Isle of Man. They undertook some excavation work there, and Childe was appointed to report on their progress. Another task which fell to him, as the result of the enlistment of the Director, A. J. H. Edwards, was the running of the National Museum of Antiquities of Scotland in Edinburgh. He spent three days a week as Director of the museum, and was very pleased with the results of his work. He felt that his displays in the museum told a story of prehistory which 'needed no quotation from Stalin or Engels' to be understood by the general public. A. J. H. Edwards died in 1944 before he could resume his duties; an expert on the preservation of antiquities, he had been on the staff of the museum since 1912 and had succeeded J. G. Callender as Director only in 1938.

Childe was released from some of his lecturing duties during the war by the appointment of H. J. H. Drummond as part-time lecturer at Edinburgh in 1939. Drummond was originally appointed to lecture on the Palaeolithic and physical anthropology, and also to take over the entire lecture course if the professor was absent abroad during the teaching term. The war put paid to Childe's plans for travelling, but Drummond was retained to give the Palaeolithic course for most of the war, though after 1942 this was in addition to a job as library assistant at the University Library.

Gordon Childe was critical of the British Government's policies during these years. In October 1939 the *Daily Worker* printed a questionnaire on peace negotiations with answers by well-known Left-wing figures, including G. B. Shaw, H. G. Wells and J. B. S. Haldane. Childe made his distrust of Chamberlain clear; in answer to the question 'are you in favour of peace negotiations?' he replied: 'Only provided such do not offer another Münich victory to Hitlerism.' He felt that a peace settlement should be guaranteed 'by a revised and strengthened League of Nations, in the establishment of which the USSR, the Scandinavian democracies, Holland, Switzerland, etc., and, if possible, the USA, should take the lead.'[25] He also advocated the abolition of colonies, and their government by an international administration. However in 1938, at a packed meeting of the Cambridge Anti-War Group held in Trinity College to discuss science and war, he had expressed himself in favour of the British government's peace-at-any-price policy.

He had little optimism to spare for the Soviet Union either at the commencement of the war. Of the German–Soviet pact he wrote: 'No doubt Stalin's action will facilitate and accelerate the spread of Communism. But however much it may have been justified by Chamberlain's past policy it does not consolidate my wavering faith that that is the best hope for humanity . . .'[26] Though he continued to apply the materialist conception of history in his works, in the world of politics he was at this time convinced that the dogmas of Fascism and of Marxism–Leninism could be equal threats to humanity. History, he suggested to his friend O. G. S. Crawford, had been moving too fast: 'A tiny majority thinking we live rationally has provided the vast mass with equipment ill adapted to their epipalaeolithic mentality but has on the whole grievously (and I think culpably) failed to sell as Yanks would say a rational mode of life.'[27]

6. Publications during the Edinburgh Years

During Childe's 19 years as Abercromby Professor he published a large number of books and papers: not only works of erudition on the lines of *The Dawn of European Civilization* and *The Aryans*, but also books designed for the general public, which sold in enormous numbers and enhanced the popularity of the study of prehistory in many countries.

His early years at Edinburgh saw the completion of his vast work of synthesis begun in *The Dawn*, with the publication of *The Most Ancient East*, *The Danube in Prehistory*, and *The Bronze Age*. These works were of a kind quite new to archaeology and firmly established his reputation. In *The Most Ancient East* (1928) he assembled the data for Mesopotamian and Indian prehistory for his lecture course at Edinburgh. Fresh excavations and discoveries every year from the Near East and India produced a wealth of archaeological evidence, but no one had yet brought the data together and related it to a broader view of the history of civilization. The importance of the Ancient East to Childe's own research was as the cradle of civilization which spread to Europe:

. . . one thread is clearly discernible running through the dark and tangled tale of these prehistoric Europeans: the westward spread, adoption and transformation of the inventions of the Orient.[1]

However *The Most Ancient East* made no explicit reference to the problem of chronology, and this was an important factor which should have been considered; for without absolute dates for prehistoric Europe neither the priority of Oriental invention nor the diffusionist hypothesis could be fully accepted.

The Danube in Prehistory was published in 1929, although it had been substantially written before Childe went to Edinburgh. He had recognized when writing *The Dawn* that the Danube river formed a natural corridor between the Near East and Europe. The main theme of *The Danube* was its importance as a channel for the diffusion of traits of civilization in the Neolithic and later periods. Childe's unrivalled grasp of the latest archaeological evidence contributed to making *The Danube in Prehistory* another exceptional work of synthesis; the impressive number of museums he had visited, listed at the beginning of the book, testifies to his indefatigable research. It was important too for its suggested chronological scheme of six Danubian periods, based on pottery styles.

One of the main problems in prehistoric archaeology is that of chronology. Thomsen's Three-Age System was the first attempt to place artefacts from the prehistoric past into some sequential order; before that, antiquarians had realized such artefacts were 'old' or even 'very old' but had not been able to say which were older than others. Once some system had been devised for arranging the artefacts in a relative chronological order, the next question to be answered was 'how old?'. Nowadays modern scientific dating techniques, such as radiocarbon dating, enable archaeologists to answer that question with a high degree of precision in many cases. Before such techniques were developed, cross-dating was the method most frequently employed by prehistorians attempting to produce a chronology; absolute dating was only possible by tying in relative chronologies to historical records. Before and during Childe's day two cultural groups were proved to be contemporary by the discovery of links between them. Childe himself made a great contribution to the study of prehistory by his exhaustive work on the chronology of Europe by cross-dating. The six Danubian periods suggested in his *The Danube in Prehistory* provided a relative chronology. The cross-dating method gave rise to one of his standard jokes—whether in a given week he was favouring a 'long' or a 'short' chronology for the European Neolithic and Bronze Age. The chronology, lacking as it did absolute dates, could be expanded or contracted like a bellows to accommodate longer or shorter time spans for the various cultures, still in the same relative order. The 'short' chronology was preferred by the Orientalists, and the 'long' chronology by the Occidentalists; though both were based on theories which assumed in advance (different) directions of culture flow between Europe and the East.

The preface to *The Danube* was in some ways as important as the main text. Here Childe made explicit some of the concepts which he (and following his lead, most British prehistorians) used in the interpretation of prehistoric data: associations, synchronisms, chronologies, and, most famous of all, the often-quoted definition of a culture:

We find certain types of remains—pots, implements, ornaments, burial rites, house forms—constantly recurring together. Such a complex of regularly associated traits we shall term a 'cultural group' or just a 'culture'. We assume that such a complex is the material expression of what today would be called a people.[2]

This definition was an original one, and was the first formulation in the English language of a concept expressed in earlier German anthropological literature as 'Kulturen sind Völker'. Such concepts are commonplace to the archaeologists of today, but in 1929 they were quite revolutionary. When Childe began his archaeological career it was usual for a pottery to be equated with a people; during the five years 1925 to 1930 he used an increasingly economic interpretation of the data. This was in line, of course, with Marxist theories; and to some extent, as Childe pointed out, most prehistorians are inclined to such a basis if only because they deal with the material remains of man's past. In *The Bronze Age* (1930) he believed he had reached a stage where the nomenclature of the Three-Age System had economic significance:

. . . each chapter heading in the archaeological record . . . became informative. If the criterion for inclusion be the *regular* use of bronze or even copper for the principal tools and weapons, that implies *regular* trade and social division of labour.[3]

Central to Childe's interpretation was his belief that metal was the first indispensable article of commerce, and he also assumed that metal-smiths were professionals who lived off the social surplus: 'The art of the smith was so complicated that prolonged apprenticeship was required. His labour was so long and exacting that it could not be performed just in odd moments of leisure; it was essentially a full-time job.'[4] This assumption was based mainly on ethnographic evidence, and so the sociological implications of the term 'Bronze Age' were less certain than its economic significance.

In the Easter vacation of 1933 Childe travelled to the Near East and India to examine at first hand the recent excavations and wealth of new discoveries which had been rapidly changing the face of prehistory in those regions. He wrote to Mary Alice Evatt soon after his return, giving his impressions of the countries he had visited:

Iraq was great fun. Besides the thrilling archaeological remains (you can climb down a shaft 60 feet deep cut through entirely prehistoric refuse to the floor of the former Persian Gulf at the biblical Erech) the land and people were pleasant—in the winter. It is intensely cold but generally sunny. You can drive anywhere (if it doesn't rain) across the desert whose flat surface is interrupted only by the banks of ancient canals or the ruins of ancient cities. The trains and hotels are bearable and fairly efficient. The English seem genuinely popular. Guards, station-masters and policemen and postmen all chatter English among themselves. It's rather comic to listen to them as you sit in the stationmaster's room at Ur Junction or Khidr. . . .

India I found detestable. It was beastly hot. You have to have a servant to carry your bedding round with you. The country is monstrously overpopulated and just swarming with miserably poor people. Among them squat the sahibs a narrow self-contained community with their golf courses and evening dress every night. They have all the defects of small isolated communities. There are no normal friendly relations with the intelligent Indians (if any). No encouragement is given to these to take responsibility. Partly as a consequence when they do get into responsible positions they are helpless and generally corrupt too. I can't see what is to happen. But the ruins were most exciting and worth the trouble.

As a result of the new discoveries *The Most Ancient East* of 1928 was completely outdated and in 1934 Childe published *New Light on the Most Ancient East*, which elaborated and consolidated his economic interpretation. In this book he first mentioned his idea of two great revolutions in human culture in prehistoric times: the change from a food-gathering to a food-producing economy, and the establishment of urban civilization based on industry and commerce. During his visit to the Near East he had seen, at Erech and Ur, how villages had grown into large townships just as English villages grew into towns as a result of the Industrial Revolution. He thought that the term 'revolution' was justified, for both changes would show up demographically in the same way in the archaeological record. This numerical criterion for the 'success' of a species he borrowed from Darwinist theory.

In 1934–5 Gordon Childe was involved in the conversion of the moribund Prehistoric Society of East Anglia into the national

Prehistoric Society. He, Stuart Piggott and the Cambridge scholar Grahame Clark got themselves onto the committee of the East Anglian Society, called a meeting at an unpopular time, and so pushed through a majority vote; Childe greatly enjoying these somewhat dubious proceedings. He was then elected President in February 1935, and gave a spirited Presidential Address entitled 'Changing Methods and Aims in Prehistory'. This important article contained the germs of several ideas which he elaborated in later books and papers. It stressed particularly the need for a systematic and significant classification as the first step towards the scientific study of prehistory. The traditional classification of Palaeolithic, Neolithic, Bronze Age and Iron Age, suggested Childe, could indicate vital stages in human progress; 'real revolutions that affected all departments of human life.'[5] He made an important contribution to archaeological thought by attempting to imbue the traditional classification of artefacts with economic significance. He wrote:

Provisionally then I would suggest that the terms palaeolithic, neolithic, etc., should be regarded as indicative of economic stages. In adopting as one method a classification by economic stages, archaeology would not be abandoning that historical character which I claimed the concept of culture gave it. We shall continue to distinguish cultures and to assign each its proper place in a framework of absolute chronology. Only then shall we consider the economic stage to which a culture should be assigned on the 'functional-economic' classification. The latter step constitutes a comparison between the material equipment, economic organization and scientific knowledge of one prehistoric people with those of others.[6]

Childe was unusual among archaeologists in that he was profoundly conscious of the theoretical basis of his thought. He adhered to Marxism as the best means of providing a framework for the study of prehistory, and after his first visit to the USSR in 1935 he gradually introduced more Marxist terms and theories into his interpretation of archaeological data. He first adopted the use of the Marxist terms 'savagery', 'barbarism' and 'civilization', which had originally been formulated by the nineteenth century anthropologist, L. H. Morgan. The Neolithic and Urban revolutions which Childe had mentioned in *New Light on the Most Ancient East*, and then in his Prehistoric Society address, separated these stages. In 1935 he clarified his conception of these revolutions and published the results in a book written not just for archaeologists but for the general public.

Man Makes Himself appeared in the Rationalist Press Association's Library of Science and Culture in 1936, and was described by O. G. S. Crawford in his *Antiquity* review as 'the most stimulating, original and convincing contribution to the history of civilization which we have ever read.'[7] *Man Makes Himself* suggested to its readers that the dichotomy usually set up between prehistory and history as conventionally understood was a false and indeed misleading one: '. . . to distinguish and unpick the thread of progress, if such there be, running through history requires a view of history very different from that set out in the formal text-books in my school-days. In the first place, a long and wide view is essential.'[8]

Viewed from a long perspective history is a documented record of man's increasing control over the non-human environment. *Man Makes Himself* aimed to make clear that this process, though discontinuous, is nevertheless progressive: 'One purpose of this book is to suggest that, viewed from an impersonal scientific standpoint, history may still justify a belief in progress in days of depression as well as in the heyday of last century's prosperity.'[9] Man's progress can be attested scientifically even before the invention of writing by the archaeological evidence for the revolutions:

They manifest themselves in the same way as the 'Industrial Revolution'—in an upward kink in the population curve. They must be judged by the same standard. . . . It is hoped that a consideration of revolutions, so remote that it is impossible to get angry or enthusiastic about them, may help to vindicate the idea of progress against sentimentalists and mystics.[10]

Up till now Childe's works had concentrated mainly on man's progress in prehistoric Europe, but in *Man Makes Himself* he explored the decline in the Orient, and concluded that the class structure, a result of the accumulation of surplus necessary for the inception of urbanism, was not conducive to further growth. Its main detrimental effect, he suggested, was the separation of theoretical from practical knowledge: 'The urban revolution, made possible by science, was exploited by superstition. The principle beneficiaries from the achievements of farmers and artizans were priests and kings. Magic rather than science was thereby enthroned and invested with the authority of temporal power.'[11]

His belief in the Materialist Conception of History, together with the inevitable bias of the archaeological record, led him to stress the economy of societies, and led in *Man Makes Himself* to a degree of technological determinism. In his autobiographical review, 'Retrospect', Childe explained that he thought *Man Makes Himself* fell short of Marxism 'in so far as it failed to emphasize that and how science can only be applied, means of production only operated, within an institutional framework that is itself not entirely economic.'[12]

Marx had said that history was determined not only by the 'means of production' but also by the 'social relations of production'; amongst the determinants of these were external stimuli such as migration or diffusion. Childe did not stress these stimuli in *Man Makes Himself*, and man's progress appeared autonomous. But he felt he had come closer to Marxism in the third edition of *The Dawn* (1939), where he made more of the role of external stimuli. Changes in the environment, internal economic progress and external stimuli, when joined together, acted as determinants of man's progress, making the process not only scientific, but also historical.

Diffusionism still played a large part in the third edition of *The Dawn of European Civilization*, and Childe emphasized 'cultural zoning' as the best possible demonstration of diffusion. In 1936 he had explained: 'To me diffusion means essentially the pooling of ideas, building up from many sides the cultural capital of humanity.'[13] He also used zoning to demonstrate that while both the 'short' and 'long' chronologies were possible in Bronze Age Europe—a chronology with a date for the Aunjetitz culture varying by as much as a thousand years could be established—for earlier periods the 'long' chronology no longer held good. This ingenious proof, however, was by no means conclusive, as it had no scientific basis. He had made the same points in his 1938 Presidential Address to Section H of the British Association for the Advancement of Science at Cambridge: 'As we pass northwestward from the Orient we descend through regular gradations from the many-sided richness of urban civilisation to the stark poverty and immediate dependence on external nature of food-gathering hordes.'[14] This is little removed from regarding the Neolithic cultures of Europe as pale imitations of the Orient, and in 'Retrospect' Childe explained that at this time

Embittered hostility to and fear of the archaeological buttresses of Hitlerism enhanced my reluctance to recognize the positive aspects of all European barbarisms.[15]

In more normal times his sense of reality led him to oppose the excesses of hyper-diffusion. Alfred Jenkin, an archivist and for many years treasurer of the British Communist Party History Group, recalled that around 1935 Gordon Childe gave a lecture to the Cambridge University Archaeological Field Club

in which he called attention to the fact that in Melbourne it was still considered correct to wear a top hat of a type which had become unfashionable in England, but that the richer citizens rode in American cars of a model which had not yet penetrated the British market. If civilization had been destroyed that night the archaeologists of the future might deduce that top hats and motor cars had been invented in Australia but that only top hats had been diffused to England and only cars to North America. Minns, a good archaeologist but conservative in his views, commented during the discussion, 'It seems that the Nazis believe in diffusionism but the Bolshies don't!'

The cessation of field work and trips abroad caused by the outbreak of the second world war, together with the lack of students, provided Gordon Childe with an opportunity to assess the results of the past decades of archaeological studies in Britain, and to publish, in 1940, a synthesis in *Prehistoric Communities of the British Isles*. His pessimistic view of the outcome of the war was one of his reasons for writing the book: he planned to synthesize the available material before libraries and museums perished in the flames. To his surprise, however, he discovered he enjoyed working on the book, even against a background of bombs and blackouts. The book was rapidly prepared and presented only a provisional view of Britain's prehistory; but it set that prehistory against the broader background of Europe and so demonstrated the relevance of regional studies. Such a synthesis was long overdue, and, surprisingly, *Prehistoric Communities of the British Isles* remains one of the very few text-books available on British prehistory. Both *Prehistoric Communities of the British Isles* and *The Prehistory of Scotland* were strongly influenced by the invasionist hypothesis which had dominated British prehistory since the beginning of the century, and in both books a series of invasions account for change

It was with strong feelings of pessimism about world politics that Childe wrote *What Happened in History* in 1942, when he was convinced that 'European Civilization—Capitalist and Stalinist alike—was irrevocably heading for a Dark Age.'[16] He wrote to convince himself that a Dark Age was only a temporary stage in man's progress:

Progress is real if discontinuous. The upward curve resolves itself into a series of troughs and crests. But in those domains that archaeology as well as written history can survey, no trough ever declines to the low level of the preceding one, each crest out-tops its last precursor.[17]

The consequent passion and purpose of the book makes it eminently readable. *What Happened in History* was a title deliberately chosen to illustrate Childe's belief that history and prehistory are a single continuous process of man's adaptation to the environment or of the adjustment of the environment to man's needs; the book actually ends with the fall of the Roman Empire, where many felt that conventional history begins. He made extensive, though culpably unacknowledged, use of the *Wirtschaftsgeschichte des Altertums vom Paläolithikum bis zur Völkerwanderung der Germanen, Slaven und Araber* (1938) by F. M. Heichelheim, a refugee scholar at Cambridge, when covering the period between his own knowledge of pre-literate societies and the fall of the Roman Empire. Indeed it is clear from a letter to O. G. S. Crawford that he intended to continue his book up to the dawn of capitalism, if he could find works comparable to the *Wirtschaftsgeschichte* from which he could glean details of the Byzantine and Arab periods. *What Happened in History* was conceived of as a continuation of *Man Makes Himself*, and was, Childe thought, a successful contribution to archaeology 'as a concrete and readable demonstration designed for the bookstall public that history as generally understood can be extracted from archaeological data.'[18] He turned down a more lucrative offer of publication from Oxford University Press in favour of Penguin Books because, as he explained to his sister Alice, 'Penguins sell at 6d on bookstalls everywhere and I feel archaeologists must now make a real effort to "sell" their knowledge to the masses as the Yanks would say or go under.'

He also took the opportunity, writing in the midst of a war against the Nazis, to clarify to his readers the proper use of the term 'Aryan': 'Because the early Hindus and Persians did really call themselves *Aryans*, this term was adopted by some nineteenth-century philologists to designate the speakers of the 'parent tongue'. It is now applied scientifically only to the Hindus, Iranian peoples and the rulers of Mitanni whose linguistic ancestors spoke closely related dialects and even worshipped common deities. As used by Nazis and anti-semites generally, the term "Aryan" means as little as the words "Bolshie" and "Red" in the mouths of crusted tories.'[19] In *What Happened in History* it is clear that Childe's revulsion from Nazism still led him to reject the Occidentalist approach. Despite its use of a basically Marxist model of change, the book was by no means typical of contemporary Marxism, for he emphasized diffusion as the main *mechanism* of change rather than internal economic progress.

In 1957 Childe criticized *What Happened in History* for the lack of advance in its conceptual framework since *Man Makes Himself* of 1936. But even in 1942 he could stand back and show his awareness of the short-comings of Marxist theories:

The 'materialist concept of history' asserts that the economy determines the ideology. It is safer and more accurate to repeat what has been stated already: in the long run an ideology can survive only if it facilitates the smooth and efficient functioning of the economy. . . . An obsolete ideology can hamper an economy and impede its change for longer than Marxists admit.[20]

Childe must have succeeded in convincing himself in *What Happened in History* that a Dark Age was not 'a bottomless cleft in which all traditions of culture were finally engulfed.'[21] His next book, *Progress and Archaeology* (1944), has been described as 'a delightfully optimistic study of "progress" in all departments of life.'[22] It was a short work describing progress which could be recognized in the archaeological record; and it was indeed optimistic in the middle of the second world war to be able to see the advantages of warfare itself: 'Warfare has, however, contributed to progress not only as a stimulant to invention, but also as an agent in diffusion, being the concomitant or condition of invasion and conquest.'[23]

Dark Ages were seen as merely temporary or local regressions, and 'in archaeological history evil appears as merely negative. Indeed an archaeologist might define evil as what is not cumulative.'[24] This conception of evil as a negation Childe took from the idealist philosophy of Benedetto Croce, which explained error too on the same lines. But the price that men pay for progress in the sense of increasing control of their physical environment is increasing dependence on their social environment:

The tragic repercussions of the American financial crisis of 1931 and of two world wars are the logical outcome of the progressive operation of tendencies observable in the archaeological record since the beginning of the Bronze Age at least.[25]

This opinion was typical of Childe's long view of man's history, and his conviction that modern society had its roots inescapably in the activities of prehistoric man. This was an important tenet of his beliefs; he had a deep desire for an orderly civilization and a deep interest in the forces shaping man's destiny.

Towards the end of the war Childe's faith in Communism appears to have revived. In 1946 he wrote to Robert Braidwood in America that he was glad an edition of *What Happened in History* had reached the New World, 'as the Old outside USSR is done for.' He had continued his close connections with Communist Party groups during the war, and in 1944 he produced a short booklet called *The Story of Tools*, published by the Cobbett Press. It was written for the Young Communist League, and a surfeit of Marxist jargon makes the book tedious reading for the layman. In the spring of 1945 he was asked by the chairman of the Marx Memorial Library, his old friend Robin Page Arnot, to lecture at the Conway Hall after the annual march in commemoration of Marx's funeral. The lecture he gave was a version of the paper he had already published as 'Archaeological Ages as Technological Stages' in the *Journal of the Royal Anthropological Institute*, the Huxley Memorial Lecture for 1944. Here he discussed the limitations of an archaeological classification based on isolating a single factor, and quoted Stalin's passage from the *History of the Communist Party of the Soviet Union (Bolsheviks)*:

The mere knowledge of bronze, the smith's presence alone, did not of itself produce even new tool types. . . . In other words, as Stalin puts it, 'the relations of production constitute just as essential an element in production as the productive forces of society'—its tools and the traditional skill of its operatives.[26]

However, a classification based on the property relations within which tools were used, upon which Soviet archaeologists had attempted to build a system, does not attain its theoretical advantages because of the scanty archaeological evidence for the social organization of preliterate communities. Childe concluded that the use of the traditional system had some justification: 'it does permit us to detect just those contradictions between the material forces of production and the relations of production on which Marxism lays such stress.'[27]

His election as Huxley Lecturer and Medallist for 1944 provided him with an example of the way that, in the academic world, honours and positions of influence tended to fall to men and women past their prime. This was a subject on which he felt very strongly, though most people did not become aware of his beliefs until 20 years after his death. The uncompromising statement he wrote in 1957 was foreshadowed by a letter to Alice in April 1943, telling her of his election as Huxley Medallist: 'This office has been conferred on many distinguished anthropologists and archaeologists like Arthur Evans, A. H. Sayce, J. L. Myres, Leonard Woolley, Arthur Keith et al but generally after they were 60 and had no new ideas. I think at 52 if alive I shall be youngest in the list—though I should like even younger people elected to this and other posts.' Characteristically he did not risk offending elderly friends and colleagues by voicing his thoughts publicly; though it does not seem to have occurred to him that Alice herself was over seventy and therefore apparently incapable of original ideas.

Gordon Childe visited the USSR again immediately after the end of the war in Europe, in June 1945. The occasion was an international meeting to celebrate the jubilee of the Academy of Sciences of the USSR, and the British delegation also included Julian Huxley, W. A. Wooster and D. M. S. Watson, who had written the bone report for Childe's *Skara Brae* in 1931. The meeting achieved some notoriety when six British and American physicists were at first refused permission to leave their countries; for reasons which became clear with the dropping of the first atomic bomb on Japan shortly afterwards. The historian of science, J. G. Crowther, recalled the feelings at that time: 'The British delegation had departed for the USSR under peculiar circumstances. At the last moment, members who might conceivably have anything to do with atomic physics were not allowed to go.

'All the members had assembled in the rooms of the Royal Society just before they were supposed to leave for the USSR, and then learned that a number would not be able to go. One of them had asked me to meet him at the Royal Society, and when I arrived, I found the atmosphere extremely excited. I learned that Sir John

Anderson was in another room, delivering the unwelcome news. I saw an eminent physicist striding up and down in a rage, and vowing that he would join the Communist Party tomorrow.'[28]

A tantalizing note in Childe's incomplete diary for the period records that he dined at the Kremlin during the visit, and suggests that he may have met Stalin on this occasion; unfortunately there is no confirmatory evidence that this meeting ever took place. He certainly returned from the conference with a strengthened conviction that in the future the original researcher in all branches of science would find Russian an essential language. Childe himself learnt to read Russian, and regarded the international exchange of scholarship as enormously important in bridging the gap between Russia and the West. The establishment of the Iron Curtain he saw as a severe blow, and a barrier to 'the natural scientists who from the days of Galileo and Newton to 1945 freely exchanged information and ideas by publication, correspondence and visits regardless of political frontiers.'[29]

As Abercromby Professor Childe did not neglect the prehistory of Scotland during his years at Edinburgh. His approach to Scottish archaeology, which would have earned Lord Abercromby's approval, was directly opposed to the smug parochialism of most Scottish antiquarians, and they regarded the 'outsider's' interference with anything but enthusiasm. He demonstrated his width of approach in 1935 when he produced a book called *The Prehistory of Scotland*. The last works in this field had been Anderson's *Scotland in Pagan Times* (1883 and 1886) and Munro's *Prehistoric Scotland* (1889), and so an up-to-date synthesis was much needed. Childe claimed in the introduction that the purpose of the book was to 'stimulate interest among the mass of the Scottish people, to suggest lines for more intensive and systematic research and to reveal the significance of Scottish prehistory to students abroad.'[30] Whether it achieved all of these aims is debatable, but the book certainly included a wealth of material and set Scottish prehistory in a wider European setting. *The Prehistory of Scotland* soon became a standard textbook for archaeology students.

When Childe published his two highly successful books, *Man Makes Himself* and *What Happened in History*, based on a Marxist model, they did more than any other work to popularize the study of prehistory everywhere. During the war he continued to examine

Marxist theories, and his Rhind Lectures at Edinburgh in 1944, entitled 'The Development of Tribal Society in Scotland in pre-Roman Times', antagonized many colleagues, who felt that his tendency to admire the work of Soviet scholars had gone too far. This lecture course, published in 1946 as *Scotland Before the Scots*, was a deliberate intellectual experiment to see how well a Marxist model fitted the facts. After the German invasion of the USSR in 1941, the CP line coincided with British Government policy and there was a sudden wave of sympathy towards Russia. During this period exchange of ideas and information between the two countries became easier, and Childe re-read the works of Soviet prehistorians. The upsurge of public interest in the Russian people and their history brought Marxist organizations into the limelight in a brief period of popularity. Childe wrote to Alice in February 1942:

I send a photo of myself with the Lord Provost opening an exhibition illustrating the Soviet's war effort and its cultural background. I have for years been branch President of the Society for cultural Relations with the U.S.S.R. a position which was anything but reputable in the past, especially during the Finnish war. But now the Society has become terribly respectable all of a sudden and Ministries and Mayors gladly assist our work. Russia is the one bright spot in the military situation at the moment and every body is quite anxious to learn how and why. Having always believed that the Soviet system was a grand and hopeful experiment at least, we can tell them something more reliable than the lies that hitherto have been dished out by most authors and papers—there are honourable exceptions like the Dean of Canterbury who wrote one of the best books on the Union available. At the same time I am reading up all the Russian archaeological literature available for a course of public lectures on Prehistory in USSR. They have done some excellent work in the last ten years though I do not agree with all their theories.

In 'Retrospect' he wrote that:

In this atmosphere I came to appreciate better the value of even the perversion of Marxism, subsequently branded as Marrism. Its principles I applied in *Scotland Before the Scots*.[31]

Marrism was the name given to the Japhetic theory of N. Y. Marr that languages necessarily develop by an autochthonous process; and Childe had first realized the possibilities of its application to prehistory on his visit to the USSR in 1935. The Soviet Communist Party supported Marrism, especially as it developed in opposition to

European scientific principles, until 1950, when Stalin himself discredited the theory in his *Problems of Linguistics*.

The reaction caused by *Scotland Before the Scots* among prehistorians was in part due to the inability of some scholars to separate Marxist philosophy and its theoretical applications from Soviet Communism. In describing the book as 'a piece of anti-establishment whimsey',[32] G. E. Daniel did not do justice to his colleague's application of working hypotheses. On the other hand it is true that Childe no doubt greatly enjoyed the predictable reaction his book caused; even the kindest reviewers were prone to remarks such as 'he has written with a red pencil and viewed his landscape through deep-rose coloured spectacles.'[33] As a theoretician, Childe loved playing with interpretations of the past; *Scotland Before the Scots* was one experiment which he enjoyed, and he often used to tell people it was his best book. On another occasion, in 1948, he wrote, at Mortimer Wheeler's request, a paper called 'Megaliths' for *Ancient India*. Here he swung to the opposite extreme and produced an extraordinary hyper-diffusionist account; the joke succeeded admirably as Wheeler was completely taken in by it.

In *Scotland Before the Scots* Childe explained that he thought British prehistorians invoked migrations and invasions too frequently as an easy way of explaining change. He felt that Soviet interpretations, based on the internal development of societies, produced more historical narratives without recourse to undocumented external factors; and he preferred *Scotland Before the Scots*, as a more realistic and historical account, to his earlier *The Prehistory of Scotland*. But however much he enjoyed experimenting with Marxist and Marrist theories, he was too honest a scholar to deny the facts. In 'Retrospect' he explained he discovered that he 'just had to admit migrations and the impact of foreign cultures: the internal development of Scottish society in accordance with 'universal laws' simply could not explain the archaeological data from Scotland; reference to Continental data actually documented the solvent effects of external factors.'[34]

Scotland Before the Scots was a gesture guaranteed to antagonize the members of the Society of Antiquaries of Scotland. Childe had become increasingly unhappy in his position at Edinburgh, isolated from his fellow-prehistorians for much of the year, and in a climate which did nothing to soothe his frequent attacks of bronchitis. As the end of the war drew near, he glimpsed a possibility of escape in the form of the directorship of the London Institute of Archaeology. He was so anxious to leave Edinburgh and return to the more congenial academic and political circles of London, he told his friend O. G. S. Crawford, that he felt obliged to keep silent over his disapproval of Government policies in case he prejudiced his chances of the job. Fortunately for Childe the authorities of the University of London were more concerned with his undisputed supremacy as a prehistorian than with his political opinions. By the summer of 1946 he was transferring all his belongings to London in readiness for taking up his appointment as Director of the Institute and Professor of Prehistoric European Archaeology in the autumn.

7. The Institute of Archaeology

Gordon Childe's ten years at the Institute of Archaeology were to be happy ones, both for himself and for his students. He found the academic, political and social contacts and possibilities of London more agreeable than the comparative isolation of Edinburgh. He was also a more inspiring teacher to the postgraduate students at the Institute, and was delighted to find himself regarded by many of them as a friend as well as a respected scholar.

The London University Institute of Archaeology was founded in 1937, mainly through the efforts of Mortimer and Tessa Wheeler, and before 1946 depended largely on a voluntary staff of lecturers and research workers. Only after the war were funds provided for an adequate complement of lecturers and administrative officers. The Institute in Childe's day was housed in St John's Lodge on the Inner Circle, Regent's Park. These spacious surroundings lent themselves to informality in teaching, and many lecturers conducted their courses with open doors. The Institute was a relatively new enterprise and was still imbued with an exciting pioneering spirit; staff and students alike found it a happy and stimulating atmosphere in which to work.

During Childe's directorship he had around him some of the leading archaeologists of the day. German-born F. E. Zeuner joined the staff along with Childe in 1946 as Professor of Environmental Archaeology and that department was later augmented by bone specialist Ian Cornwall. Cornwall had previously held the post of Secretary at the Institute, and in 1951 Edward Pyddoke took over that job. The chair of Indian Archaeology was held by K. de B. Codrington, and from 1947 the Professor of Western Asiatic Archaeology was Max Mallowan, whose excavations at Nimrud are famous. His wife was Agatha Christie, the novelist, with whom Childe often played bridge. Kathleen Kenyon had been Acting-Director during the war, and her work in the Middle East and especially Jericho is well-known. She and Childe were both strong personalities and occasional friction was inevitable, though each had a great deal of respect for the other. Another colleague wrote of her: 'though often offensive in confrontation she spoke good behind one's back, and belied an occasional rough manner by great kindliness of heart, for which an inclination to bossiness is readily overlooked.'[1]

One difference of opinion between Childe and Kathleen Kenyon was over the latter's dogs. She had a number of these, which she brought to the Institute where their barking got on Childe's nerves. He was always rather frightened of dogs, though he loved cats, and eventually introduced a ban (never very effective) on dogs in the Institute. Two women students used to sneak in their small dogs to keep their feet warm when working in the virtually unheated library at St John's Lodge. One recalled a day shortly before the ban was due to be enforced: 'I was coming across the courtyard, *carrying* my dog (so that he should be even less obvious) and out came Childe. Instead of the usual 'good morning' or other greeting, he came right up to me, peering at the bundle in my arms, which was a poodle with a rather fine moustache. He stood and wagged his finger under my dog's nose, saying two or three times: '*silly* little dog, *silly* little dog'—and then moved on, both of us laughing! Fortunately my poodle remained mute, and thoroughly disdainful of the whole performance.'

From 1948 to 1955 a third dominant personality, in the person of Sir Mortimer Wheeler, joined Childe and Kenyon on the staff of the London Institute, and became Professor of Archaeology of the Roman Provinces. A more different person from Gordon Childe would be difficult to imagine: Wheeler was the typical Regency buck in appearance and manners, fitted into the world of the Athenaeum Club like a duck into water, and was admirably efficient at organizing whatever projects he had afoot. Unlike Childe he was intolerant of others' shortcomings and could be very high-handed; in this way he gained enemies. He also loved the limelight, and Childe certainly never became as well-known a figure as Wheeler, whose frequent television appearances and extrovert personality made him a household name. Wheeler had developed scientific methods of archaeological excavation, following the traditions of Flinders Petrie and

Pitt-Rivers, and these methods, coupled with his outstanding ability as an administrator, made him one of the best known British field archaeologists of the twentieth century. He re-excavated the great cities of the Indus civilization, Harappa and Mohenjo-Daro, while he was Director-General of Antiquities in India from 1942 to 1948. Prior to 1944 these cities were thought to be devoid of fortification, and therefore indicative of a society differing radically from those of Mesopotamia, Anatolia and Egypt. Childe himself had stressed the apparently peaceful nature of the Indus civilization after his visit to India in 1933.

No multiplication of weapons of war and battle scenes attests futile conflicts between city-states as in Babylonia nor yet the force whereby a single king, as in Egypt, achieved by conquest internal peace and warded off jealous nomads by constant preparedness. We cannot even define the nucleus round which accumulated the surplus wealth of capital involved in the conversion of the village into the city . . . no temple nor palace dominates the rest . . . The visitor inevitably gets an impression of a democratic bourgeois economy, as in Crete, in contrast to the obviously centralized theocracies and monarchies hitherto described.[2]

Mortimer Wheeler's excavations were to dramatically contradict such a view. Both Harappa and Mohenjo-Daro were in fact dominated by citadels, and walls were revealed of an astonishing height. Wheeler lost no time in telling his colleague of his discoveries: 'I sat down and wrote to Gordon Childe in London that the bourgeois complacency of the Indus civilization had dissolved into dust and that, instead, a thoroughly militaristic imperialism had raised its ugly head amongst the ruins. To his credit he accepted the retrogression with a good and unhesitating grace, and in due course re-wrote his book.'[3]

When Wheeler joined the staff of the Institute of Archaeology he found Childe's lack of skill in administrative matters an affront to his own efficient nature: though many people deemed it an advantage that affairs at the Institute were run with the minimum of red tape. Wheeler later wrote of Childe: 'his failing lay in the matters of administration, which crowded upon him in his later years and were admittedly distasteful to him.'[4] The truth was that Childe made research and the promotion of prehistory primary; petty details of the day to day running of the Institute were settled by his secretaries. People, especially the future generation represented by the students, took precedence. Undoubtedly he saw his administrative duties as a chore, and he had no flair for them, although he was always conscientious in Management Committee meetings. One Secretary of the Institute recalled uncomfortable moments when financial estimates had to be presented to the University Court. 'For Childe, an "estimate" was a hard-and-fast figure to be strictly adhered to. In his view it was just as disastrous not to spend up to the sum estimated as to overspend under any head.'

Gordon Childe's inaugural lecture at the Institute was delivered on his official installation as Professor of European Prehistoric Archaeology in the autumn term of 1946. The occasion afforded a demonstration of his somewhat ponderous humour. Ian Cornwall recalled: 'we were all dressed up in academic finery and he was to be introduced to the gathering by the Vice-Chancellor or some other bigwig. The latter, delayed by fog and a taxi which could not find the Inner Circle, Regent's Park, never turned up, so Childe, after a decent interval, rose, wearing his Director's "hat", to introduce himself as the new Professor and proceed with his inaugural lecture! Very embarrassing to everyone save (apparently) the man chiefly concerned.'

The inaugural lecture itself, entitled 'Archaeology as a Social Science', immediately introduced a fresh perspective. Few of the students would have thought of describing archaeology as a classificatory science, and some felt apprehensive at the thought of future studies under these auspices. Childe stressed too the need for the integration of disciplines:

I have talked such a lot about the help archaeology needs from natural sciences and the contribution it can make to the social sciences, that the inaugural lecture of a prehistoric archaeologist may seem like a discourse on sociology. Yet the discussion will not have been irrelevant if it has helped to clarify the nature and aims of archaeological studies.[5]

He explained that his conception of history had changed during the 19 years since he began his academic career. The definition of cultures and the movement of peoples no longer played such an important part in the 'nature and aims of archaeological studies' he had in mind. He continued:

. . . archaeology may be able to provide knowledge, practically useful knowledge, of the course of human affairs that eludes the literary historian. I am in fact going to suggest that archaeology in an indispensable element in the social sciences as they have recently been defined by the British Association's Committee on 'the Scientific Study of Human Institutions'. Archaeological data can and must provide the reliable basis requisite for the study of what that Committee terms 'the dynamics of social change' and can alone furnish evidence on 'the long-range trends in the life of societies' . . .[6]

Prehistorians who studied under Childe at the Institute include Sinclair Hood, Paul Ashbee, Humphrey Case, Nancy Sandars, Isobel Smith, Peter Gathercole, John Alexander, Henry Hodges and many others. Childe was successful in conveying to his students that the past societies they studied were composed of people, and that this fact should never be forgotten. His profound intellect together with his incredible knowledge made him an inspiring teacher for the postgraduates studying for the two-year Diploma course. He was a conscientious teacher, and took the trouble to cover fields in which he personally had little interest; much more so than many of his colleagues, and this was appreciated by his students. He knew that his interpretations of prehistory were only theories, readily admitted earlier mistakes, and always talked to his students as equals. This scholarly humility was very attractive in so great a man, and almost without exception his students from these ten years were devoted to their eccentric professor. However, it seems probable that Childe never fully realized how much he was appreciated by his students. When Max Mallowan asked Marjorie Maitland-Howard to make a bust of Childe for the Institute, he only consented to sit if she would also do one of his predecessor, Mortimer Wheeler. He seemed to feel it was a tribute not to him personally, but to his position as Director. His only comment on the finished bust, now in the library of the Institute of Archaeology, was that it looked like a Neanderthal Man! When visiting the home of a student who had acquired a copy of the bust, he always tossed his famous hat onto the head of his likeness with a jocular remark.

As a lecturer Childe was often difficult to follow, for he tended to sit down and mumble into his chest, or wander out into another room to fetch something, talking all the way. He expected students to find the facts for themselves from his own and other people's publications; yet students never willingly missed a lecture, for they were exciting exercises in interpretation. It required close attention to attempt to follow his agile mind, but after students had had time to think, they often discovered exciting ideas thrown in at a tangent.

Especially difficult to cope with was Childe's own familiarity with
foreign languages, for he threw in outlandish place-names with no
help in the matter of spelling, with the result that the most peculiar
mutations turned up in essays. This was particularly the case as he
made a point not only of referring to East European countries as 'the
People's Democratic Republic of . . .', but of using Slavonic rather
than Germanic names of towns: Praha for Prague, Plzni for Pilsa and
Wroclaw for Breslau, for example. Added to this, he thought
nothing of demanding that a student should learn, say, Danish,
Rumanian or Serbo-Croat in order to read some obscure reference!

His sense of humour could be very dry, and if an essay had not
come up to his expectations, he would innocently enquire whether
the writer had been suffering from 'flu at the time. Usually his
written comments on essays were kept and referred to by his
students for years; though occasionally this was impossible because
of his writing, as a former student recalled: 'Once I had a comment
on an essay and had to ask him what it was. He took it—looked at
it—turned the sheet sideways—turned it upside down, set it back,
and said "It's quite clear—it says 'illegible'"'! Often he chose to
lecture from 5 to 7 p.m. and could therefore drone on at interminable
length. A former student recalled: 'These lectures were awful
and it was commonplace to fall asleep and wake up half an hour later
to find him still stuck not only on the same Danubian site, but
apparently on the same phase or level.' However Gordon Childe was
not an archaeologist to lose sight of the human element in the study
of prehistory. During one lecture on the Lower Palaeolithic, he
reminded his students, 'But you must never forget that a day in the
life of one of those people was just as full of important incident and
meaning as a day in your own lives.' Remarks like that deeply
impressed his listeners, struggling to note down every find and its
provenance, and all too likely to miss the wood for the trees.

As always Childe enjoyed experimenting with theories to fit the
archaeological data, and Henry Hodges recalled a typical lecture the
Director gave on the dating of the European Bell Beaker: 'He began
with a beaker found in a Minoan context in, I think, Sicily. On this
one piece of evidence he created a huge inverted pyramid of beaker
typology. It took an hour and twenty minutes, and in his last
sentence he admitted that many people were doubtful about the
precise context of his first vessel. As he left the room a small voice

was heard asking, "What are we to believe?". The answer was a chuckle.'

Childe used a large number of slides for his lectures, and several students felt that his Marxism in teaching was limited to pointing out 'primitive communistic societies', even if there did seem to be one hut larger than the rest. These comments were not taken very seriously by his audience, and indeed he usually brought them in to tease people. His Marxism was of the intellectual rather than the emotional variety, and he was quite capable of poking fun at Russian propaganda of the cruder sort. One student, David Kelly, remembered such an occasion: 'We were once shown a Russian film of some excavations in the Caucasus or Black Sea area, Childe translating as necessary. The monuments laid open and interpreted by the Soviet archaeologists recorded the miseries of a land conquered by warlike leaders and a population exploited over the centuries by greedy capitalists; "but now," cried Childe, beaming all over his face, "thanks to J. V. Stalin . . ."'.

Practical classes were included in the Diploma course at the Institute, with photography and surveying, pot-mending and metal cleaning; experimental archaeology also played a part. Childe himself fired some 'prehistoric' pottery in the garden of St John's Lodge, whilst several students attempted the manufacture of flint implements and 'Bronze Age' metal objects. He demonstrated how to flake flint using a large potato and sharp knife; but his demonstrations of primitive technology were not always crowned with success —on one occasion the mould in which he was attempting to cast lead fell apart.

Every year he continued to spend time travelling to visit excavations in progress around Britain, and he frequently spent his holidays walking in the Scottish Highlands. However the only digging he directed in his London years was work at Maes Howe, a huge burial mound at Stenness, Orkney, in 1954–55. This impressive megalithic tomb had already been plundered by the Vikings in the twelfth century and excavated by Farrer in 1861, so nothing of the original burials or furniture remained. Childe's excavations, carried out on behalf of the Ministry of Works, were designed to clarify some details of construction of the earthworks surrounding and covering the exceptionally well-built stone chamber. He discovered that the chamber had been built on the levelled crest of a natural ridge and that, contrary to the assumption made by the compilers of the Royal Commission on Ancient and Historical Monuments' Orkney Inventory, the howe was not supported by built retaining walls comparable to those at other Orcadian chambered tombs such as Quoyness.

It was in tutorials and seminars that Gordon Childe was at his best as a teacher, for he took enormous trouble with his students individually. Any serious student, regardless of ability, benefited from his patient and inspiring tuition; he never, as his colleague Wheeler was apt to do, singled out his less bright students as targets for sarcasm. However he did tend to assume that his students, especially once they reached their second year, were as familiar with his interpretations of the archaeological data as he was himself. One student recalled a traumatic tutorial when 'he came in and dramatically announced that he was about to recant (and it obviously cost him a lot to do so) and then he plunged into a long tale about this dagger from the Orkney Islands, which he had previously thought was something or other, but had now decided was something else—all fearfully vital and we felt sure we should get it in the exam, but as none of us knew what he was on about and didn't catch the name, we couldn't take a single note or follow a word.'

He was prepared to go to great lengths when it came to assisting students in financial trouble. One student's source of cash was cut off part-way through his Diploma course at the Institute because of the sudden death of his father. He recalled with gratitude the Director's immediate and exhaustive efforts to raise funds from the University to enable him to continue; and this was typical of the infinite care Childe took of his students. He also concerned himself with placing his former students in suitable jobs, and in this he was a shrewd judge of character. Whenever he could help he liked to do so, though sometimes the help offered was a little eccentric. During one series of oral examinations, Childe's technique had obviously improved from his early days at Edinburgh, for he had a great bowl of strawberries by him and offered one to each student as they entered. Clearly most kindly meant and supposed to put them at their ease, the strawberries were actually a source of great embarrassment, leaving the nervous student uncertain whether to eat it then and there, and if so, how to talk while munching and where to dispose of the stalk.

In spite of his commitments as Director and a prolific writer, Childe was always available to students in his spacious room in the Institute overlooking the park. His remarkable personal library was housed there on enormous bookshelves and contained a large number of books in several languages, including an English and a Russian edition of Marx's *Capital*. His successor at Edinburgh, Stuart Piggott, recalled how 'I once asked him from which bookseller he ordered his foreign archaeological books and he answered with some surprise, "I don't *buy* the books—I expect the authors to send them to me!"'.[7] Of course they did, for Gordon Childe was acknowledged all over the world as the leading prehistorian of his day.

However he was also a lonely man, and one who was extremely sensitive. His delight in the company of his students was not just because they enormously respected and admired him, but because they confided in him and made him feel wanted and loved. This meant as much to him as the world-wide acclaim he received as a prehistorian. Often Childe and a group of students would sit chatting at tea time in friendly companionship and he would be as happy on these occasions as he ever was. His special tin labelled 'Childeish Sugar' (it was in the days of rationing and he had a very sweet tooth) would be on the table, and he used to stir his cup, beam at the assembled group, and say: 'Well, I think I'll have a long chronology this week.' This standing joke emphasized that he was always aware that the archaeological data did not at that time permit any certainty in dating.

The famous professor had a great sense of humour which was not appreciated by all his acquaintances; his enjoyment of jokes and pranks could be very childlike. Apparently he used to keep a halfpenny in his pocket to fool pickpockets: and once in Spain this trick was worth his while. On another occasion he deliberately packed his large suitcase with the bare essentials—plus a large pillow, to annoy the Spanish customs. He hated the Franco régime in Spain and always referred to the uprising as the revolution, a habit which did little to endear him to some Spanish colleagues. His sense of humour often had more than a touch of irony in it, and his verbal jokes, which were long and elaborate and produced with a dead-pan expression, often failed because his audience did not realize they were supposed to be funny. At one Prehistoric Society conference in the early '50s Childe came up with the theory that Woodhenge was a copy of Stonehenge created by a *nouveau riche* capitalist/chieftain; more than one of his audience failed to realize it was a hoax.

This irony was characteristic of Childe's detachment, and it remained true throughout his life that colleagues and students found it impossible to get really close to him. Human relationships had always been difficult for him, and in the '50s he remarked to a friend how contact with another person involved a great expenditure of energy. He inspired deep affection nevertheless and enjoyed the company of his students. During his first year at London a few students were planning a trip to Avebury and one of them, Sinclair Hood, on the spur of the moment asked Childe to join them. To their amazement, and almost horror, he said, 'I'd love to, and I'll take you in my car.' This nerve-racking trip in his huge old-fashioned Ford was the forerunner of what became a regular feature at the Institute. In the summer term everyone travelled down to Avebury and stayed there for a weekend, visiting museums and monuments in the vicinity. There was some competition to avoid being driven there by Childe in his open-roofed car, as his driving had not improved with age. Everyone enjoyed these weekend trips, in spite of the long distances covered—for Childe was still an indefatigable walker and could easily outdistance much younger men.

The professor also provided his students with some amusement on these trips, as they observed the expressions on the faces of country hotel keepers as he charged in at the head of a straggling procession to order afternoon tea in his extraordinary voice. Whatever the weather, Childe rarely wore trousers, and insisting on sticking to his famous short shorts, together with the large black hat and oilskin coat. Sometimes he would walk along holding his jacket out in front to prevent his legs becoming sunburnt. When this inevitably failed he would borrow a female student's best face-cream to soothe the burning—and set off the next day in the same style regardless! On one memorable trip to Maiden Castle a cow took fancy to his oilskin and persisted in licking it throughout his exposition on the famous site. His futile attempts to prevent this (for he was rather scared of cows) presented a spectacle which reduced his students to silent hysterics.

All year round Childe loved to take to the Downs in his car, sometimes showing the sites of Wessex to visiting foreigners, or just taking a couple of students on a weekend's strenuous walking. He also had other more sedentary relaxations. He patronized the Left-wing Unity Theatre, which staged suitable plays, heavy with political significance, and was sometimes accompanied by an unsuspecting student. Often the fervent ideals of the audience were not matched by the quality of the performances on these occasions. He was also extremely fond of classical concerts in both Edinburgh and London, though he was not an executive musician like many other members of his family. He often visited the Festival Hall—he admired both the architecture and the acoustics—and sometimes invited students to join him, for he enjoyed the company of other people on such occasions. He always had one of the best seats for a concert or the opera; and it did not seem to occur to him that others were not so fortunate. One friend remembers Childe's horror at her admission that she had never been to the Festival Hall, and his apparent inability to imagine the practical difficulties which might have prevented her. On another occasion he overheard a student mentioning that she too had never heard a concert at the Festival Hall; he was shocked and told her she should never have admitted it. The result this time was that she was soon on her way to the Hall to hear Beethoven's Ninth Symphony, accompanied by Professor Childe and an acquaintance from his block of flats. Not long before he left England for Australia in 1957, he attended a performance of Wagner's 'Ring' at Covent Garden and described to a friend how the principal female singer had left the stage in a shower of gold. The explanation for this unusual phenomenon was that Childe had clapped so enthusiastically that his gold signet ring had fallen onto the stage.

In 1948 he met for the first time his half-brother Laurence's daughter Mary, who arrived in London to spend the next three years studying music. She found her famous uncle kind in his own rather prickly way, and the two frequently dined together and visited the theatre or attended concerts or the opera. His shyness sometimes made him appear brusque, but he was always thoughtful and generous. On one occasion he told Mary that his father's third wife, Monica, now in a mental home in England, was selling off the family silver, and he presented his niece with a set of beautiful cutlery marked with the Childe 'C', which he had purchased specially for her.

Gordon Childe was frequently a kind and generous host to colleagues and students alike. He disliked doing things on his own and would happily seize the nearest student to accompany him. One former student recalls being whisked out of the library to see 'La Bohème', and on another occasion being treated to lunch at the Fellows' dining room at Regent's Park Zoo to celebrate the professor's successful visit to the dentist. He was proud to have been elected a Fellow of the Zoological Society in March 1950, and remained one until the end of 1956. Childe loved good food and drink, and often invited friends to join him for a meal at the Athenaeum, the Festival Hall, or one of a variety of restaurants which he frequented. His lectures on European prehistory were punctuated with advice on the local delicacies to be sampled when visiting various archaeological sites. He loved food in general, but had a great weakness for sweet and sticky cream cakes in particular. Woe betide the unwary student who had the misfortune to take from the plate the very cake on which the professor had his eye! Once when Childe and a friend were lunching in Wiltshire in a hotel then in Postgate's *Good Food Guide*, the frozen vol-au-vents were obviously insufficiently thawed and the customers' feet were overrun by a troupe of affectionate puppies. Childe exclaimed in loud and piercing tones, 'You should pay more attention to your customers' food, and less to your little dogs!'

In contrast to his years as Abercromby Professor, at London Childe found himself on terms of real friendship with many of his postgraduate students, and he was enormously pleased if they invited him out socially. At one students' party he made valiant attempts to join in the games, even when requested to sing 'Waltzing Matilda' as the Australian national anthem. His students were delighted to be regularly remembered by a postcard signed familiarly 'Gordon', when he was away on his summer travels. One Christmas he sent out cards which were reproductions of a photograph he had taken of a view from his hotel window on a recent trip behind the Iron Curtain. So carried away was he that on these cards both greeting and signature were in Cyrillic script.

Whilst in London for his last ten years Childe lived at Lawn Road Flats, near Hampstead. These were rather spartan and functional service flats, fashionable with various intellectual groups at the time, and possibly recommended by his colleague's wife, Agatha Christie, who lived there during the war. The building contained a small restaurant for the residents, where he could dine well with a good bottle of wine and entertain guests. On his own rooms he left hardly any trace to betoken the personality of the occupant: there were no obviously personal pictures or ornaments, and no books. There was on one shelf a small range of battered blue files—and these contained the sum of his incomparable knowledge of European prehistory. Most of his work that required reference to libraries he did in his book-lined room at the Institute.

Childe had been elected a Fellow of the Society of Antiquaries in 1927 but his opinion of the Society had never been particularly high, and in 1949 he, O. G. S. Crawford and other prehistorians fell into disagreement with the main body of Fellows. The occasion was the disputed election of the Presidency after Cyril Fox had retired from office. They violently objected to the election of James Mann (then Keeper of the Tower's Armouries), believing that the prehistorian Mortimer Wheeler should have been chosen instead to promote the growing science of prehistoric archaeology. Childe and Crawford resigned their fellowships of the Society; though continuing their subscriptions to the *Journal* to keep their sets complete. Childe felt that their names were valued by the Society and their public resignation would have some effect; however he urged younger colleagues, who had more need of the facilities of the Society, to remain members.

Also in 1949 the American physicist, W. F. Libby, was invited to London to talk to the Royal Society. Childe arranged for Libby to lecture at the Institute of Archaeology in the afternoon before his address to the Royal Society; the first time he had spoken about the revolutionary method of radiocarbon dating in this country. This method of dating, suggested by Libby in 1946, provided the first universal means of absolute dating, independent of subjective archaeological methods, and enabled prehistorians to fix their relative chronologies in terms of calendar years. The technique is based on the fact that all living matter contains minute quantities of carbon-14, a radioactive isotope of carbon, in a fixed proportion to ordinary carbon, carbon-12. When an organism dies, the carbon-14 diminishes at a known rate, and so the age since death of organic material can be calculated. When the first reliable radiocarbon dates began to appear they often surprised archaeologists, whose carefully constructed theories vanished overnight. Glyn Daniel recalled the problems when the dates became available: 'for years in the fifties and sixties, archaeologists used to meet each other, rather like the proverbial Stock Exchange operator with the latest dirty joke, and say, "Have you heard this one?", as he produced some startling early C14 date.'[8] Radiocarbon dates, almost all of which appeared after Childe's death, proposed a much earlier chronology for prehistoric Europe than the traditional one, advocated by Childe and others in the footsteps of Montelius and based on cross-datings with Egypt and Mesopotamia. However, in the pre-radiocarbon age in which Childe lived, the diffusionist model was really the only one which made it possible to use the historically recorded dates of the Near East to make sense of the events of European prehistory. The assumption of a gradual outward spread from some south-eastern source allowed a reasonably coherent chronological structuring of prehistoric Europe; and without such a structure any interpretations were impossible.

Childe constantly stressed the overriding need for a firm chronology for pre-literate sites, and strove towards such a pattern. Before the technique of radiocarbon dating was refined, the early results even tended to confirm his model, and it was not until after his death that it became apparent how much of the theoretical relative dating he had assumed was in fact wrong. Childe himself was well aware of the importance of an independent and reliable chronology, if this could be achieved. In the posthumously published 'Valediction' he wrote, 'Long before an archaeological frame has been fitted by cross-datings firmly onto Europe and the Near East . . . a more trustworthy chronology, independent of archaeology and of any historical assumption, may well have been provided by radiocarbon.'[9]

During his decade at the Institute Gordon Childe was the acknowledged leader in the study of European prehistory and greatly admired all over the world. However his interest in Socialist politics did not lessen during this period, although his participation in the activities of Left-wing societies was known to few of his colleagues. He was respected as an expert on the prehistoric stages of man's development by Marxist historians, and he had attended meetings of Communist Party historians since before the war. When the periodical *Past and Present* was formed by Marxist historians in 1952 Childe joined the editorial board, for he saw *Past and Present* as a progressive and forward-looking journal of historical studies. A member of the Rationalist Press Association, he was one of the

Association's panel of Honorary Associates from 1941 until his death, and also one of the Association's distinguished authors. Apart from *Progress and Archaeology* (1944) and *Social Evolution* (1951), his revised edition of *Man Makes Himself* (1941) was one of the most successful books in their Thinker's Library. The Rationalist Press Association, prominent in the humanist movement and founded as it is on free-thinking and secular principles, had Childe's good opinion for many years.

He was also a member of the board of *The Modern Quarterly* in the early '50s. This journal, later called *The Marxist Quarterly*, was not formally an organ of the Communist Party, but became so in reality. The chairman of the board for some years was none other than Rajani Palme Dutt, and the board meetings took place in the CP's headquarters in King Street. Both here and on the board of *Past and Present* Childe's natural reticence prevented his playing any prominent part in discussion. As in earlier years, the fact that he seemed detached from his Left-wing beliefs and frequently played them up persuaded some colleagues that they were not sincerely held. However, his presence on the *The Modern Quarterly* editorial board is sufficient indication that he took his Marxism seriously and was taken seriously by other Marxists. Palme Dutt was an exceptionally staunch Communist Party supporter and Marxist scholar, and would certainly not have tolerated a board member whose Marxist ideals were merely an anti-Establishment pose.

Childe kept in close touch with Palme Dutt all his life, though the paths of their careers had diverged after 1925. Palme Dutt later wrote of Childe's continued interest in Marxism: 'During his later years we planned to publish together a joint edition of Engels' *Origin of the Family*, in which he would add the archaeological notes to supplement the necessarily limited information at that time available to Engels, and I would add a political preface. We had proceeded some way with this project, but unfortunately time defeated it for both of us.'[10] It is interesting that Childe's first impressions of Engels' book were that it was 'horridly outfashioned' and 'filled with cheap polemic'. He came round eventually to accepting that it had value for his own discipline: 'In archaeology and ethnology an appreciation of Engel's (sic) Origin of the Family, Private Property and the State is a great help. . . . Engel's own contributions are by the way a lot better than the large slice he cribbed from Morgan because he really knew something of German history and archaeology.'[11] In some respects, he believed, Engels was 'remarkably far-sighted, insisting, for instance, that bronze did not normally replace stone for tools, a fact which his contemporaries and many more recent investigators have been inclined to overlook.'[12]

In 1921 R. Palme Dutt had founded a Left-wing journal called *Labour Monthly*, which he edited for over 50 years; Childe contributed an occasional article. In 1956 the Communist leadership in Hungary, threatened by revolt, was sent aid by Russia. In the outcry which followed this act and Kruschev's attacks on Stalinism, the Communist Party came under fierce criticism. In Britain Palme Dutt was the target of attack for many months, as the result of his notorious article in the May issue of *Labour Monthly*, in which he referred to Stalin's errors as mere 'spots on the sun' which 'would only startle an inveterate Mithras-worshipper'. Childe took the opportunity of the 35th anniversary celebrations of the *Labour Monthly* in July 1956 to indicate his own continuing friendship with Palme Dutt. He volunteered to move the resolution of greetings—a speech in praise of Palme Dutt, dealing with their early association at Oxford and his friend's later work as editor of the journal.

However Childe's speech did not imply that he condoned Palme Dutt's defence of Stalin. The Soviet invasion of Hungary precipitated a crisis in the world Communist movement, and resulted in many CP members leaving the Party. The *New Statesman* published a famous letter signed by some leading British Communists or pro-Communists, dissociating themselves from the Russian action. Childe did not sign this letter; he explained later that to have done so would have given too much satisfaction to his life-long enemies. But he was deeply upset by the Russian action, and he lost his faith in Soviet Communism, though not his faith in communism itself, which was still his ideal. His shock over the 1956 action was all the greater because of his previous admiration of Soviet Russia. On his visits to the USSR he had gone wanting to see only the positive side of Communist life, and as an official guest of the Russian government, he had been carefully guided to do just that; though he was not blind to its deficiencies. Writing to his cousin Alexander Gordon on 20 November, he said:

The world situation in 1956 is distinctly unpleasant—but probably not really worse than in 1956 B.C. say under Shulgi of Ur. In the later period one would hardly have expected an exhibition of incompetent idiocy such as has blocked Suez and made Britain so unpopular in India and the Near East. Nor despite my devotion to the CCCP can I really regard events in Hungary with equanimity. (I was there just over a year ago and am particularly worried about the fate of my charming colleagues in the National Museum and the scientifically irreplaceable treasures [most still unpublished] it contained.) But of course one must not believe anything one reads—not even in the Daily Worker!

Childe's political activities were not confined to sitting on the boards of Marxists journals. He was a member of the Executive Committee of the Association of Scientific Workers, and a Vice-President of the Association during the 1950s. The AScW was a trade union now within the Association of Scientific, Technical and Managerial Staffs. One of the Association's founders was Hyman Levy, whom Childe had known from the 'Tots & Quots'. Childe had been active in the founding and building of the Edinburgh branch of the AScW, and served as its Chairman from 1939 to 1946. In London he contributed to the work and publications of the Science Policy Committee, and also lectured at branch meetings.

He was also actively involved with the Society for Cultural Relations with the USSR, and as well as being President of the Edinburgh branch, he was President of the National History and Archaeology Section from the early '50s until his death in 1957. The Society was nominally independent of the Communist Party, though it was in reality a 'satellite' body controlled by it. The President of the SCR was the prominent Left-wing lawyer, D. N. Pritt, who was later denounced as a secret CP member. Childe's acquaintance with Pritt began as a result of his work on the committees of the SCR.

The Chairman of the SCR during Childe's involvement with it was a Classics Professor at the University of London, Robert Browning. He admired particularly the endless correspondence and exchange of publications in which Childe engaged; this international co-operation was an aspect of scholarship whose importance the prehistorian thought could not be overstressed. His own contribution in this field was great, beginning in the early '20s when he had travelled extensively abroad and helped to build up the library of the Royal Anthropological Institute. He was one of the very few scholars who had acquired at least a reading knowledge of Russian and other

East European languages, and deliberately kept up his contacts with archaeologists behind the Iron Curtain. In 1945 he wrote, 'in all domains of science the original research worker will in future find Russian as essential as German was in the past and the sooner students know this the better.'[13]

He also visited the Soviet Union at least three times as well as frequently travelling to other Communist countries, and, as Browning remembers, he certainly entered into the spirit of the 'cultural relations': 'I well recall him once, because I had to chair the meeting, giving a lecture at the SCR on his return from such a visit. He had been in central Asia visiting, I think, the Khorezm sites and he turned up to give his lecture in central Asian national costume.'

Childe's last visit to the USSR was in 1953, and his trip combined a careful blend of scholarship and culture. He left London on 22 August, travelling via Brussels, Prague and Minsk to Moscow. By the 26th he was in Leningrad, and here he visited the Astoria and the Hermitage Museum, as well as seeing a production of *King Lear* performed by the Minsk Company. Apparently he was one of the honoured few for whom the Russians opened the famous Gold Room of the Hermitage; though, as he later maintained, he was only interested in a well-preserved copper axe of around 2000 B.C. Returning briefly to Moscow, he continued over the Urals to Tashkent and on to nearby Stalinabad, where he spent some time at the University. On his return to Moscow on 5 September he was shown not only the Foreign Languages Publishing House, the university and a Lenin exhibition, but also visited a circus and a performance of *Romeo and Juliet*.

Gordon Childe was an extremely hospitable host to colleagues from all over the world when they visited Britain. On the radio programme broadcast a year after his death Max Mallowan told how Childe's foreign colleagues 'never failed to go and see him when they passed through London, and many of them have written to say how much they miss him.'[14] He was one of the few British prehistorians who knew many of the Soviet scholars personally. He was very active in organizing the visits of two leading Russian archaeologists, S. P. Tolstov and A. V. Artsikhovskij, in 1956. The occasion of Tolstov's visit provided Childe with an opportunity, which he did not neglect, to denounce the policy of the British government towards the Russians. He allowed an audience to assemble at the

Institute for a lecture by Tolstov, only to tell them that because of the obscurantism of the British Foreign Office, Professor Tolstov was not there. Ironically, the Russians themselves were in fact responsible for this delay, and Tolstov appeared later to deliver his lecture.

Although Childe's many publications and his duties at the Institute occupied much of his time, he still loved to travel, and attended numerous international conferences during the vacations. The third International Congress of Prehistoric and Protohistoric Sciences, scheduled for Budapest in 1940, had been postponed because of the war. Childe was particularly keen that the Congresses should bring together scholars from both sides of the Iron Curtain, and welcomed the renewed offer to act as host from Hungary. He wrote to his Hungarian friend and colleague, J. Banner:

all European archaeologists know the great wealth of prehistoric antiquities that have been collected in Hungary and appreciate the leading role that Hungary played in the development of civilization throughout Europe in prehistoric and early historic times. . . . It is . . . with the highest expectations that archaeologists even in the remotest parts of Europe have welcomed the renewal of the invitation for 1949.[15]

However the Congress was postponed again, and Childe's next long-term visit to Hungary was to be in September 1955, when he attended an archaeological conference of the Hungarian Academy of Sciences. Childe also loved Czechoslovakia, especially Prague, which he always referred to as Praha, and frequently stayed there for short visits in the years after the second world war. On one occasion he stayed in the country home of his friend and colleague, Jan Filip, and particularly liked the sandstone configurations of the Jicín-Turnov area, which reminded him of the Australian landscapes of his youth.

Childe was a gifted linguist and had taught himself most European languages during his early travels; in later years he also learnt Russian. He was extremely proud of his accomplishments, and insisted on speaking to foreign colleagues in their own languages. This could cause problems, as the Czech archaeologist, Jiri Neustupný recalled: 'Everybody knows him with the inseparable pipe in his mouth which he did not put aside even while speaking. So we always had, first of all, to distinguish the right language when he started speaking. This was not an easy task as he changed the language frequently and unexpectedly.'[16] Once having distinguished the correct language, all was not plain sailing. French and German scholars implored him to speak in English rather than in their native tongues, so that they might have some chance of understanding him. Once Childe's Polish colleague in London, Professor Sulimirski, who was himself a fluent Russian-speaker, received a telephone call from Childe. He recognized the distinctive voice, but could not understand a syllable. When he eventually persuaded him to converse in English, it emerged from a highly annoyed Childe that he thought he had been speaking Russian! Nevertheless he commanded enormous respect in foreign countries, for his books, translated into French, Russian, Czech, Japanese and many other languages, had made a world-wide impact on archaeological thought. His eccentricities made him something of a mascot at international meetings, and he was held in great affection by colleagues all over the world.

His Czech friend, J. Neustupný, paid his first visit to England in 1956, and on Childe's invitation lectured at the Institute of Archaeology on the chronology of the Eneolithic of Central Europe. Childe introduced him to some prominent scholars at the Athenaeum, and set off in his car with Neustupný to spend two days visiting sites in southern England. Two days' driving with Childe must have been a nerve-racking experience, for his driving had if anything got worse with time. He was not only very short-sighted but also red/green colour-blind; and on occasion was so absent-minded that he apparently thought his passenger was driving. Max Mallowan was the witness to one incident after he had dined with Childe at the Athenaeum: 'when we stepped into Pall Mall he found that his car was inconveniently parked between two others and that there wasn't enough room for him to manoeuvre it out easily so he proceeded to get in and treat it exactly like a steam engine. Instead of trying to find a gradual way out he simply shunted back and forth until he buffeted the two vehicles in front and behind enough to get them out of the way.'[17]

However, Neustupný survived his travels with Childe, and the two of them took part in the television programme 'Animal, Vegetable, Mineral' on 3 April 1956. Childe probably felt that the programme was a good means of bringing archaeology to the public, and afterwards he was delighted to be recognized in the street as a participant. However he always stressed that the serious study of archaeology would earn it 'a more secure position than can be earned by sensational finds and even witty wireless programmes.'[18] Perhaps a touch of envy for some of his colleagues who were more popular radio and television personalities can be detected in this statement from his 'Valediction' of 1957.

Whilst he was in England on this visit Neustupný suggested that his colleague should re-write his famous book, *The Danube in Prehistory*, incorporating material which had come to light since 1927. But Gordon Childe replied that it would have been necessary to visit many countries and museums and that he was now too tired to undergo such travels. In 1956 too the era of wide overall syntheses was coming to an end and with the vastly increased amount of archaeological data available, specialization was inevitably beginning to take over. He had already decided to retire from the London Institute a year early, and his Czech friend was left with a strong impression that he felt his academic life was nearing its end and that he did not want to embark on any new projects.

8. Publications: the Last Decade

Childe's years at London between 1946 and 1957 were exceptionally prolific in terms of publications. *History* (1947) testifies to his continued interest in the theory of the study of history, which for him included prehistory. But during the years following his London appointment he was particularly occupied by the problems of diffusionism and evolutionism, and wrote many papers dealing with these topics. These papers, as well as *Prehistoric Migrations* (1950), show clearly his own position as a moderate diffusionist. However he did not consider this to be opposed to evolutionism; in his view, archaeology and anthropology should work together in the best interests of prehistory. His concern with the possibilities of an analogy between organic and social evolution were to culminate in the popular but in some ways unsatisfactory book, *Social Evolution*.

The final years of his life saw important developments in Childe's own philosophy, and his arrival at an explanation of the phenomena of European prehistory which he thought satisfactorily fitted the facts. *Society and Knowledge* (1956) is a purely philosophical book, and of interest particularly as an exposition of Childe's own theories of epistemology. *Piecing Together the Past* is equally important as a rare study of methodology in the field of prehistory. However the book which Childe himself considered his final and most satisfactory contribution to the study of prehistory was *The Prehistory of European Society*, published two years after his retirement from the Institute. Although later scholars may not agree with his own assessment of his writings, his books published between 1946 and 1958 are clearly significant works in the discipline of prehistoric archaeology, and refute the suggestion made by J. G. D. Clark in the first Childe Memorial Lecture that 'he had achieved what he was going to achieve in this genre essentially by 1930.'[1]

Prehistorian

The decade after the second world war was an important one for prehistoric archaeology as a whole. A new generation of scholars, brought up on Childe's *The Dawn*, *The Danube* and other early works, were not only excavating but producing new methods and theories. Christopher Hawkes was a prehistorian of whom Childe himself had a very high opinion. He had just left the British Museum and in 1946 became Professor of European Archaeology at Oxford, a research school which he was to build up over the next 30 years. His wife Jacquetta, later married to J. B. Priestley, wrote many books on archaeology and ancient history and was also a friend of Childe's.

At Cambridge, the Disney Professor of Archaeology from 1952 to 1974 was Grahame Clark. He was followed in this post by Glyn Daniel, who also took over the editorship of *Antiquity* after Crawford's sudden death in 1957. Grahame Clark and E. S. Higgs were to become known as the principal British exponents of the economic approach to prehistory. Clark's excavation of the Mesolithic site of Star Carr in Yorkshire was soon recognized as a classic example of the retrieval of economic data to reconstruct the prehistoric environment, whilst his *Prehistoric Europe: the Economic Basis* (1952) was the forerunner of a new breed of books and papers concentrating on the economy and environment of pre-literate communities. Childe reviewed the book in the *Antiquaries Journal* and was favourably impressed by the younger man's methods: 'Dr Clark here gives a new interpretation of archaeological data—or perhaps we should say revives a mode of interpretation, familiar last century, but with far richer material, enlarged technical resources, and profounder vision. The theme is not the interaction of human societies, as represented by typologically distinguishable cultures, but the interaction of society and environment as expressed in material culture. Attention is accordingly focused not on the arbitrary formal peculiarities of tools that serve typologists for the definition of groups and periods, but on the activities which the use, manufacture and distribution of the implements imply. Culture is conceived as action, not as the fossilized results of action. The latter, of course, alone survive as archaeological data.'[2] He could not refrain from slipping in a few Marxist phrases, knowing that these would be like a red rag to a bull as far as the politically Right-wing Grahame Clark was concerned: 'Nowhere does the author allow himself to speculate on "social organization" or "relations of production", though house types and settlement patterns are ably described.'³

Also at Cambridge, Eric Higgs and others explored the technique of site catchment analysis which provided archaeologists with some idea of the potential population of a prehistoric site or area. Recently there has been a tendency to criticize Childe for a lack of concern over the environmental evidence in his interpretation of prehistoric societies; however, his many excavation reports invariably included experts' evaluations of the economic and environmental evidence, and it was he who first integrated the study of the environment with the study of prehistory at the London Institute. Meanwhile Stuart Piggott, replacing Childe at Edinburgh, built up the department there in a way which his predecessor had failed to do, whilst continuing to carry out the spirit of Lord Abercromby's deed of bequest.

Shortly before he took up his appointment as Director of the Institute of Archaeology Childe admitted to the man who was to be his successor there, W. F. Grimes, that he was coming to London to get on with his research. This statement was amply borne out by his publications within the first few years of his appointment. In 1946 a paper entitled 'Archaeology and Anthropology' was published in the *Southwestern Journal of Anthropology*. Childe wrote: 'My thesis is that archaeology and anthropology (or, if you will, ethnography) are two complementary departments of the science of man related in the same way, and as mutually indispensable, as palaeontology and zoology in the science of life.'⁴ The Marxist historian George Thomson later wrote of this introduction that 'as a statement of Marxist attitude, that leaves nothing to be desired'; repudiation of the comparative method would, according to some Marxists, be 'bourgeois'.

Childe's paper castigated equally the extreme of 'diffusionism' and of 'evolutionism'. He frequently claimed, as he did here, that the antithesis between the two theories was illusory. In his view, a revision of the sequence of culture stages could best be effected by an alliance between archaeology and ethnography which would reconcile functionalism, diffusionism and evolutionism. Since most of the evidence for human history lay in the realm of prehistory, this method was, he claimed, the best hope for reaching general laws indicative of the direction of historical progress. In this way the study of prehistory was vindicated, for Childe regarded 'as a legitimate ideal a history or science of culture that shall "be able, to a degree at least, to forecast the future and to guide our steps towards it".'[6]

Also published not long after Gordon Childe's appointment to the London chair was a work of historiography. *History* (1947) was a critical discussion of man's attempts to disclose an order in the sequence of human events. Childe reviewed and rejected various theories of history—theological, naturalistic and comparative—and decided in favour of the Marxist conception of history as a creative process. Barbara McNairn has pointed out, however, that Childe did not deal with the laws of the dialectic in *History*; and indeed it was only by ignoring them, and their exalted position as eternal laws to which Soviet Marxists at least had raised them, that he could present 'Dialectical Materialism' as 'a view of history freed from transcendentalism and dependence on external laws.'[7] The creativity of reality and of history was an important tenet of Childe's beliefs, clearly stated in the later years of his life. Archaeology's contribution to knowledge viewed in this light had much to offer:

. . . if history be not following a prescribed route but is making its path as it proceeds, the search for a terminus is naturally vain. But a knowledge of the course already traversed is a useful guide to the probable direction of the next stage of the way.[8]

But while he thought that Marxism was the most realistic and adequate approach to the interpretation of history, he was not dogmatic about its use: '. . . Marxism goes on to assert that all constitutions, laws, religions and all other so-called spiritual results of man's historical activity are in the long run determined by the material forces of production—tools and machines—together with, of course, natural resources and the skills to operate them. Thus the Materialist Conception offers a clue for the analysis of the data of history and opens up the prospect of reducing its phenomena to an easily comprehensible order. This clue is not to be used slavishly.'[9] Gordon Childe believed that some Marxists *had* used the materialist conception slavishly and had re-instated a preconceived goal, such as world communism, to man's progress:

Marx himself escaped this prejudice not so much by leaving the content of 'Communism' exceedingly abstract and attenuated, but by wisely asserting that its attainment would mark the end, not of history, but 'of the prehistoric stage of human society.' . . . It is not the historians' business to imagine an absolute value, approximation to which is then labelled 'progress', but rather to discover in history values to which the process is approximating.[10]

Childe came in for criticism for his opinion of Stalin at the end of *History*: 'One great statesman of today has successfully foreseen the course of world history and him we have just quoted as an exponent of Marxist historiography.'[11] One reviewer pointed out that Stalin had notoriously failed to foresee the German invasion of Russia in 1941. *History* did not escape criticism from Communist scholars either, and the book is a good example of Childe's ambiguous position in society: on the one hand criticized by hard-line Marxists for an atypical Marxist attitude, and on the other labelled as 'Communist' by Right-wing colleagues. In spite of his consistent championing of Soviet archaeology, he did not earn unqualified praise from some Russian scholars. Soviet archaeological literature of the post-war period had a sharply political character, and A. Mongait's paper 'The Crisis in Bourgeois Archaeology' (1951) contains an example of such criticism:

Among bourgeois scholars there are not only our ideological enemies. There are also progressive scholars who are friends of our country who understand very well the universal significance of our science. One of these persons among the English archaeologists, for example, is Gordon Childe. Childe has not yet succeeded in overcoming many of the errors of bourgeois science. But he understands that truth is in the socialist camp and is not ashamed to call himself a pupil of Soviet archaeologists.[12]

During the late '40s, as well as being much concerned with the conflict between diffusionism and evolutionism, Childe began to explore the possibility of an analogy between organic and social evolution, and to examine the precise meaning of 'knowledge' as perceived by society. These themes were eventually discussed at length in his book *Social Evolution* (1951), but he wrote a number of papers dealing with such topics in 1949 and 1950.

In 'Social Worlds of Knowledge' (a Hobhouse Memorial Lecture delivered in 1949) and 'The Sociology of Knowledge' (1949) Childe began to realize that 'the environment to which a society actually adjusts itself is not the material environment that natural science can reconstruct and observe as an external object, but the society's collective representation of that environment—that is, part of its culture.'[13] 'The Sociology of Knowledge' carried the discussion further into the realms of epistemology, and Marx's contribution to this field: '. . . Marx, in founding a new science of society, observed that categories and "laws of thought" are neither absolute nor eternal but conditioned by the productive forces used by society and must change with the appropriate relations of production.'[14] Childe thought that Durkheim's theory of scientific knowledge, derived from his sociological studies, was complementary to Marxist theory. Childe's own philosophy as expounded in *Society and Knowledge* in 1956 owes a great deal to the influence of both Durkheim and Marx.

He denied that the function of the historian was to attempt to rediscover the thoughts and emotions of men of past societies. In November 1949 he delivered the Frazer Lecture at Liverpool, under the title 'Magic, Craftsmanship and Science'. Here he emphasized that the progress of science included not only pure, but also applied science: that is, craftsmanship. It was, he suggested, as much a shedding of errors and superstitions as the accumulation of new skills and facts.

So the corresponding development in logic must have involved not only the emergence of new categories and the recognition of new 'laws of thought', but also the transcendance of old categories and the amendment of habits of thinking. In other words the prehistory of sciences would reveal, not a linear addition, but a dialectic comprising the negation of error just as much as the achievement of truth . . . the generative contradiction would be that between theory and practice, between the reflective thought of cloistered priests or philosophers and the successful activities of farmers, craftsmen and experimentalists.[15]

Though not published until 1951, *Social Evolution* was based on a series of lectures delivered by Childe in 1947–8 at the University of Birmingham. The Josiah Mason Lectureship was established in 1946 by the Rationalist Press Association, and the lectures were intended to fall within the field of the social sciences, and to illustrate the scientific method of approach to the problems of civilized society. *Social Evolution* was a theoretical work, and aimed, like *Man Makes Himself* and *What Happened in History*, at the general public as well as the archaeologists.

Childe had already explained his view of the relevance of archaeology to anthropology, and now reiterated it: 'in anthropology archaeology must play the same role as palaeontology does in zoology.'[16] *Social Evolution* documents the successive steps through which barbarian cultures passed on the road to civilization in contrasted natural environments. The evidence is examined to see how far it fits with abstract theories of social evolution, such as Spencer and Morgan's, and whether an analogy with biological evolution can be drawn. Childe was forced to admit that such a analogy was not supported by the facts gleaned from the archaeological evidence. The variation and differentiation of Darwin's evolutionary theory can be compared with an analogous process in cultural evolution: the splitting of large homogeneous cultures into a multitude of distinct local cultures, and documented archaeologically. But equally conspicuous in the archaeological record is convergence and assimilation, to which phenomena it is difficult to find an analogy in organic evolution.

This brought Childe to his important point: the unique role played by diffusion in social evolution.

Now, just as convergence distinguishes social from organic evolution, so diffusion is peculiar to social adaptation—that is, to evolution; so diffusion is culture. For of course culture represents the means by which societies adapt themselves to their environments so as to survive and multiply . . .[17]

He continued by pointing out that at the root of the mechanism of change in organic evolution is mutation; while change occurs in cultures by inventions being passed on by diffusion. But if culture is the means by which societies adapt themselves 'so as to survive and multiply', then he must have believed that culture is biologically profitable as well as socially acceptable. This was always his thesis: his 'revolutions' offer cases of such profitability showing in the demographic record. However culture need only be socially acceptable; and Childe himself knew this. An example is to be found in every edition of *The Dawn of European Civilization* in his description of the French megalithic culture:

. . . superstition absorbed all their energies; the cult of the dead overshadowed all other activities. Its votaries, preoccupied with their gloomy ritual and fettered by sacerdotal conservatism, originated nothing. Neither the advent of the bell-beaker folk nor the civilizing currents of commerce roused the western megalith-builders from their ghostly preoccupations to the creation of an original bronze age. . . . Thus the legacy left by the 'Children of the Sun' was only a dark superstition which retarded progress.[18]

This clearly reveals a discrepancy in his thought at this time. For the 'gloomy ritual' and 'cult of the dead' were all inventions, though, according to Childe himself, totally unprofitable. Furthermore he had assumed, and not explained, inventions and their social acceptance, upon which rested his whole theory that 'the concept of cultural evolution as a rational and intelligible process has been vindicated'.[19] In *Social Evolution* he explicitly rejected the analogy between cultural and organic evolution. But he wished to believe that 'cultural change is an orderly and rational process that can be understood by the human intellect without invoking any necessarily incalculable factors and miracles';[20] and he was selective in the data he produced for the expression of this theory.

In 1950 Gordon Childe had made a clear statement of his position as a diffusionist in *Prehistoric Migrations in Europe*. Although this book was published in 1950 it contained a number of themes reminiscent of his pre-war interests. It was based on a course of ten lectures delivered at Oslo in 1946 before the Institutet for Sammenlignende Kulturforskning. The lectures formed part of a series arranged in 1925 by the Norwegian Institute for Comparative Research in Human Culture on 'the importance of the great Migrations to the evolution of European culture during late Antiquity and the early Middle Ages.' With such a clearly stated outline of his subject Childe abandoned the Marrist model he had used in *Scotland Before the Scots* (published the same year he gave the Oslo lectures), and concentrated instead on the traditional British diffusionist thesis. He had learnt from his experiment in *Scotland Before the Scots* that external influences could not be entirely ignored in writing the prehistory of Europe. He wrote:

I am a diffusionist in the following senses: I assume that major technological inventions and discoveries—the wheeled cart, the potter's wheel, intelligent copper smelting, the rotary quern, the scythe—were usually made but once and diffused from a single centre. In prehistoric archaeology this seems to be a useful working hypothesis or heuristic principle unless there are objective grounds against it . . . I am a diffusionist too in that I assume, that minor but quite arbitrary changes or devices occurring or current in more or less adjacent areas and about the same time are not likely to be independent but to reflect diffusion.[21]

Childe accepted diffusion, then, as a working hypothesis; but he was well aware of the dangers of subjective interpretation of culture change: 'Still more debatable is the mechanism of diffusion. How far should it be explained by cultural borrowings between two independent societies and how far by migration, the replacement or conquest of one society by another?'[22]

He had not forgotten his original philological interests and devoted some space in *Prehistoric Migrations* to considering the archaeological evidence for the Indo-European speaking peoples. He was less sure of the plausibility of the task in 1950 than he had been 25 years earlier, and he realized that in spite of the additional data accumulated since 1926 he had no more proof of his thesis. By 1957 he was convinced that a search for the Indo-European speaking peoples was not a fruitful problem for archaeological research: 'I no longer believe that the problem can be solved archaeologically with the available data, nor that any strictly archaeological research, not even excavation, can profitably be directed simply to its solution.'[23]

Gordon Childe paid his last visit to the USSR in 1953, and his interest in Russian sites and museums continued. His article contributed to the *Anglo-Soviet Journal* in 1952, 'Archaeological Organization in the U.S.S.R.', contains a particularly interesting statement on the issue of 'Marrism', written only two years after its denunciation by Stalin. Childe reminded his readers that 'Marxism does not mean a set of dogmas as to what happened in the past (such would save you the trouble of excavating to find out!), but a method of interpretation and a system of values.'[24] Dialectical materialism seeks to explain change as far as possible in terms of internal development. However,

. . . the first converts to Marxism among former bourgeois prehistorians after the Revolution were more enthusiastic than profound. Intoxicated by their success in making a superficial, literal application of Engels's scheme yield a more satisfying interpretation of archaeological data than had the old migrationist postulates, they never took the trouble to master the deeper implications of the method. This was particularly true of N. Y. Marr . . .[25]

His own experiment in *Scotland Before the Scots* had taught Childe that external stimuli could not be ignored as a factor in cultural development. Although he always warmly supported Russian archaeology, he was aware too of the fluctuation of Soviet theories with the Party line. He was not a dogmatic Marxist, and was always critical of any tendency in fellow Marxists of any country to go beyond what the facts would bear. It was his insistence on the primary need to ascertain the facts which led him in 1957 to refuse an invitation to write a volume on Russia for the *Ancient Peoples and Places* series. He wrote to the editor, Glyn Daniel:

Even if one did explore the unpublished collections in remote museum magazines . . . I shouldn't find the evidence to produce a coherent story that would convince me, for I don't believe it yet exists. One cannot just enumerate a number of archaeological 'facts' in any old order; they must be set at least in a chronological frame. But the relative and absolute chronology for the neo- and palaeometallic stages is just hopelessly vague. The official Russian schemes are really just guesses that do not attract, still less convince me.[26]

During Childe's last few years he wrote a considerable number of new books. *Piecing Together the Past*, subtitled 'The Interpretation of Archaeological Data', was published in 1956 and was based on lectures given over the preceding decade at the Institute every alternate year, devoted to principles of archaeological classification, implicit interpretative concepts and current terminology. A former student of Childe's recalled that he was uncertain about publishing the material of these lectures in book form, but as a study of archaeological theory and method at the time, *Piecing Together the Past* is a significant book. Childe defined concepts which had been widely used and assumed in archaeology but rarely explicitly formulated, such as 'artefact' and 'culture-cycle'. However he did not have a positive contribution to make to all the methodological and theoretical problems of archaeology. The *Antiquity* review of the book pointed out that 'He is critical of the inconsistencies in current archaeological nomenclature and practice and points out how confusing and ambiguous they may be; yet he has refrained from proposing any ideally logical system of classification and terminology, largely on the ground that nobody would adopt it if he did.'[27]

Childe's discussion of the term 'culture' in *Piecing Together the Past* is unsatisfactory in two ways. Firstly, although he is clearly aware of a problem arising through the many different usages of the term, including the general ethnographers' sense as well as his own specialized sense defined in *The Danube in Prehistory* in 1929, he does not attempt to solve the difficulty. Ten years earlier, writing to American prehistorian Robert Braidwood, he had discussed this more fully:

As to the terminology the use of 'culture' by archaeologists is I admit open to a number of objections, but I would not include among them the anthropologists' usage of the term; this to my mind is one of the main advantages of it. The Beaker culture or the Dimini culture to my mind represent precisely the same sort of entity as the Plains culture or Maori culture albeit less perfectly known. Maori culture is not only social organization and supersititions (about which archaeologists can say practically nothing) but also woodworking, adzes, agriculture, etc. about which the archaeologist can say quite a bit. Archaeologist's (sic) cultures should therefore be comparable to the ethnographers'. This does not explain away the objection that culture is used in such a lot of other senses. But assemblage, though descriptively correct, tends to foster what R.B. called the 'threads and patches theory' that a culture is a collection of disparate traits brought together by historical accident.[28] . . . And archaeologists now try to describe their cultures 'functionally' as much as ethnographers do. The term complex would be better, but is I think wanted for the traits that cluster about a given item of culture and are functionally related thereto, like the tobacco complex in American ethnography or the malachite complex in Egyptian prehistory. So I am inclined for the present to stick to 'culture'.[29]

The second weak point in his discussion of 'culture' in *Piecing Together the Past* was that he did not face up to the problem, becoming increasingly evident as archaeological data amassed, of the subjective nature of the classification of archaeological groups. In *The Danube* in 1929 he had believed that a culture was a definite entity whose components were waiting only to be discovered; in *Social Evolution* in 1951 he was aware that the problem was more complex:

Culture and society are abstractions. No two products of handicraft are strictly identical. Every family of craftsmen, and every member of such a family, have their own tricks of style. No two villages yield precisely the same complex of relics and traits. The subjective element comes in in deciding which idosyncrasies should be ignored in defining a culture. Frankly, it is hard to say which should be disregarded as purely individual and which should be taken as social traits, the differentiae of new cultures.[30]

Childe was concerned to bring scientific precision to archaeology, and *Piecing Together the Past* indicated the complex problems involved in the interpretation of data. The book was designed not so much for the public as for archaeologists and student archaeologists. The apparent banality of the chapter headings is really deceptive simplicity. Childe's point is just that there is no one-sentence answer to 'What is the "archaeological record"?'; 'How long ago did that happen?'; 'What happens in prehistory?'. The title of the final chapter of the book, 'What is the good of archaeology?', does not necessarily imply that he was justifying the usefulness of archaeology to himself; he had devoted a life-time's study to archaeology, and knew its uniquely important contribution to historical knowledge. He suggested here that archaeology can recover prehistoric thoughts, in so far as they were translated into action and left a material expression in the archaeological record. What did not remain in the record were expressions of 'ideological delusions'. These delusions played no part in man's progress; their loss, Childe suggested, is of no great importance. Certain aspects surrounding, for example, the building of a megalithic tomb—its economic and social role or its contribution to practical science—were not 'at all likely to have been present to the consciousness—a "false conscious-ness"—of the architects and builders . . . their motives, like their emotions, have been lost forever, just because they were illusions.'[31]

Also published in 1956 was a small volume entitled *A Short Introduction to Archaeology*. Designed for the general public, the book was an introduction to the limitations and possibilities of archaeology and the first two chapters contained a précis of his theoretical arguments expounded in *Piecing Together the Past*. Childe was at pains to point out that as an important source of history, archaeology differed from the mere collection of objects: 'All archaeological data are expressions of human thoughts and purposes and are valued only as relevations thereof. This differ-entiates archaeology from philately or picture-collecting.'[32]

Whilst many of Gordon Childe's books had some philosophical content, *Society and Knowledge* (1956) was a work dealing specifi-cally with problems of epistemology. He had been fascinated by philosophy since his introduction to it at Sydney University in 1911. *Society and Knowledge*, first published in America, was a personal statement of his beliefs. He was well aware that they did not fall easily into any accepted category, as he explained in a letter to his cousin Alexander Gordon: 'I'm sending you a copy of a book I published in USA (despite MacCarthy!). It is not archaeological and not Marxist (at least my Soviet colleagues would not recognize it as such though old Marx might have) so should not be too repellent.'

Knowledge, as he described it, is a sort of map or pattern of ideas which should correspond to the external world. As knowledge is derived from experience, Childe believed the degree of correspondence should become greater as man progresses through time: 'The construction of a known world, an ideal reproduction of the external world, is a cumulative process, and the result at any time represents the pooled experience of mankind.'[33] But knowledge, besides being dependent on society, must at the same time be useful—that is, 'capable of being translated into successful action.'[34]

Society and Knowledge can be criticized on philosophical grounds; and this is not surprising, for after all Childe admitted that he was a prehistorian, and not a 'professional' philosopher. An example is that he describes some characteristics of 'ideas', but cannot define them or distinguish them clearly from 'symbols'. On the other hand the book is written in a style refreshingly free from jargon and is much easier for the layman to understand than most philosophical works. In *Society and Knowledge* Gordon Childe expressed his belief in a dynamic view of reality:

Henceforth I shall state what I believe, not what I claim to know, and shall enunciate beliefs that may not be truths. I believe then that the pattern of Reality—I do know that it is patterned—is at least four-dimensional. Reality is an activity, a process that is neither repeating itself over and over again nor yet is approximating to a predetermined goal or to the realization of a preconceived plan. It is on the contrary genuinely creative, constantly bringing forth what has never been produced before, genuine novelties.[35]

With his arrival at belief in a creative reality, Childe had now finally left behind him, as he noted in 'Retrospect', the need for 'transcendental laws determining history and mechanical causes, whether economic or environmental, automatically shaping its course.'[36] His interpretation of European prehistory could now be both scientific and historical. What is more, he believed that all society needed was enough knowledge to act successfully, and to progress. He said: 'I am not in the least perturbed if my description of Reality as a creative activity of process makes perfect knowledge and absolute truth unattainable.'[37] This belief was surely relevant, near the end of Childe's life, to convincing him that his own contribution to prehistory, however imperfect his interpretations might be, could still be of practical help to future archaeologists.

When Childe wrote the sixth and final edition of *The Dawn of European Civilization* in 1956 he said that he began to recognize 'how right Hawkes had been in 1940 when in his *The Prehistoric Founda-*

tions of Europe he had insisted that, by the Bronze Age, Europe had achieved a kind of culture distinctively its own.'[38] It is rather puzzling why he attributed his enlightenment of this fact to Hawkes, when Childe's *The Dawn* of 1925 testifies to his own earlier expression of it. It seems probable that with the rise of Nazism in the early '30s he became so dissatisfied with his *explanation* of that uniqueness, expounded in *The Aryans* in 1926, which could be linked to Kossinna's racialist doctrines, that he denied, certainly to others and possibly even to himself, that he had recognized the distinctive culture. Now, however, he had a radically different explanation to offer which depended on causes within the socio-economic structure of Bronze Age society: 'The startling tempo of progress in European prehistory thus documented is not to be explained racially by some mystic property of European blood and soil, nor yet by reference to mere material habitat, but rather in sociological and historical terms.'[39]

By now the traditional format of *The Dawn* was too restrictive for a clear exposition of the sociological and historical explanation. Childe included in the sixth edition all the latest archaeological evidence collected since the edition of 1950, but he wrote an entirely new book, *The Prehistory of European Society*, to be 'the final answer to those who told us: "the true prelude to European prehistory was written in Egypt, Mesopotamia and Palestine while the natives of Europe remained illiterate barbarians." '[40]

So *The Prehistory of European Society* (1958) answered the question 'How could European barbarians outstrip their Oriental masters as they have done?' Childe acknowledged his debt to C. F. C. Hawkes' book of 1940, which insisted that the European Bronze Age was not just a degradation, but exhibited progressive and distinctively European innovations. But Hawkes, thought Childe, did not explain clearly why this was so. *The Dawn* of 1957 did offer an explanation, but buried under a mass of data and references; *The Prehistory of European Society* attempted to present the argument more simply. Writing to Hawkes from Australia in June 1957, Childe summed up his answer:

Because the Urban revolution, the precondition of getting a metallurgical industry—a system for the extraction and distribution of metals—*started*, took place in the Ancient East (where alone it *could*) and not Europe (where it couldn't) but that Europe could profit by the distributive system created for the oriental market without having to accumulate the requisite reserves. So in Europe the bronze smiths, the first full-time specialists, were not reduced to the lower class since the fission of society had not yet occurred in Europe and was not necessary.

In 'Retrospect' Childe made it clear that he believed *The Prehistory of European Society* presented an explanation of the distinctive European culture which was both scientific and historical. He wrote: 'I invoke no agencies external to the observed data, no eternal laws transcending the process as empirically given, but historical conjunctures[41] of well-established environmental circumstances and equally well-known patterns of human behaviour legitimately inferred from their archaeological results.'[42] External stimuli, such as environmental circumstances or the movement of peoples, together with internal economic progress, make the process of change 'historical'. The explanation was also 'scientific' because it explained particular events in terms of known universal factors or general laws of human behaviour. Childe believed that the roots of modern European culture lay as far back as the Bronze Age:

The national states that eventually emerged were indeed enormously larger than our Bronze Age tribes and fewer in number. But they have all shown themselves just as mutually jealous in policy and as competitive economically. All have been increasingly dependent on a supra-national economic system for vital raw materials as well as for the disposal of their own products . . . craftsmen, the exponents of applied science, have preserved their traditional freedom of movement within a supra-national economy. The metics at Athens, the wayfaring journeyman of the Middle Ages, and the migrant craft unionist of the nineteenth century are the lineal descendants of the itinerants just described. But so were the Natural Philosophers and Sophists in Classical Greece, the travelling scholars of medieval Europe, and the natural scientists who from the days of Galileo and Newton to 1945 freely exchanged information and ideas by publication, correspondence, and visits regardless of political frontiers.[43]

Childe's final thesis rested mainly on his belief that craftsmen in Bronze Age Europe were, unlike their counterparts in the totalitarian régimes of the Orient, free to travel and free to work for whomsoever they chose. But direct evidence for the unique status which he claimed for these craftsmen can be found nowhere in the archaeological record. Childe was in fact appealing to hypotheses outside the material evidence. This is a major flaw in his last book, for it is the premise on which his whole case rests.

9. Homecoming

A change of premises for the Institute of Archaeology was planned for the academic year beginning in autumn 1956. Childe decided to resign his directorship in the summer of 1956, one year ahead of his official retirement date, so that his successor, W. F. Grimes, could have a fresh start in the new building in Gordon Square.

Characteristically Childe introduced his final lecture course with the same touch of individual humour which he had displayed at his inauguration ten years earlier. The series was called 'A reconsideration of the dawn of European civilization', and dealt with his major work which he had just revised for the fifth time. Daryll Forde recalled the opening lecture on the BBC broadcast of 1958: 'he came onto the platform to an audience composed mostly of students and colleagues of the Institute . . . and spoke as Director of the Institute, saying it would give him great pleasure to introduce Professor Childe to deliver this series of lectures and he would like to say a few remarks about Professor Gordon Childe's work before asking him to speak. He then gave a lecture for an hour as Director Childe making a critique of the background from which Professor Childe had developed his views on the dawn of European civilization a quarter of a century ago, what silly mistakes he had made, the naive interpretation he had adopted at certain points and so on. . . . He carried the whole thing off—a tremendous *tour de force* and the audience of course was delighted.'[1]

On Childe's last day as Director of the Institute there appeared a *Festschrift* edition of the *Proceedings of the Prehistoric Society* with contributions from many of his friends all over the world. He was deeply moved by this gesture, and wrote personally to thank each contributor. He was also honoured on 23 April 1956 by the award of the Gold Medal of the Society of Antiquaries for distinguished services to archaeology. Childe was not without a touch of vanity and despite his unfavourable opinion of the Society, the award—the highest distinction the Society can confer—was not unappreciated. The words with which Mortimer Wheeler closed his Presidential Address to the Antiquaries reflected the world-wide esteem in which Gordon Childe was held: 'When, not long ago, I was invited to take part in a symposium in the University of Chicago, the first request addressed to me was, "Tell us about Professor Childe." In another distinguished university I am assured that undergraduates, in selecting their courses of study, first ask, "Has Gordon Childe written a book about it?" He generally has.'[2]

Childe's farewell party at the Institute was a memorable occasion, attended by his students and colleagues of many nationalities; those who were unable to come sent gifts and messages. Edward Pyddoke was Secretary at the Institute at the time, and recalled that 'upon his retirement the students decided they must have some extra form of celebration . . . and they got in touch with park keepers who produced banks of flowers with which the whole of the entrance hall was filled, and they presented him with a number of things which they thought were suitable for his future career: airweight luggage, and hairbrushes.'[3] A small group consisting mainly of the staff of the Institute had arranged to take Childe out to dinner after the official farewells. They had spent a considerable time waiting for him in the hall of St John's Lodge before he eventually sauntered in, dressed as usual in his shabby and none too clean clothes, unperturbed and apparently quite surprised to find everyone waiting for him to appear.

Many of Childe's friends asked him what his plans for retirement were. He replied that he wanted to go back to Australia, see his native land again, and visit his two surviving half-sisters and his old friends. He also stated unequivocally to several people on separate occasions that he intended to find a suitable cliff and jump off it. Recently he had visited an aged and learned friend and had been struck by his senility, and the reason he gave for wanting to end his own life was that he had a horror of growing old and useless and ending his days with no one to look after him. He feared too that he had cancer and that his doctors were concealing the fact from him. This dislike of old age was not a new idea, thought up in a fit of depression: fifteen years beforehand he had written to O. G. S.

Crawford that he thought suicide would be the only answer in the end. No doubt he dreaded that with retirement his active part in the academic world of prehistoric archaeology would lessen, and with it the friendship and companionship of students which meant so much to him. As an atheist and rationalist there was nothing that Childe considered reprehensible in such a deed; though his Communist acquaintances would have disagreed, and he did not reveal his intentions to them. His personal philosophy was that his works were more important than himself: 'Society is immortal, but its members are born and die. Hence any idea accepted by Society and objectified is likewise immortal. In creating ideas that are thus accepted, any mortal member of Society attains immortality—yes, though his name be forgotten as completely as his bodily form dissolve. Personally I desire no more.'[4]

In the months following his retirement Childe sorted out his papers and gave a large proportion of his vast personal library to the Institute of Archaeology; the remainder was sold through the antiquarian booksellers, Holleyman and Treacher of Brighton. His last will, drawn up in 1953, left all his estate and the income from his royalties to the Institute of Archaeology, with the exception of an annuity to be paid to his sister Ethel in Queensland for her lifetime. Edward Pyddoke, then Secretary of the Institute, was appointed his personal executor, with Grahame Clark of Cambridge as his literary executor.

Gordon Childe gave up his flat at Lawn Road in December 1956, and travelled by air (the Suez Canal was still closed) to spend the winter as the guest of the Indian Government at a Science Congress. He broke his journey at Athens where he arrived late for a Christmas dinner with his former student Sinclair Hood, now Director of the British School of Archaeology at Athens. On his return to England he lived at the Athenaeum and spent a good deal of time playing bridge there. *The Prehistory of European Society* was in the final stages of planning, though it was written mainly on his voyage to Australia and concluded on arrival in his native land. It was seen through the press in England by his ex-student and secretary, Isobel Smith, and copies of his last book were distributed to friends and colleagues after his death from a list he sent to his publishers.

On 10 February 1957 Gordon Childe set off for Gibraltar to spend a fortnight with his student, Celia Topp, whose husband was stationed there. They visited numerous archaeological sites in nearby Spain and Childe gave a lecture to the local archaeological society on Bronze Age Europe, embodying the theme of *The Prehistory of European Society*. He had written before his visit, 'Please remember how stupidly deaf I am—the sort of deafness that prevents my hearing what is said to me in a train or at a party or committee meeting where lots of people are talking . . . Remember too that I've no small talk.'[5] But in spite of his doubts, he greatly enjoyed the social life at Gibraltar, played a lot of bridge and also went to several parties. His friends in London had been worried about his frame of mind in recent months, and Edward Pyddoke had written to Celia Topp in January:

I gather that Gordon will be visiting you on his way back from India, and should like to whisper in your ear. When he was on the point of leaving London he was in very low spirits and was talking of how poor he felt now that he is retired; also he was remembering all his friends who live permanently in nursing homes or lead solitary lives in out-of-the-way cottages. He said he did not relish his own prospects and that it was all very well for folks like me who were married and had a wife and a child to look after me if I became unfit, but what about him etc etc.

This all arose from my question as to what plans he had for accommodation when he returned from Australia—he having surrended his flat in Hampstead. He replied that he doubted if he would return from Australia and that he would in all probability throw himself over some convenient cliff.

Now can you, without appearing to know anything of these words of gloom, cheer him up with some suggestion that he is now Emeritus Professor in the University and that he will have a room in our new building (which goes on apace) and that we shall probably still need him to lecture on Eastern Europe etc?

However his beliefs on the futility of old age were not so easily overthrown, and he left Gibraltar giving the firm impression that he would not return.

Childe sailed again from England on 17 March on the Orient Line ship, the SS Oronsay, travelling back to Australia along the same route that he had traversed on his way from Sydney to Oxford in 1914. He had an enjoyable journey, and wrote to Edward Pyddoke on 29 March off the coast of South Africa: 'We crossed the equator without a jerk—I was actually asleep: it is as hard to plot as the Iron Curtain but 3 nights and 2 days were excessively hot. Fortunately the dining room and lounge are air conditioned to quite Icelandic temperatures and my Australian hock is kept refrigerated. This will go from Cape Town tomorrow. If allowed to enter this police state I hope to ascend (in a train) Table Mountain and deposit there a stone hammer and tangential sickle of ox horn.'

Gordon Childe arrived in Sydney on his 65th birthday, 14 April 1957. Ironically the University of Sydney, which had been so keen to get rid of him in 1918, now awarded him an honorary degree of Doctor of Letters. In true 'Childeish' style, he attended the presentation ceremony dressed in a bright green shirt. Later he was elected a temporary member of the University Club; and after his death he was further honoured at St Andrew's College, for an antique clock was presented in his memory to the Senior Common Room by a famous judge, Legay Brereton. In Sydney he stayed for some time with Dr H. V. Evatt and his wife Mary Alice, with whom he had kept in touch over the years and seen occasionally in Britain. Evatt was the leader of the Australian Labour Party, which in 1957 was disintegrating; politically Childe could not have chosen a more unfortunate time to return to his native land. It seems that Evatt's despair may have influenced his old friend and coloured his impressions of political development in Australia. In August Childe wrote to John Morris, editor of the Marxist journal *Past and Present*:

The Australian Labor Party is in a parlous plight. Evatt is a man of great ability and unusual vision especially on international affairs and he has now cleared the Federal Party of the Roman Catholics who once dominated it to an extent I could never have thought possible. But the party's prospects are not at all bright and the State Parties are still either secretly clerical or split . . .

During the six months he spent in Australia he visited towns and cities all over Eastern Australia as well as Tasmania, but wherever he went he was bitterly disappointed by what he considered to be the lack of cultural and social development. Leaving Australia in 1921, after a period of rapid and innovative changes in social welfare, Childe apparently expected to find great democratic advances by the year 1957. However he had kept in touch with developments in Australian politics and culture over the years through his friends, in particular the Evatts and William McKell, and so his expectations should not have been so impossibly high. He expressed himself shocked and disappointed at the general lack of interest in museums, in Australian prehistory and in current affairs. As an old man accustomed to the best in travel and hotels, he commented unfavourably on those aspects of Australian life which fell short of his standards: 'Australia is rather more uncomfortable than USSR. The standard of public service—hotels trains etc—used to be set by commercial travellers and they didn't like bugs and did demand hot water and porters and quiet writing rooms. The standard is now set by shearers and miners. I don't think they like bugs either but they'll shave (if at all) and bathe (regularly) in cold water don't mind lumping their bags upstairs but demand spacious bars with jazz bands which have accordingly replaced the comfortable Commercial Rooms. Everybody has his own little house and plot and of course a car and does all his own housework and gardening. The result is that suburbs have swallowed up all the country I used to know as wild for miles and miles round Sydney and the traffic congestion is worse than London (but not yet as bad as Istanbul). Still about 50 ms out the Blue Mountains begin to be more or less unspoiled save for a narrow belt of bungalows along the newly electrified railway line. They are just as good as remembered and to me compare favourably with West Highlands or Tyrol . . .'[6] Although he loved Australian scenery, his reaction to Australians, he explained, was still the same as D. H. Lawrence's in *Kangaroo*. His disappointment caused him to over-react, and he came to regard Australia as a cultural desert with no likelihood of becoming, like Britain, a place where intellectuals could be happy. He wrote to John Morris about his feelings:

Australian society is dominated today by the values that Zweig takes as typical of the *British* working class. What is demanded by people who stay in hotels and what is offered by advertizers in the beastly papers is sport and beer and new motor cars. The front page news consists of crimes, divorces and accidents. There is nothing else offered, no hotels where even commercial travellers could work in peace, no decent intelligent daily papers . . . funnily enough no labor papers, still less communist. The only dailies are extremely reactionary and the only European papers they quote are *Express* and *Daily Mail*!

Not long after his arrival Childe travelled to Queensland to visit his two surviving half-sisters, Alice and Ethel. Marion, or 'May' as she was always known, had followed a career as a nurse, holding positions of responsibility in hospitals in Sydney and Brisbane, but had died unmarried around 1948. His elder brother Christopher was a professional pianist and organist who, after his marriage to a woman his father considered unsuitable, had left Australia for good and became the organist for a large Christian Scientist church in

Pasadena, California. Laurence Childe, the father of Mary, had died comparatively young, as the result of a fall from a horse, in January 1939. After leaving Sydney Church of England Grammar School he became a bank clerk, specializing in pastoral work, and finally setting up in business as an inspector and valuer of pastoral properties.

Both Alice and Ethel had connections with the Society of the Sacred Advent, Brisbane, a religious community founded in 1892 by two Church of England Sisters from England. Ethel, who was a gifted musician, was well-known to the Society and taught music at All Saints, one of their hostels for schoolchildren in Charlesville, a small town in south-western Queensland. She was considered something of an invalid throughout her life, a gentle and timid woman, whose happiest memories were of her childhood at the rectory. In 1957 she was living in Toowoomba, 85 miles west of Brisbane, as was her niece Mary. Gordon Childe visited them both and took his sister for long drives to local beauty spots. As always he was unobtrusively kind and thoughtful where his relatives were concerned: he gave Mary a sum of money to bank to be spent on treats for Ethel—more drives and cream cakes, which both she and her brother loved—and also to buy her an oil heater to provide a little more luxury in the home where she lived.

Alice Vernon Childe, Gordon's other half-sister, had entered the Society of the Sacred Advent not long after its foundation, and was known for most of her life as Sister Vernon, though she was always Alice or 'Lala', his special pet name for her, to her younger brother. She was a woman of exceptional personality with a great talent for teaching, and had a considerable impact on education in Queensland. In 1917 Sister Vernon and another Sister of the Sacred Advent were sent by their Mother Superior to establish C of E schools in North Queensland. Sister Vernon became headmistress of St Anne's, a boarding and day school for primary and secondary pupils in Townsville. Her main subject was English literature, but she also taught Scripture, History, Art of Speech and French. She was a particularly inspiring teacher of both History and English, and during her 21 years at St Anne's she produced a play each year on the natural tree-bordered stage in the school grounds. These plays—often Shakespeare, but sometimes Sheridan or Barrie—were acted by pupils, staff and old girls, and were famous far and wide. After she left Townsville, Sister Vernon taught English and Elocution at a small primary school, St Michael's, in Clayfield, Brisbane. By 1957, when

Gordon Childe visited her, she was in her 80s and being cared for by another Sister of the Sacred Advent. Perhaps this brought home to her brother what his own position might be in another 20 years—with the difference that he had no religious faith to sustain him.

Childe visited several old friends in Australia besides his relatives. He stopped briefly in Adelaide to see his friend and associate for many years, J. Fitzherbert, Classics Professor at Adelaide University, who had been a flyer in world war one, and something of a national hero. Childe dined at Adelaide with archaeologist N. B. Tindale, who remembered that Childe was beginning to think in terms of a Far Eastern origin for agricultural civilizations: 'He told me of his surprise in finding side-pebble implements, so characteristic of South East Asia, as far west as the Caucasus Mountains, and was coming to see that the early Hoabinhian of the Far East had a definite relationship with the early Australian tools.'

Another friend from earlier days was the Sydney Professor of Archaeology, James Stewart. Childe visited him and his wife, Eve, a number of times, for a week or so, at Mount Pleasant, their estate near Bathurst, just west of the Blue Mountains. He met there another guest, a young woman student of classical archaeology, and was greatly intrigued by the fact that she smoked a pipe. He insisted on teaching her how to clean a pipe with a blade of grass, as the most economical method. Great was his embarrassment when the blade broke and got stuck in the pipe stem, and had to be removed with fine wire! Childe also talked to her about his ideas for the endless possibilities for the study of Australian prehistory. He felt there was much to do in this neglected field, and he wrote to Mary Alice Evatt in August:

I could not at my age work up an interest in it myself but I'm sure it's something worth studying and preserving. There are only 3 or 4 people working on it at all seriously with rather inadequate training and hopelessly inadequate resources. One university—probably ANU—ought to have a professorship or at least a readership in Australian or Oceanic archaeology. And antiquities ought to be preserved—particularly the 'Aboriginal' rock pictures.

Childe had visited the Australian National University at Canberra, where he gave lectures and seminars. A colleague remembers that he was 'deeply depressed at what he saw of Australian society which appeared to him to be over-fed, culturally destitute and totally suburban. At one point he remarked that there was less socialism in people's consciousness than when he left it more than 30 years before'. Both at Canberra and at the University of New England at Armidale Childe emphasized that he had done all his work, had written all he ever would on his particular field, and had no plans for the future. At Armidale in early August he stayed with Russel Ward, Professor of History, who had, like Childe in 1918, suffered a set-back to his career a year or two before because of his Left-wing views. The two men discussed the state of communism in Iceland, China and other parts of the world, and Childe seemed keenly interested in its progress. He was especially delighted at the successful stand the Icelanders were making at that time over American bases for NATO. From Armidale he travelled to Stonehenge Station, where he had tutored the young Harold Simpson in 1914, and surprised his former pupil with a visit from the now world-famous professor.

Childe paid two visits to Melbourne in 1957, but the last was in September, exactly a month before his death. He had been invited to lecture to a Left-wing literary society called the Australasian Book Society, and it was only a week before his arrival that the prehistorian D. J. Mulvaney became aware of his impending visit. Mulvaney and representatives of the Book Society met the famous prehistorian at the airport, and both offered him accommodation. Mulvaney was able to offer him a room at the exclusive Melbourne Club and this proved most tempting to Childe, bereft of the comforts to which he had become accustomed at the Athenaeum.

Childe's two lectures on prehistory delivered at the University of Melbourne were fitted into the timetable at short notice, and were, like most of the lectures he gave during his last months, largely on the theme of *The Prehistory of European Society*. However his address to the Australasian Book Society, which summed up his impressions of his native land after his long absence, was altogether more controversial and sardonic. He compared the achievements of Australians with those of Icelanders, and concluded that Iceland's culture in the tenth century was more vital than that of Australia in the twentieth. He pointed out, for example, that although Australia's population was almost 40 times that of Iceland, the smaller country had more Nobel prize winners. The only place in Australia for which he seemed to have any respect was Broken Hill, a New South Wales mining town. He had visited Broken Hill and thought that the miners showed more enterprise and cultural interest than people in the big cities like Sydney, Adelaide or Canberra.

At Melbourne Childe was reluctant to discuss world politics with members of the Left-wing book society; but he left its members with the strong impression that he felt he had finished his work as a scholar. One of the audience of Childe's ruthless speech was Brian Fitzpatrick, who later wrote: 'After the speeches, Childe told me he intended to return, two months thence, to Europe. He had done all he intended to do on prehistory. . . . He said, "Now I am going back to my first love, epistemology. . . . I shall see whether I am still capable of thinking about Thinking." '[7]

During the last week of his life Childe broadcast a talk in the 'Guest of Honor' series on Australian radio. The talk consisted mainly of the argument presented in his last book, but was aimed, for his Australian audience, at exposing the probable falsity of the viewpoint that 'the true prelude to Australian history was written in the British Isles and Continental Europe, while the aborigines stagnated in illiterate savagery.'[8]

However Gordon Childe had not travelled to his native land after an absence of 35 years with the primary purpose of suggesting what a systematic examination of the archaeological data might do for Australian history. He had returned to Australia to visit remembered scenes and friends, and that is how he spent most of his time. It must have seemed strange to him to be reading tourist brochures on places which he had known well 35 years ago, but which had since grown out of all recognition. At the end of August he travelled to Wentworth Falls, where the current occupants of 'Coronel' showed him round the house built by his father. He wrote to his niece Mary: 'Really I found I had forgotten it altogether and would not have recognized it but for the name on the gate. . . . It now strikes me as a ridiculously extravagent house with all that useless basement; my poor dear father never was any good at economizing.'

He spent a lot of time staying at Katoomba, near Wentworth Falls, delighted to be again among the Blue Mountains he remembered from his boyhood. Returning to his early interest in geology, he employed the unaccustomed leisure of retirement in making hundreds of sightings from the peaks and 'Look Outs' of the mountain ranges. On the three occasions he visited Katoomba in these last months he stayed at the Carrington, a hotel he thought greatly superior to most in Australia. There he wrote a number of final letters to his closest friends and formers students; letters which were relaxed and informal in tone, with a greater degree of personal detail than his usual correspondence. In early October he wrote to Humphrey Case, who had studied at London Institute:

I have employed the past couple of months with enormous zest satisfying my youthful craving to understand the complicated arrangement of the pale blue ranges that bounded the wide valley on the precipitous edge of which we had a summer house. Now I have reached most of the vantage points in taxis and climbed to some.[9]

The manner of Gordon Childe's death caused speculation at the time and is still the subject of dispute among those who knew him. One of his last actions at Katoomba was to post to Professor W. F. Grimes, his successor at the Institute, a statement of his beliefs on old age—his own and other people's. He requested that it should not be opened until January 1968, explaining in an accompanying letter to Grimes that it contained 'matter that may in time be of historical interest to the Institute. But now it may cause pain and even provoke libel actions. After ten years it will be less inflammable.'[10] In fact the statement was published for the first time in March 1980 in an editorial of the journal *Antiquity*. It seems to clarify both that Childe did indeed commit suicide, and some of his reasons for doing so. The statement is more than an expression of personal beliefs: it is also a thoughtful essay on the problem of old age; but it is the unusual revelation of his own feelings which make it a moving and even disturbing document:

> THE CARRINGTON
> KATOOMBA
> BLUE MOUNTAINS, N.S.W.

The progress of medical science has burdened society with a horde of parasites—rentiers, pensioners and other retired persons whom society has to support and even to nurse. They exploit the youth which is expected to produce for them and even to tend them. While many are physically fit to work and some do, others are incapable of looking after themselves and have literally to be kept alive by the exertions of younger attendants who might be more profitably employed otherwise. And in so far as they do work, they block the way to promotion against younger and more efficient successors. For all in all persons over 65—there are of course numerous exceptions—are physically less capable than their juniors and psychologically far less alert and adaptable. Their reactions are slowed down; they can only gradually and reluctantly, if at all, adopt new habits and still more rarely assimilate fresh ideas. I am doubtful whether they can ever produce new ideas. Compulsory retirement from academic and judicial posts and from the civil services has of course done something to open the rewards of seniority to younger men, and has rescued students and subordinates from inefficient teachers and incompetent administrative chiefs. In British universities the survival of the old system during my lifetime has provided cautionary examples of distinguished professors mumbling lectures ten years out of date and wasting departmental funds on obsolete equipment. These instances probably outweigh better publicized cases of scientists and scholars who in their colleagues' opinion are 'forced to retire at the height of their powers'. But even when retired, their prestige may be such that they can hinder the spread of progressive ideas and blast the careers of innovators who tactlessly challenge theories and procedures that ten or fifteen years previously had been original and fruitful (I am thinking for instance of Arthur Evans).

In fact if the over-age put 'their knowledge, experience and skill at the service of society' as honorary officers or counsellors of learned societies, public bodies, charitable institutions or political parties, they are liable to become a gerontocracy—the worst possible form of leadership. In a changing world their wisdom and maturity of judgement do not compensate for their engrained prejudices and stereotyped routines of behaviour. No doubt the over 65s are competent to carry out routine investigations and undertake compilations of information, and may be helped therein by their accumulated knowledge. Yet after 65 memory begins to fail, and even well-systematized information begins to leak away. My personal experience is confirmed by observations on senior colleagues. And new ideas, original combinations of old knowledge, come rarely if at all. Generally old authors go on repeating the same old theses, not always in better chosen language.

I have always considered that a sane society would disembarrass itself of such parasites by offering euthanasia as a crowning honour or even imposing it in bad cases, but certainly not condemning them to misery and starvation by inflation.

For myself I don't believe I can make further useful contributions to prehistory. I am beginning to forget what I laboriously learned—forget not only details (for these I never relied on memory), but even that there is something relevant to look up in my note-book. New ideas very rarely come my way. I see no prospect of settling the problems that interest me most—such as that of the 'Aryan cradle'—on the available data. In a few instances I actually fear that the balance of evidence is against theories that I have espoused or even in favour of those against which I am strongly biased. Yet at the same time I suspect this fear may be due to an equally irrational desire to overcome my own prejudices. (In history one has to make decisions on inadequate evidence, and, whenever I am faced with this necessity, I am conscious of such opposing tendencies.) I have no wish to hang on the fringe of learned societies or university institutions as a venerable counsellor whose authority may slow down progress. I have become too dependent on a lot of creature comforts—even luxuries—to carry through some kinds of work for which I may still be fitted; I just lack the will-power to face the discomforts and anxieties of travel in the USSR or China. And, in fact, though I have never felt in better health, I do get seriously ill absurdly easily; every little cold in the head turns to bronchitis unless I take elaborate precautions and then I am just a burden on the community. I have never saved any money, and, if I had, inflation would have consumed my savings. On my pension I certainly could not maintain the standard without which life would seem to be intolerable and which may be really necessary to prevent me becoming a worse burden on society as an invalid. I have always intended to cease living before that happens.

The British prejudice against suicide is utterly irrational. To end his life deliberately is in fact something that distinguishes *Homo sapiens* from other animals even better than ceremonial burial of the dead. But I don't intend to hurt my friends by flouting that prejudice. An accident may easily and naturally befall me on a mountain cliff. I have revisited my native land and found I like Australian society much less than European without believing I can do anything to better it; for I have lost faith in all my old ideals. But I have enormously enjoyed revisiting the haunts of my boyhood, above all the Blue Mountains. I have answered to my own satisfaction questions that intrigued me then. Now I have seen the Australian spring; I have smelt the boronia, watched snakes and lizards, listened to the 'locusts'. There is nothing more I want to do here; nothing I feel I ought and could do. I hate the prospect of the summer, but I hate still more the fogs and snows of a British winter. Life ends best when one is happy and strong.[11]

Early in the morning of 19 October Gordon Childe set off walking near the beautiful Bridal Veil Falls, and fell 1,000 feet to his death below Govett's Leap at Blackheath in the Blue Mountains. He had gone to the Leap by taxi at eight o'clock, and told his regular driver, a Mr Harry Newstead, that he was walking along the cliff top to study the ranges and would be going back to the Carrington for lunch. Mr Newstead became concerned about noon when the professor had not returned, and started a search for him. A Sydney visitor to the Leap eventually found Childe's compass, mackintosh, pipe and spectacles at the top of the cliff and notified Blackheath police. The coroner's verdict was that he had died as a result of injuries 'accidentally received when he fell from a cliff top', and it was generally believed that he had missed his footing whilst studying the ranges and rock formations of the Blue Mountains.

His funeral service was arranged by his cousin Alexander Gordon and his friend H. V. Evatt, and was held at his father's old church, St Thomas's, North Sydney, on 23 October. Gordon Childe had lived for many years in Britain, and had established a reputation all over the world, but he preferred to end his days in Australia near the place of his birth.

Epilogue

A few weeks before his death Childe drew together 'the conclusions of forty years as to the main tasks confronting archaeology in Britain.'[1] Arriving in London a few days after the news of his death, this article was given the title 'Valediction' and published by the Institute of Archaeology. It provides an unusual statement on the future of his discipline by a scholar at the end of his life, and is reprinted here in full in Appendix I. But in the weeks before his death Gordon Childe had been reviewing his life's work as well as looking to the future of his chosen discipline. In September he had sent an autobiographical piece describing his intellectual career as a prehistoric archaeologist to J. G. D. Clark, and this was given the title 'Retrospect' and printed in the 1957 edition of *Antiquity*. As the only autobiographical statement which he left the article is of particular interest, though of course it has the limitation that it was written with hindsight. At the age of 65, and once more in an Australia which he had found disappointing, he described his work for Labour Premier John Storey as 'a sentimental excursion into Australian politics'.[2] However, it has been shown that in 1921, at the age of 29, he was seriously intending a career in the political field. Similarly, he claims that it was in 1940, and from Hawkes' *The Prehistoric Foundations of Europe*, that he realized that 'by the Bronze Age, Europe had achieved a kind of culture distinctively its own';[3] whereas he had stated this quite clearly in his own *The Dawn of European Civilization* as early as 1925.

'Retrospect' is illuminating, though, in that it tells us what influences Childe felt affected him at various stages throughout his career. It tells us too what he felt in 1957 had been his most useful contributions to mankind. The *Prehistory of European Society* has already been discussed, and it was his opinion that his final book achieved some of the aims set out in 'Valediction': 'It exemplifies better than any other work I know how what everyone will accept as history could be extracted from archaeological finds; whether the particular extract be accepted or no, it should help to confirm the status of archaeology among historical disciplines. At the same time it illustrates what scientific archaeology ought in my opinion to be like.'[4] He believed that prehistoric phenomena should be described in such a way as to be seen as instances of general familiar principles; but that historians should not forget they had to explain individual events. These could be made intelligible by presenting them as historical conjunctures of general and familiar processes and patterns.

The archaeological data are interpreted as the fossilized remnants of behaviour patterns repeatedly illustrated in ethnography and written records. Together with the relevant features of the non-human environment they are presented as instances of more general known processes. So the specific events are explained as individual and perhaps unique conjunctures of known universal factors. Such explanation is scientific as well as historical. It is just so that a geologist would explain the peculiarities of a particular site, where a dam is to be built or a mine shaft sunk, as the resultant of general characters of the minerals exemplified there and the equally general processes of folding, faulting, erosion . . . to which they have been exposed at this precise spot. For natural, like human, history explains particulars by describing them as exemplifying universal laws, and these laws are no longer regarded as imposed upon nature from outside, but as generalized descriptions of what has been observed inside; so 'laws of nature' are not necessary but very highly probable. At the same time, as soon as an event is seen to conform to such a law, it is recognized as rational and logically necessary, or, in a word, understood. Admittedly laws of human behaviour are so far less highly probable than the laws of chemistry and physics that the term law is deceptive. Yet they are or would be of the same kind.[5]

Childe's advice to future archaeologists was soundly based on his own experiences of a life-time devoted to the study of the prehistory of Europe. There is no doubt that his death robbed the world of a man of great erudition and unusual ability. Childe himself was of the opinion that his most original and useful contributions to prehistory were: 'certainly not novel data rescued by brilliant excavation from the soil or by patient research from dusty museum cases, nor yet well founded chronological schemes nor freshly defined cultures, but rather interpretative concepts and methods of explanation.'[6] Though characteristically underestimating his contribution to prehistory—his early research in the museums of Europe and his exhaustive work on relative chronologies were of immense importance—the main truth of this statement is borne out by the debt which prehistoric archaeologists all over the world still owe to many of Childe's basic principles. It is easy to overlook that it was he who first used and made explicit many now-familiar concepts in the interpretation of prehistory—associations, cultures and synchronisms, to name a few. Such concepts are now so familiar they are taken for granted, but when Childe introduced them into the largely typological archaeological world of the 1920s, they were revolutionary. So too it was Childe, almost alone, who between the wars brought British prehistoric studies out of provincialism and into a wider European setting.

Archaeology in the early years of this century was considered very recondite, though important steps had been taken from the dilettante methods of many eighteenth century antiquarians. Childe built on the conceptual and geological advances of the nineteenth century to make the study of prehistory internationally recognized as a serious scientific discipline, and demonstrated the uniquely important role of archaeology in the study of history. He realized that the surviving elements of material culture were to be interpreted as the fossil remains of human behaviour, and that through them prehistorians should perceive communities and societies. His study of Marxism helped him to approach the archaeological data in a way which made this possible. Through his many publications Childe conveyed to specialists and the general reader alike that prehistory was not just a list of pottery types or daggers, but a continuously changing pattern of human life. He was also unique among his contemporaries in that he was profoundly conscious of the philosophical basis of archaeological methods and aims. Although his views on this were not expounded in any detail until the mid-'50s, they nevertheless underlay all his work, and foreshadowed some aspects of the 'New Archaeology' of the '60s and '70s to a surprising extent.

However Gordon Childe was not mourned solely as an eminent prehistorian, for he inspired deep affection as well as respect amongst those who knew him. After his death many of his friends regretted that they had been unable to break through the barrier which in some way prevented Childe from feeling close to his fellow human beings. He was a man of complex personality, and although he was unable to establish relationships on an intimate footing, he loved the company of others. The lack of intimacy in his life may well have led him to devote himself so whole-heartedly to scholarship, and have contributed to his unparalleled impact on the study of European prehistory.

An examination of Childe's life reveals that, whilst his philosophical ideas were never static, his Marxism was not just an individual brand of casuistry applied to his works, but an unobtrusive faith. R. Palme Dutt wrote shortly after Childe's death that 'his philosophical Marxism, reached along the classic royal road through Hegel, helped to give him his strength in the forefront of archaeologists of our time.'[7] This is true: Marxism, as a way of thought, guided his choice of questions, not only his solution to problems. The wife of one of his former students once remarked illuminatingly that she had never particularly noticed any Marxism in his books; this was because his work, though often based on Marxist principles, is never filled with polemic. He differed from other, more orthodox, Marxists of the day in that he did not degenerate into anti-capitalist propaganda, and his work endures better for that reason.

While the main contribution of Marxism to archaeology lay in the interpretative field, Childe always insisted on the primary need for substantiating data; and the scope of the data he presented was unique. Quite apart from Gordon Childe's incalculable influence on archaeological thought in this century, it is unlikely that one man would now be able to produce a work with the exhaustive informational qualities of *The Dawn of European Civilization*. Stuart Piggott's 'Ballade to a Great Prehistorian', written around 1934–5, expresses this sentiment:

BALLADE TO A GREAT PREHISTORIAN

When sounds of verbal conflict fill the air,
    And archaeologists, that curious few,
Debate some problem or in turn prepare
    To build whole cultures on the slightest clue,
    Then soon or late is heard the speaker who
Says to the questing novice—shy, forlorn
    And diffident—'I can't explain to you:
You'll find it in a footnote in The Dawn'.

Are Frankfort's views on Erösd really fair,
    And what says Peet of Anghelu Ruju?
What kind of necklace did the Minyans wear,

And what did Blegen find at Korakou?
  Is *Studie o českém neolithu*
The book to read on harpoon-heads of horn?
  Is Tallgren's Fatynovo theory true?
You'll find it in a footnote in The Dawn.

All secrets of the past are here laid bare—
  What beer the Beaker Folk were wont to brew,
The answer to a Lausitz maiden's prayer,
  The recipe for Maglemose fish-glue,
  What style of beard the Michelsbergers grew,
The songs they sang when gathering in the corn
  At harvest-homes in late Danubian II—
You'll find them all in footnotes in The Dawn.

Envoi

Prince—to your learning be all honour due!
  How will eternity treat man, its pawn?
Leaving the past, do you then turn and view
  Man's end as but a footnote to his dawn?

STUART PIGGOTT
(c. 1934–35)

Notes and References

The following abbreviations have been used in the notes:

BBC broadcast   British Broadcasting Corporation radio programme, 'The Archaeologist', no. 58, broadcast on 17 June 1958.
R   Childe, V. G. (1958) Retrospect. *Antiquity*, 32, 69–74.
V   Childe, V. G. (1958) Valediction. *Bull. Lond. Inst. Arch.*, 1, 1–8.

Where no author is cited, the work referred to is by V. Gordon Childe.

Chapter 1
1. Fink, D. P. J. (1954) *Queen Mary's Grammar School 1554–1954*, 283.
2. *ibid.*, 283.
3. Wright, E. H. Unpublished note quoted in D. A. Dobbyn, 'A look at St Thomas' Parish 1870–1913', unpublished address delivered Sydney, 26 October 1976.
4. Frazer, A. J. A. (1977) Unpublished notes on Sydney clergy.
5. Portus, G. V. (1953) *Happy Highways*, 63–64.
6. Tennant, K. (1970) *Evatt: Politics and Justice*, 24.

Chapter 2
1. Mallowan, M. (1977) *Mallowan's Memoirs*, 26.
2. R, 69.
3. Evans, J. (1964) *Prelude and Fugue*, 73.
4. Evans, J. (1943) *Time and Chance*, 367.
5. (1915) Letter to Stephen H. Childe.
6. Dutt, R. P. (1957) *Daily Worker*, 22 October, 3.
7. (1918) Letter to the Chancellor, University of Sydney.
8. Wilson, H. W. and Hammerton, J. A. (1916) *The Great War*, vol. 7, 37–38.
9. (1917) Letter to the High Commissioner for Australia, London.

Chapter 3
1. (1918) Letter to Dr Harper, St Andrew's College, University of Sydney.
2. *N.S.W. Parliamentary Debates, 1918*, 2nd Series, vol. 72, 1453.
3. (1918) Letter to the Chancellor, University of Sydney.

4. Lindsay, J. (1958) *Life Rarely Tells*, 132.
5. *ibid.*, 132.
6. *ibid.*, 135.
7. *ibid.*, 135.
8. *ibid.*, 135–6.
9. *Daily Standard*, Brisbane, 19 September 1919.
10. Evatt, H. V. (1945) *Australian Labour Leader*, 489.
11. (1964) *How Labour Governs*, 131.
12. (1921) Letter to David Blelloch.

Chapter 4
1. Kelly, V. (1971) *A Man of the People: from Boilermaker to Governor-General*, 36.
2. Childe, S. H. (1922) Letter to Sir George Fuller.
3. Goldring, D. (1945) *The Nineteen-Twenties*, 145.
4. Crowther, J. G. (1970) *Fifty Years with Science*, 20.
5. Undated letter to David Blelloch.
6. Crowther, J. G., *op. cit.*, 20.
7. (1922) The Present State of Archaeological Studies in Central Europe, *Man*, 22, 119.
8. (1964) *How Labour Governs*, 181.
9. Gollan, R. (1964) Review of *How Labour Governs*, 2nd edition. *Labour History*, 7, 61.
10. (1924) A Labour Premier Meets his Masters. *Labour Monthly*, 6, 285.
11. Wheeler, R. E. M. (1955) *Still Digging*, 87.
12. R, 70.
13. (1925) *The Dawn of European Civilization*, xiii.
14. R, 69.
15. (1926) *The Aryans: a Study of Indo-European Origins*, 4.
16. *ibid.*, 211.
17. *ibid.*, 3.
18. *ibid.*, 212.
19. Forde, D. C., BBC broadcast.
20. Extract from Lord Abercromby's Trust Disposition and Settlement dated 10 April 1916.
21. Dutt, R. P. (1965) The Pre-Historical Childe. *Times Literary Supplement*, 539.

Chapter 5
1. V, 3.
2. Powell, D. (1973) *The Villa Ariadne*, 50.
3. Cruden, S. (1957) Memorial of Professor V. Gordon Childe. *Proc. Soc. Antiq. Scotland*, 90, 258.
4. (1939) Some Results of Archaeological Research in Scotland 1932–7. *Lond. Univ. Inst. Arch. Second Ann. Rep.*, 42.
5. Bridge, A. (1949) *And Then You Came*, 172.
6. Piggott, S. (1958) Vere Gordon Childe. *Proc. Brit. Acad.*, 44, 308.

7. (1932) Chambered Cairns near Kilfinan, Argyll. *Proc. Soc. Antiq. Scotland*, 46, 415–16.
8. Cruden, S., *op. cit.*, 257.
9. (1946) *Scotland Before the Scots*, 33.
10. *ibid.*, 33.
11. Cruden, S., *op cit.*, 258.
12. Lawrence, D. H. (1923) *Kangaroo*, 387.
13. Undated letter to O. G. S. Crawford.
14. Zuckerman, S. (1978) *From Apes to Warlords*, 87.
15. *ibid.*, 393–394.
16. Piggott, S., *op. cit.*, 312.
17. (1947) *History*, 37.
18. (1979) Prehistory and Marxism. *Antiquity*, 53, 93–95.
19. (1945) Rational Order in History. *Rationalist Ann.*, 24–25.
20. (1933) Is Prehistory Practical? *Antiquity*, 7, 410.
21. *ibid.*, 418.
22. (1936) International Congresses on the Science of Man. *Nature*, 137, 1074.
23. (1946) Letter to R. J. Braidwood.
24. Crawford, O. G. S. (1957) Prof. V. Gordon Childe. *The Times*, 5 November, 13.
25. (1939) Answers to questionnaire. *Daily Worker*, 14 October, 1 and 6.
26. (1939) Letter to Sir W. Lindsay Scott.
27. (1940) Letter to O. G. S. Crawford.

Chapter 6
1. (1928) *The Most Ancient East*, 1.
2. (1929) *The Danube in Prehistory*, v–vi.
3. R, 71.
4. (1930) *The Bronze Age*, 4.
5. (1935) Changing Methods and Aims in Prehistory. *Proc. Prehist. Soc.*, 1, 7.
6. *ibid.*, 9.
7. Crawford, O. G. S. (1936) Human Progress: a Review. *Antiquity*, 10, 404.
8. (1936) *Man Makes Himself*, 4.
9. *ibid.*, 2.
10. *ibid.*, 16.
11. *ibid.*, 268.
12. R, 72.
13. (1937) A Prehistorian's Interpretation of Diffusion. In *Independence, Convergence and Borrowing in Institutions, Thought and Art*, 4.
14. (1939) The Orient and Europe. *Amer. J. Arch.*, 43, 21–22.
15. R, 72.
16. R, 73.
17. (1942) *What Happened in History*, 252.
18. R, 73.
19. (1942) *What Happened in History*, 150.
20. *ibid.*, 16–17.
21. R, 73.

22. Ravetz, A. (1959) Notes on the Work of V. Gordon Childe. *The New Reasoner*, 10, 60.
23. (1944) *Progress and Archaeology*, 73.
24. *ibid.*, 109.
25. *ibid.*, 114.
26. (1944) Archaeological Ages as Technological Stages. *J. Roy. Anthrop. Inst.*, 74, 21–23.
27. *ibid.*, 23.
28. Crowther, J. G. (1970) *Fifty Years with Science*, 246.
29. (1958) *The Prehistory of European Society*, 173.
30. (1935) *The Prehistory of Scotland*, xi.
31. R, 73.
32. Daniel, G. E. *A Hundred and Fifty Years of Archaeology*, 373.
33. Davidson, J. M. (1950) Review of *Scotland Before the Scots*. *Antiquity*, 24, 56.
34. R, 73.

Chapter 7

1. Mallowan, M. (1977) *Mallowan's Memoirs*, 239.
2. (1934) *New Light on the Most Ancient East*, 207.
3. Wheeler, R. E. M. (1955) *Still Digging*, 192.
4. Wheeler, R. E. M. (1957) Prof. V. Gordon Childe. *The Times*, 23 October, 13.
5. (1946) Archaeology as a Social Science. *Inst. Arch. Ann. Rep.*, 3, 57.
6. *ibid.*, 50–51.
7. Piggott, S. (1958) Vere Gordon Childe. *Proc. Brit. Acad.*, 44, 312.
8. Daniel, G. E. (1975) *A Hundred and Fifty Years of Archaeology*, 356.
9. V, 1.
10. Dutt, R. P. (1965) The Pre-Historical Childe. *Times Literary Supplement*, 539.
11. (1945) Letter to R. J. Braidwood.
12. (1946) Letter to C. H. Desch.
13. (1945) Letter to R. J. Braidwood.
14. Mallowan, M., BBC broadcast.
15. (1948) letter to J. Banner, quoted in J. Banner (1958) Vere Gordon Childe. *Acta Archaeologica*, 8, 322.
16. Neustupný, J., BBC broadcast.
17. Mallowan, M., BBC broadcast.
18. V, 8.

Chapter 8

1. Clark, J. G. D. (1976) Prehistory Since Childe. *Bull. Lond. Inst. Arch.*, 13, 4.
2. (1952) Review of *Prehistoric Europe: the Economic Basis*. *Antiq. J.*, 32, 209.
3. *ibid.*, 210.
4. (1946) Archaeology and Anthropology. *S.W.J. Anthrop.*, 2, no. 3, 243.

5. Thomson, G. (1949) Review of *History*. *The Modern Quarterly*, N.S. 4, 267.
6. (1946) Archaeology and Anthropology. *S.W.J. Anthrop.*, 2, no. 3, 251.
7. (1947) *History*, 68.
8. *ibid.*, 68.
9. *ibid.*, 72.
10. (1956) The Past, the Present and the Future: review article. *Past and Present*, 10, 4.
11. (1947) *History*, 83.
12. Quoted in Miller, M. (1956) *Archaeology in the U.S.S.R.*, 151.
13. (1952) Social Worlds of Knowledge: Hobhouse Memorial Lecture no. 19. *Hobhouse Memorial Lectures 1941–50*, 23.
14. (1949) The Sociology of Knowledge. *The Modern Quarterly*, N.S.4, 303.
15. (1950) *Magic, Craftsmanship and Science*, 19.
16. (1951) *Social Evolution*, 7.
17. *ibid.*, 168–169.
18. (1925) *The Dawn of European Civilization*, 284–285.
19. (1951) *Social Evolution*, 179.
20. *ibid.*, 175.
21. (1950) *Prehistoric Migrations*, 9.
22. *ibid.*, 9.
23. V, 2.
24. (1952) Archaeological Organization in the USSR. *Anglo-Soviet J.*, 13, no. 3, 25.
25. *ibid.*, 26.
26. Quoted in G. E. Daniel (1958) Editorial. *Antiquity*, 32, 66.
27. Addison, F. (1957) Review of *Piecing Together the Past*. *Antiquity*, 31, 52.
28. Childe is here referring to the 1935 paper by the structural-functionalist A. R. Radcliffe-Brown in *American Anthropology*, 37, 394–402, 'On the Concept of Function in Social Science', which criticized the particularist or '*shreds* and patches' theory of culture originally so described by Robert Lowie in *Primitive Society* in 1920.
29. (1946) Letter to R. J. Braidwood.
30. (1951) *Social Evolution*, 40.
31. (1956) *Piecing Together the Past*, 177.
32. (1956) *A Short Introduction to Archaeology*, 11.
33. (1956) *Society and Knowledge*, 61.
34. *ibid.*, 4.
35. *ibid.*, 123.
36. R, 73.
37. (1956) *Society and Knowledge*, 126.
38. R, 74.
39. (1973) *The Dawn of European Civilization*, 6th edition, 396.
40. R, 74.
41. 'conjectures' in the original is surely a misprint for 'conjunctures'. C. F. C. Hawkes has suggested that Childe took the term (*Konjunktur* in

German) from Nils Åberg's five-volume work, *Bronzezeitliche und Früheisenzeitliche Chronologie*, published in Stockholm (1930–35).
42. R, 74.
43. (1958) *The Prehistory of European Society*, 172–173.

Chapter 9
1. Forde, D. C., BBC broadcast.
2. Wheeler, R. E. M. (1956) Presidential Address. *Antiq. J.*, 36, 171.
3. Pyddoke, E., BBC broadcast.
4. (1956) *Society and Knowledge*, 130.
5. (1956) Letter to Celia Topp.
6. (1957) Letter to Celia Topp.
7. Fitzpatrick, B. (1958) In Memoriam: V. Gordon Childe. *Overland*, 11, 22.
8. (1957) Australian Broadcasting Commission radio programme, 'Guest of Honor', broadcast on 13 October.
9. (1957) Letter to Humphrey Case, quoted in H. Case (1957) Prof. V. Gordon Childe. *The Times*, 13 November, 13.
10. (1957) Letter to W. F. Grimes, quoted in G. E. Daniel (1980) Editorial. *Antiquity*, 54, 1.
11. (1957) Quoted in G. E. Daniel (1980) Editorial. *Antiquity*, 54, 2–3.

Epilogue
1. V, 1.
2. R, 69.
3. R, 74.
4. R, 74.
5. R, 74.
6. R, 69.
7. Dutt, R. P. (1957) Prof. V. Gordon Childe. *The Times*, 24 October, 14.

APPENDIX I: Valediction

*by V. Gordon Childe**

Having reached the age at which a university professor is bound to retire, it may be useful to sum up the conclusions of 40 years as to the main tasks confronting archaeology in Britain.

1. First a truism that is hardly a task for archaeology: our most urgent need is still a reliable absolute chronology or at least a global temporal frame within which events in different cultural provinces may be compared, i.e. seen as earlier, contemporary or later. It is theoretically feasible to correlate the several relative chronologies, established stratigraphically in the different provinces, so that the horizontal lines dividing each of the vertical columns should run continuously across the whole page, dividing it into truly global periods. But reliable correlations can only be effected by 'cross-datings', by this I mean the observed interchange of type-fossils, manufactured articles each distinctive of a province and a period in it. That alone can establish synchronisms; typological homotaxy or stadial equivalence must never be mistaken for contemporaneity as it was so long by those who believed that 'Aurignacian' or 'Neolithic' designated a precise span of sidereal time. In so far as the net of periods, thus duly established, embraced provinces in which written records were available, some periods would then receive limiting dates in years and so acquire duration. But before the Bronze Age such interchanges of archaeologically usable articles must have been exceedingly rare. Before 3000 B.C. no periods whatsoever could be given 'historical' dates. Finally the dates extracted from written texts

* This essay was received in London after Professor Childe's death, having been posted by surface-mail early in October, 1957. It has been given a title but is otherwise printed as received.

166

are often very unsatisfactory. Estimates for the first of these, the unification of Egypt under 'Mena', range over at least 300 years; in Mesopotamia all dates before Sargon of Agade are little more than guesses, and his date, dependent on that of Hammurabi, may be put anywhere between 2350 and 2270 B.C.; in Scotland not a single size or type can be confidently and precisely located between A.D. 400 and A.D. 800! In fact long before an archaeological frame has been fitted by cross-datings firmly on to Europe and the Near East (*sensu Americano et Europaeo sed non Anglico*) a more trustworthy chronology, independent of archaeology and of any historical assumption, may well have been provided by radio-carbon, and that is already being invoked to check historical dates in Egypt and Mesopotamia. In other words, archaeologists will abandon responsibility for chronology or themselves become nuclear physicists. In any case every prehistorian must master enough mathematics, physics and chemistry to appreciate the limitations of the information the latter can provide.

Nor can I now regard as an immediately fruitful direction for archaeological research the problem that originally led me into archaeology—to identify the 'primitive culture' of the Indo-Europeans and to locate their *Urheimat*. I still believe that this is a legitimate question. An Indo-European culture must have existed as much as an Indo-European language and should be identifiable by archaeological means, and to it should be traceable distinctive traits in some cultures of India, Iran, Greece and Italy. But I no longer believe that the problem can be solved archaeologically with the available data nor that any strictly archaeological research, not even excavation, can profitably be directed simply to its solution. A thorough study of the animal bones from excavated sites by a competent zoologist might contribute to a solution; Indo-European familiarity with horses is certain and distinctive, while the diagnosis of equine bones—and often their stratigraphical position—at Anau and Sialk, in Anatolia and Greece is very unsatisfactory. But that is a task for zoology rather than archaeology as usually conceived. And careful collection of animals bones in future excavations especially in India, Iran and the Near East will surely be needed before conclusive results are to be expected. In museum cases there may still be lying about unrecognized some bits or models of wheeled vehicles that were just as certainly familiar to Indo-Europeans though not so distinctive, but such unknown examples must be very few, and there is no use digging just to find more; for wheeled vehicles are preserved only under quite exceptional circumstances and will turn up as an uncovenanted bonus in the course of excavations directed to other ends as at Storozhevaya Mogila.

The economic, sociological and ultimately historical interpretation of archaeological data has, I believe, now become a main task that can contribute enormously to human history and should enhance the status of archaeology.

2. (i) A deeper analysis and ecological description of recognized cultures directed towards disclosing the functional integration of their surviving constituents and reconstituting the economic and sociological linkages between the latter are suitable themes for doctorial theses, though even these demand botanical and zoological diagnoses of food refuse and petrological and metallographic analyses of artifacts and a reconstitution of the environment with the aid of pedology and palaeobotany.

So soon as a reasonable culture sequence be available (as now over most of Europe and the Near East) the immediate task is first to clarify the economy and sociology of the constituent cultures, or rather of the societies they represent in the archaeological record. What did they live on? Here botanical and zoological reports on food refuse will be requisite. In what environment? But remember that the effective environment was that known to and exploited by the society with its available equipment and applied sciences. How was the land exploited—from lone-steadings, dispersed hamlets or nucleated villages? How old is the lone-steading so characteristic of the British Iron Age? Air-photography has revealed it in 'Neolithic' Apulia and Calder's 'Neolithic' farms in Shetland, each on its own distinct plot of arable, belong to this category rather than to that of Skara Brae, Barkaer, Koln-Lindental and other villages. The answers will, of course, illumine the sociological issues connected with land tenure and incidentally the Indo-European problem if Palmer's thesis be accepted. The issues just raised can hardly be settled without some further excavation, and that total excavation, even in North-Western Europe. In the Balkans and on the Anatolian plateau all the relevant and revealing excavations remain to be done; it is conceivable that some Turkish *hüyüks* or Thessalian *toumbas* might turn out to represent just lone-steadings. And finally, how many households in each village or in each natural unit area (a block of downland or a single löss-clad slope might be more profitably considered than *n* square miles of mixed land)? In brief, what sort of population density has to be reckoned with? For this sort of issue a fully excavated cemetery would be nearly as good as a totally excavated village, but in either case we must be able to estimate the total number of graves or houses and in the former instance we need some idea of the age at death and the duration of the cemetery's use.

Note that not only for prehistoric phases but also for periods fitfully illuminated by written texts is archaeological evidence needed for the elucidation of economic and demographic as well as technological problems. Even Domesday Book can profitably be supplemented, not just illustrated, by excavation of village sites. Archaeological evidence alone indicates the use of water-power in Roman Britain that would never have been suspected from a study of ancient authors or inscriptions. The excavations at Olynthos have brought us nearer to an estimate of the population of a fifth-century Greek city than all the erudite studies of texts and inscriptions. In so far as the above questions can be answered, a reasonable account of the culture's (i.e. the society's) economy can be offered; the culture can be described as a functioning economic organization.

(ii) From this basis it is worth while and indeed obligatory, however perilous, to attempt some sociological inferences. After all, the division of the product, what Marxists call the relations of production, is really an integral moment in the economy. From cemeteries and totally excavated settlements we have some hope of recognizing not only a *de facto* distinction between richer and poorer households—that on ethnographic evidence might be taken for granted—but also a division of society into rich and poor as classes. Bernabó Brea's recent account of Poliochni, where large and small houses were juxtaposed indiscriminately, represents a 'pre-class' society as surely as the distinction between artisans', 'merchants'' and ruler's *quarters* at Harappa illustrates class division. In the funerary record too class divisions should be reflected in qualitative as well as quantitative differences in architecture, ritual and furniture. 'Royal Tombs' are not merely larger and more richly furnished than the vast majority of contemporary graves, but exhibit also qualitative differences in structure and ritual (*mastaba*, tholoi, human sacrifices, burial of funerary barques or hearses); they perhaps illustrate the elevation of a *king* above society rather than a division within it. But to distinguish such *kings* from the more familiar barbarians' *chiefs* who remain subject to all a tribesman's customary obligations despite pre-eminence in wealth and prestige, experts rather than professionals, may overtax archaeological information. Classes or ranks we may infer confidently but only from contrasts in funerary practice and contrasts that are both quantitative and qualitative; for the qualitative contrast between cremation and inhumation burials in ancient Rome had nothing to do with rank or wealth. By these criteria Dvŏrak could distinguish three classes in some Bylany cemeteries. In the sepulchral record for Mycenaean Greece we cannot find evidence for a three-class system (allegedly implied in some texts) unless we find in addition to tholos tombs (surely attributable to *dioi basilees*) and chamber tombs (belonging perhaps to Palmer's *telestai*) a third kind of grave in which perhaps simple peasants, like the villagers of Korakou and Zyguries, would have reposed. So too the rich Bronze Age barrows of Wessex, Brittany and Jutland cannot be attributed to a pastoral aristocracy—what Australians would call a squattocracy—with real confidence until contemporary commoners' graves have been identified. Unless other Neolithic burials are recognized, long barrows and Megalithic tombs are liable to appear as communal ossuaries to which every member of the local group would eventually be consigned—an inference which reacts terribly on demographic conceptions. This kind of deficiency in the funerary record could, of course, be corrected by reference to settlement sites; but at present no Middle Bronze Age settlements have been identified in Britain or Denmark and no regular village associated with a known long barrow in England or Scotland!

(iii) I believe foredoomed to failure any attempt to recapture the subjective motives or emotions that inspired the overt acts the results of which alone survive in the archaeological record. Archaeologists must resign themselves to adopting a behaviourist position as much as students of animal psychology. It is no more legitimate to impute to Palaeolithic hunters or Neolithic farmers the motives and values of twentieth-century Europeans and Americans than to birds or ants. We can, of course, recognize the utilitarian purposes (not necessarily conscious) underlying the confection of tools, weapons, traps, field systems, dwelling houses and clothes; not, however, the intentions inspiring their ornamentation or the erection of temples, ceremonial burial of the dead, the execution of works of art in inaccessible caves. We should deceive ourselves if we attributed to them equally utilitarian motives. It is fun to find the same pattern on an Arunta churinga and an Irish grave slab. Let us not waste our time in deciphering such sepulchral carvings by reference to the recorded meaning of similar patterns in aboriginal Australia. The value of such ethnographic comparisons is just to show the funny kinds of meanings or purposes that may be attached to the queerer kind of archaeological data. The collection and interpretation of mother-goddesses is just a harmless outlet for the sexual impulses of old men. It can hardly ever throw any real light on the religion or even the sexual behaviour of preliterate societies. The large range of 'ritual' objects deserves the most scrupulous study, but only to extract therefrom the technical capacities, scientific knowledge and aesthetic values of their makers.

(iv) Archaeology can offer authentic documents for the history of science provided it be admitted that Science is just systematized social experience that can be applied—i.e. that works. In reconstituting the techniques used for producing fire, locating minerals, firing pots, smelting ores, laying out a rectangle or subdividing a circle's circumference we are reconstituting the genuine science of the age. Now it may well happen that the best evidence for applications of exact science is to be found in very unscientific ritual monuments. Very probably ideological, rather than utilitarian, motives in the first instance inspired barbarians to lay out accurate right angles or to divide circles symmetrically. True geometrical constructions may be inferred from the dimensions of ritual monuments or actually observed as temporary auxiliary features incorporated in them. The discovery of such applied geometry rather than details of ritual ceremonies or mystic lore justifies and demands the minutest observation, the most scrupulous excavation and the most accurate measurement of 'ritual monuments'.

(v) At least one aspect of ideology is directly, if imperfectly, documented in the archaeological record. The decoration on pots or weapons, paintings or engravings on cave walls or naked rocks, the carving of statuettes or the moulding of figurines may have been executed with a 'magical' intent and so could be interpreted as utilitarian. But that is a guess. Even if it be correct, such products can be more profitably interpreted and evaluated as expressing or approximating to the aesthetic standards and ideals of the artists' societies.

3. No prehistorian can be content with describing, however functionally, his culture as a finished and static organism. It must not only function; it must change, and the observed changes must be described and explained. In so doing it is all too easy to appeal to external factors, to influences from foreign cultures or even migrations. A prehistorian would be well advised to employ a version of Occam's razor and invoke external factors only when compelled by cogent concrete evidence. (It was quite illegitimate to infer 'Mycenaean influence' on Britain or Denmark from such vague similarities as spiral patterns when not a single Mycenaean import had been found in Britain or Denmark and no Danish or British manufacture even suspected in Greece.) As far as possible, changes should be explained by internal development including thereunder adjustments to documented changes in the non-human environment. Of course universal laws of social development are far fewer and far less reliable than Marrists before 1950 thought. Generalizations descriptive of the directions in which societies tend to develop have, however, been inferred albeit from a regrettably few instances. It should be one of the aims of prehistory to examine these and to establish new ones.

4. A tendency to modify tools and weapons in the direction of greater efficiency, to adjust the rural economy to secure higher productivity may provisionally be accepted as common to all progressive societies. Hence all observed changes in those directions could be interpreted as a result of independent inventions provided the postulated inventions are compatible with the observed equipment and technology of the culture. One could thus explain a shift of emphasis from cultivation to pastoralism given cereals and stock or the development of the socketed celt, given bronze-casting and knee-shafting. Even when these conditions are fulfilled, the possibility of diffusion cannot and should not be excluded. How many societies, left quite to themselves, were or are progressive? It is arguable that all progress, indeed all change, is due to the stimulus

of contact with other societies, the cross-fertilization of divergent traditions. Indeed, one ground for demanding a reliable chronological framework is just to see whether there be not a correlation between the rate of change and the intensity of intercourse with other societies. The prehistorian will seek eagerly for any concrete sign of foreign influence without attributing all changes thereto or accepting as evidence therefore rather vague similarities with, say, the pottery of remote regions. How fallacious the 'Mycenaean' inspiration of Iberic pottery has turned out to be! Before diffusion can be invoked to explain an innovation, we must in the first place have found in the archaeological record one society where the device was current earlier, once more requiring a global chronology, and then look for other less ambiguous indications of contact with the culture thus established. And if invasion is to be admitted as the mechanism, the invading culture must be well defined in its home land and must bring with it a substantial number of its distinctive archaeological traits.

5. A prehistorian, like any other historian, should aim not only to describe, but also to explain; historical description should be at the same time explanatory. Phenomena should be so described that they are seen as instances of general familiar principles. In the most successful natural sciences such principles are uniformities, so constant and universal that they are termed laws of nature. In geology, however, their place is taken by processes familiar from many instances—folding, faulting, erosion—and recurrent properties of minerals, rocks, and soils. Historians are provided with a far more restricted equipment of generalizations. The recognizable behaviour patterns common to all societies are virtually those common to all mammals. Despite Spencer and Morgan few, if any, patterns are necessarily associated with evolutionary stages of culture. Still, ethnography does suggest that certain patterns are very frequently associated with specific basic economies—the pursuit of gregarious game, hoe-cultivation in woodlands, grassland or parkland pastoralism, plough cultivation, and so on. A reference to such a pattern is therefore to some extent explicative too.

6. But the historian has to explain the individual and possibly unique event. Uniformities of behaviour just will not do. The

Marrists' appeal to 'uniformities of social evolution' while it seemed to make intelligible the development of each individual culture to which they applied it, completely failed to explain the differences between one culture and another and indeed obliterated or dismissed as irrelevant the differences observed. So it made prehistory unhistorical. To restore historicity it is needless and illegitimate to appeal to undemonstrable genetic factors or to a mechanical determination by the non-human environment on the one hand, or to the unpredictable genius of Great Men or interpositions by an inscrutable providence on the other. The individual and unique can be made intelligible by presentation as an historical conjuncture of general and familiar processes and patterns. Given the general character of Neolithic rural economy and knowing the relative productivity of different environments, it is clear that maximum yields would be obtainable in alluvial river valleys. Noting at once the transport facilities offered by such rivers and the well-illustrated tendency for gods or chiefs, credited with supernatural powers, to accumulate wealth, the observed accumulations in Egypt and Sumer appear logically inevitable. Then appreciating the economic prerequisites for the establishment of a regular machinery for the extraction, distribution and processing of metal, it ceases to be surprising that a true Bronze Age (which implies such a machinery) was achieved first in Egypt and/or Sumer; and finally the observed quite totalitarian concentration of wealth is disclosed as rational, justified as making the technological advance actual. Here without appealing to any written documents an archaeologist can offer a truly historical explanation. It is certainly incomplete and may not be correct, but it does illustrate what archaeology can offer history.

7. The Institute of Archaeology is peculiarly fitted to contribute to the fulfilment of all the above tasks, including even the first. For in all help is needed from disciplines outside the normal curricula or archaeological courses and employing equipment not regularly provided in archaeological institutes—botany, geology, chemistry, physics and zoology. Our Environmental Department constitutes a unique link with these branches of Natural Science and some of the Institute's students are required to master the rudiments of the relevant techniques. This requirement should be extended beyond students of Prehistoric Archaeology to those of Classical, Indian,

Roman and Western Asiatic, since, as I have insisted above, those techniques are no less essential in converting into history the data provided by these branches of archaeology—and other branches not yet covered by distinct Departments in London such as Anglo-Saxon. Nevertheless the future of archaeology lies, I believe, with the historical rather than the naturalistic disciplines. It is a source of history rather than of generalizations claiming the dignity of natural laws. No doubt the archaeologist is predisposed to a sort of materialism. A prehistorian may legitimately excuse his foredoomed failure to recapture 'the thoughts and motives of his agents' by the pleas that they do not matter; it is the results actually achieved that reveal the 'objective will' directing the action and that have to be judged and justified. But every historian is really in the same plight or worse—for he may be taken in by the false and distorted imputations of the agents, their friends or their enemies! More seriously, a prehistorian must be so materialistic as to rank the intuition of Reality achieved by a naked mystic through contemplation of his own navel as of incomparably lower historical value than say the discovery of Pythagoras' Theorem or its converse. And he will be a materialist too in assuming that the value system dominating American society today was at least included in that of every preliterate society. He cannot, however, logically be a complete materialist; for bits of dead matter become even archaeological data only in so far as they are expressions and symbols of human thought and volition, of ideas and purposes that transcend not only each particular embodiment in an archaeological datum, but also each individual actor or thinker being social and therefore eminently immaterial! Archaeology must achieve the status as an university discipline that now it so sadly lacks by integration with the historical disciplines. And thus it will in the end attain a more secure public position than can be earned by sensational finds and even witty wireless programmes.

I.X.57.

APPENDIX II: Bibliography of Childe's Works*

* This bibliography is based largely on the one compiled by Isobel F. Smith and published in 1955 in the *Proceedings of the Prehistoric Society*, 21, 295–304.

Note: For convenience of reference, articles in journals have been listed under the years to which the volumes in question refer and, with the exception of the *Annual Reports of the University of London Institute of Archaeology*, not necessarily under the years of publication. Only the more important book reviews have been included.

ABBREVIATIONS

Acta Arch.	*Acta Archaeologica*, Copenhagen.
A.J.A.	*American Journal of Archaeology.*
Ant.J.	*Antiquaries Journal*, London.
Arch. J.	*Journal of the Royal Archaeological Institute*, London.
Arch.	*Archaeologia*, London.
B.S.A.	*Annual of the British School of Athens.*
D.A.J.	*Derbyshire Archaeological Journal*, Derby.
I.L.N.	*Illustrated London News.*
J.H.S.	*Journal of the Hellenic Society*, London.
J.R.A.I.	*Journal of the Royal Anthropological Institute*, London.
J.R.S.A.I.	*Journal of the Royal Society of Antiquaries of Ireland*, Dublin.
L.A.A.A.	*Liverpool Annals of Archaeology & Anthropology.*
M.A.G.W.	*Mitteilungen d. anthropologischen Gesellschaft in Wien.*
P.P.S.	*Proceedings of the Prehistoric Society*, Cambridge.
P.P.S.E.A.	*Proceedings of the Prehistoric Society of East Anglia*, Norwich.
P.S.A.S.	*Proceedings of the Society of Antiquaries of Scotland*, Edinburgh.
U.J.A.	*Ulster Journal of Archaeology*, Belfast.
W.P.Z.	*Wiener Prähistorische Zeitschrift.*

1915
'On the Date and Origin of Minyan Ware', *J.H.S.*, XXXV, 196–207.

1922
'The East European Relations of the Dimini Culture', *J.H.S.*, XLII, 254–75.
'The Present State of Archaeological Studies in Central Europe', *Man*, XXII, no. 69.

1923
'Some Affinities of Chalcolithic Culture in Thrace', *Man*, XXIII, no. 2.
Obituary: Jaroslav Palliardi, *ibid.*, no. 64.
How Labour Governs, Labour Publishing Co., London.

1924
'A Gold Vase of Early Helladic Type', *J.H.S.*, XLIV, 163–5.
'The Stone Battle-axes from Troy', *Man*, XXIV, no. 51.
'A Labour Premier Meets his Masters: *Labour Monthly*, VI, 282–5.

1925
The Dawn of European Civilization; Kegan Paul, Trench, Trubner & Co.,
     Ltd., London; XVI, 328.
'When did the Beaker-folk arrive?', *Arch.*, LXXIV, 159–78.
Obituary: Dr Ferencz Laszlo, *Man*, XXV, no. 110.
'National Art in the Stone Age' (review of *Urgeschichte der bildenden Kunst in
     Europa* . . . by M. Hoernes), *Nature*, 116, 195–7.
'Greek Myths and Mycenaean Realities' (review of *The Ring of Nestor* . . .
     by A. Evans), *ibid.*, 635–6.

1926
The Aryans: a study of Indo-European Origins; Kegan Paul, Trench, Trubner
     & Co. Ltd., London; XIII, 221.
'Traces of the Aryans on the Middle Danube', *Man*, XXVI, no. 100.
'The origin of European Civilization' (review of *The Aegean Civilization*, by
     G. Glotz), *Nature*, 117, 716.
'Zur Chronologie der älteren Bronzezeit', *W.P.Z.*, XIII, 38–42.

1927
The Dawn of European Civilization (2nd edition).
'The Minoan Influence on the Danubian Bronze Age', in *Essays in Aegean
     Archaeology presented to Sir Arthur Evans in honour of his 75th birthday*, ed.
     S. Casson; Clarendon Press, Oxford; 1–4.
'The Danube Thoroughfare and the Beginnings of Civilization in Europe',
     Antiquity, I, 79–91.

1928
The Most Ancient East: the Oriental prelude to European prehistory; Kegan
     Paul, Trench, Trubner & Co. Ltd., London: XIV, 258.
Translation from the German: *Scythian Art*, by G. Borovka; E. Benn Ltd.,
     London; III.
'Capsians and Badarians', *Ancient Egypt*, 1928, 6–7.
'The Lausitz Culture', *Antiquity*, II, 37–42.
'Relics of Human Sacrifice in the Orkneys', *I.L.N.*, 15 September 1928.
'The Origin of some Hallstatt Types', *Man*, XXVIII, no. 140.

'Lausitzische Elemente in Griechenland', *Mannus*, Ergänzungsband VI: *Festgabe für den 70 jährigen Gustaf Kossinna*; 236–9.
'Nouvelles fouilles au Lapos Halon, près de Tószeg (Hongrie)', *Rev. Mus. Coll. archaeol.*, 13, 3 pp.

1929

The Danube in Prehistory; Clarendon Press, Oxford; XX, 479.
'The Decorative Art of the Prehistoric Village of Skara Brae, Orkney', *I.P.E.K.*, 1929, 53–5.
'Provisional Report on the Excavations of Skara Brae, and on finds from the 1927 and 1928 campaigns', *P.S.A.S.*, LXIII, 225–80.

1930

The Bronze Age; Cambridge University Press; XII, 258.
'New Views on the Relations of the Aegean and the North Balkans', *J.H.S.*, 50, Part 2, 255–62.
'The Origin of the Bell-beaker', *Man*, XXX, no. 142.
'Second Baltic Archaeological Congress: Riga, 18–23 August 1930', *ibid.*, no. 157.
'The Roots of Hellenism' (review of *Who were the Greeks?* by J. L. Myres), *Nature*, 126, 340–1.
'The Early Colonization of North-eastern Scotland', *Proc. Royal Society of Edinburgh*, 50, 51–78.
'Operations of Skara Brae during 1929', *P.S.A.S*, LXIV, 158–90.
'Excavations in a Chambered Cairn at Kindrochat, near Comrie, Perthshire', *ibid.*, 264–72.

1931

Skara Brae: a Pictish Village in Orkney (with chapters by T. H. Bryce and D. M. S. Watson); Kegan Paul, Trench, Trubner & Co. Ltd., London; XIV, 208.
'Skara Brae: a "Stone Age" village in Orkney', *Antiquity*, V, 47–59.
'The Continental Affinities of British Neolithic Pottery', *Arch. J.*, LXXXVIII, 37–66.
'The Forest Cultures of Northern Europe: A study in Evolution and Diffusion', *J.R.A.I.*, LXI, 325–48.
'The Chronological Position of the South Russian Steppe Graves in European Prehistory', *Man*, XXXI, no. 135.
Review: 'Early Man in North-east Yorkshire', by F. Elgee, *Nature*, 128, 776–7.
'Final Report on the Operations at Skara Brae', *P.S.A.S.*, LXV, 27–77.
'The Chambered Long Cairn at Kindrochat, near Comrie, Perthshire', *ibid.*, 281–93.

1932

'A Chronological Table of Prehistory' (with M. C. Burkitt), *Antiquity*, VI, 185–205, folding table as supplement.
'Chronology of Prehistoric Europe: a Review',* *ibid.*, 206–12.
'The Danish neolithic pottery from the coast of Durham', *Arch. Aeliana*, 4th series, IX, 84–8.
'Glacial Geology of East Anglia' (letter to the Editor), *Man*, XXXII, no. 36.
'Russia: a new anthropological museum', *ibid.*, no. 53.
'The Dates of the Beaker Invasions' (letter to the Editor), *ibid.*, no. 102.
'Age of Skara Brae', *ibid.*, no. 225.
'Comparative Notes on a Series of Neolithic Potsherds from Larne' (with S. Piggott), *P.P.S.E.A.*, VII, Part 1, 62–6.
'Scottish Notes', *ibid.*, 129–30.
'Excavations in Two Iron Age Forts at Earn's Heugh, near Coldingham' (with C. D. Forde), *P.S.A.S.*, LXIV, 152–82.
'Chambered Cairns near Kilfinan, Argyll', *ibid.*, 415–25.

1933

Ancient Dwellings at Skara Brae. Official Guide; Ancient Monuments and Historic Buildings, HM Office of Works; HMSO, Edinburgh; 24.
'Notes on some Indian and East Iranian Pottery', *Ancient Egypt and the East*, March–June 1933, 1–11.
'Is Prehistory Practical?', *Antiquity*, VII, 410–18.
'Excavations at Castlelaw, Midlothian, and the small Forts of North Britain', *Ant. J.*, XIII, 1–12.
'Races, People and Cultures in Prehistoric Europe', *History*, NS, XVIII, no. 21, 193–203.
'Die Bedeutung der altsumerischen Metalltypen für die Chronologie der europäischen Bronzezeit'. *M.A.G.W.*, LXIII, 217–22.
'Painted Fabrics from India and Iran' (substance of a paper read to Section H (Anthropology) of the British Association, 1933), *Nature*, 132, 790.
'Notes on Excavations in Scotland in 1933', *P.P.S.E.A.*, VII, Part 2, 269.
'Trial Excavations at the Old Keig Stone Circle, Aberdeenshire', *P.S.A.S.*, LXVII, 37–52.
'Excavations at Castlelaw Fort, Midlothian, *ibid.*, 362–88.
'Scottish Megalithic Tombs and their Affinities', *Trans. Glasgow Arch. Soc.*, NS VII, 120–37.

1934

New Light on the Most Ancient East; the Oriental prelude to European prehistory; Kegan Paul, Trench, Trubner & Co. Ltd., London; XVIII, 327.
'Eine Hirschgeweihaxt aus der Mittelsteinzeit Schottlands', *Altschlesien*, 5: *Festschrift zum 70. Geburtstag von Hans Seger*, 13–14.
'Eurasian Shaft-hole Axes', *E.S.A.*, IX: *Minns Volume*, 157–64.

* *Bronzezeitliche und früheisenzeitliche Chronologie.* III, *Kupfer- und Frühbronzezeit*, by N. Åberg.

'The Chambered Tombs of Scotland in Relation to those of Spain and Portugal', *Annuario del Cuerpo Facultativo de Archiveros, Bibliotecarios y Arqueólogos*, I, 1–13.
'Notes on Excavations in Scotland during 1934', *P.P.S.E.A.*, VII, Part 3, 413–14.
'Final Report on the Excavation of the Stone Circle at Old Keig, Aberdeenshire', *P.S.A.S.*, LXVIII, 372–93.
'Neolithic Settlement in the West of Scotland', *Scottish Geographical Magazine*, 50, 18–25.

1935
New Light on the Most Ancient East (2nd edition, revised); Kegan Paul, Trench, Trubner & Co. Ltd., London.
L'Orient préhistorique; translation by E. J. Lévy of *New Light on the Most Ancient East*; Payot, Paris.
The Prehistory of Scotland; Kegan Paul, Trench, Trubner & Co. Ltd., London; XV, 285.
'Some Sherds from Slieve na Caillighe', *J.R.S.A.I.*, LXV, 320–4.
'Man Conquers the Desert' (review of *The Desert Fayum* by G. Caton-Thompson and E. W. Gardner), *Nature*, 136, 353–4.
'Changing Methods and Aims in Prehistory: Presidential Address for 1935', *P.P.S.*, I, 1–15.
'Notes on Excavations in Scotland during 1935', *ibid.*, 142–4.
'Excavation of the Vitrified Fort of Finavon, Angus', *P.S.A.S.*, LXIX, 49–80.
'Notes on Some Duns in Islay', *ibid.*, 81–4.
'Le Rôle de l'Ecosse dans la civilisation préhistorique de l'atlantique', *Préhistoire*, IV, 7–21.

1936
Man Makes Himself; Watts & Co., London; XII, 275.
'The Antiquity of Nordic Culture', in *Die Indogermanen*; *Wien Beitr. Kulturgesch. und Linguistik*, 4; 517–30.
'A Promontory Fort on the Antrim Coast', *Ant. J.*, XVI, 179–98.
'The Axes from Maikop and Caucasian Metallurgy, *L.A.A.A.*, XXIII, 113–19.
'The Antiquity of Nordic Culture' (summary of communication presented to the Royal Anthropological Institute on 24 March 1936), *Man*, XXXVI, no. 83.
'International Congresses on the Science of Man', *Nature*, 137, 1074.
'Man and Forest in Prehistoric Europe' (review of *The Mesolithic Settlement of Northern Europe*, by J. G. D. Clark), *ibid.*, 138, 95.
'Notes on Excavations in Scotland during 1936', *P.P.S.*, II, Part 2, 224–6.
'Scottish Tracked Stones and their Significance', *ibid.*, 233–6.
(i) 'Carnminnow Fort; (2) Supplementary Excavations at the Vitrified Fort of Finavon, Angus; and (3) Some Bronze Age Vessels from Angus', *P.S.A.S.*, LXX, 341–62.

1937

Man Makes Himself (2nd impression).

'Neolithic Black Ware in Greece and on the Danube', *B.S.A.*, XXXVII: *Papers presented to Professor J. L. Myres in honour of his 70th Birthday*; 26–35.

'Adaptation to the Postglacial Forest on the North Eurasiatic Plain', in *Early Man*, ed., C. G. MacCurdy; J. B. Lippincott, Philadelphia; 233–42.

'A Prehistorian's Interpretation of Diffusion'; in *Independence, Convergence and Borrowing in Institutions, Thought and Art*; Harvard Tercentenary Publications, Harvard University Press, Cambridge, Mass.; 3–21.

'The Antiquity of the British Bronze Age', *American Anthropologist*, 39, 1–22.

'The Indus Civilization', *Antiquity*, XI, 351.

'Symposium on Early Man, Philadelphia', *ibid.*, 351–2.

'On the Causes of Grey and Black Coloration in Prehistoric Pottery', *Man*, XXXVII, no. 55.

'Symposium on Early Man in Philadelphia; some impressions', *ibid.*, no. 162.

'Notes on Excavations in Scotland during 1937', *P.P.S.*, III, 454–5.

'A Round Cairn near Achnamara, Loch Sween, Argyll', *P.S.A.S.*, LXXI, 84–9.

1938

'The Orient and Europe: Presidential address to Section H (Anthropology) of the British Association', *The Advancement of Science*, 1938, 181–96. Reprinted in *Nature*, 142, 557–9 and 600–3.

'The Oriental Background of European Science', *The Modern Quarterly*, I, 105–20.

'Notes on Excavations in Scotland during 1938', *P.P.S.*, IV, 323–4.

'The Vitrified Fort at Rahoy, Morvern, Argyll' (with W. Thorneycroft), *P.S.A.S.*, LXXII, 23–43.

'The Experimental Production of the Phenomena distinctive of Vitrified Forts', *ibid.*, 44–55.

'Excavations carried out by H.M. Office of Works in the Bronze Age Levels at Jarlshof in 1937', *ibid.*, 348–62.

'Doonmore, a Castle Mound near Fair Head, Co. Antrim', *U.J.A.*, 3rd S, I, 122–35.

1939

Man Makes Himself (3rd impression).

The Dawn of European Civilization (3rd edition, revised and reset), XVIII, 351.

'The Orient and Europe', *A.J.A.*, XLIV, 10–26.

'India and the West before Darius' (substance of a lecture before the Warburg Institute, 10 October 1938), *Antiquity*, XIII, 5–15.

'Double-looped palstaves in Britain', *Ant. J.*, XIX, 320–3.

'Notes on Excavations in Scotland during 1939', *P.P.S.*, V, 256–7.

'A Stone-age Settlement at the Braes of Rinyo, Rousay, Orkney (First Report)' (with W. G. Grant), *P.S.A.S.*, LXXIII, 6–31.

'Rock Scribings at Hawthornden, Midlothian' (with J. Taylor), *ibid.*, 316–17.

'A Beaker Burial from Innerwick, East Lothian', *ibid.*, 318.

'Some Results of Archaeological Research in Scotland, 1932–7', *University of London Institute of Archaeology, Second Annual Report*, 29–45.

1940
Prehistoric Communities of the British Isles; W. & R. Chambers Ltd., London and Edinburgh, XIV, 274.
'Archaeology in the USSR', *Nature*, 145, 110–11.
Prehistoric Scotland; Historical Association, London, 24.

1941
Man Makes Himself (slightly revised edition); now first published in The Thinkers' Library; Watts & Co., London.
'The History of Civilization', *Antiquity*, XV, 1–14.
'Horses, Chariots and Battle-Axes', *ibid.*, 196–9.
'Rock Engravings in Scotland', *ibid.*, 290–1.
'A Bronze Dagger from Hungry Bentley', *D.A.J.*, 62, 29–30.
'Prehistoric Iron' (letter to the Editor), *Man*, XLI, no. 99.
'The defences of Kaimes Hill-fort, Midlothian', *P.S.A.S.*, LXXXV, 43–54.
'Examination of the Prehistoric Fort on Cairngryfe Hill, near Lanark', *ibid.*, 213–18.
'Man and Science from Early Times', *University Forward*, VI, no. 5, 4–7.

1942
Prehistoric Communities of the British Isles (2nd printing).
What Happened in History; Pelican Books; Penguin Books Ltd., Harmondsworth and New York; 256.
'The Antiquity and Function of Antler Axes and Adzes', *Antiquity*, XVI, 258–64.
'Ceramic Art in Early Iran' (a review of *The Comparative Stratigraphy of Early Iran*, by D. E. McCown), *ibid.*, 355–8.
'Prehistory in the USSR. I. Palaeolithic and Mesolithic. A. Caucasus and Crimea', *Man*, XLII, no. 59.
'Prehistory in the USSR. I. Palaeolithic and Mesolithic. B. The Russian Plain', *ibid.*, no. 60.
'Prehistory in the USSR. II. The Copper Age in South Russia, *ibid.*, no. 74.
'Further Urns and Cremation Burials from Brackmont Mill, near Leuchars, Fife' (with D. Waterston), *P.S.A.S.*, LXXVI, 84–93.
'The Chambered Cairns of Rousay', *Ant. J.*, XXII, 139–42.
'The Significance of Soviet Archaeology', *Labour Monthly*, XXIV, 341–343.

1943
What Happened in History (new impression).
'The Prehistoric Archaeology of North-east Scotland'; in *The Book of Buchan*, ed. J. F. Tocher; The Buchan Club, Aberdeen; 62–80.
'Rotary Querns on the Continent and in the Mediterranean Basin', *Antiquity*, XVII, 19–26.

'The Study of Anthropology', *ibid.*, 213–14 (reprinted from *The Scotsman*; contributed on the occasion of the centenary of the Royal Anthropological Institute of Great Britain and Ireland).
'Archaeology in the USSR. The Forest Zone', *Man*, XLIII, no. 2.
'The Mesolithic and Neolithic in Northern Europe', *ibid.*, no. 17.
'Directional Changes in Funerary Practices during 50,000 Years', *ibid.*, no. 91 (summary of a communication to the Royal Anthropological Institute on 15 June 1943).
'Archaeology as a Science', *Nature*, 152, 22–3.
    'Another late Viking House at Freswick, Caithness', *P.S.A.S.*, LXXVII, 5–17.
'Some Notable Prehistoric and Medieval Monuments Recently Examined by the Royal Commission on Ancient and Historical Monuments of Scotland' (with A. Graham), *ibid.*, 31–49.
'A Hoard of Bronzes from Ballymore, Cowall, Argyll', *ibid.*, 184–6.
'An Encrusted Urn from Aberlemno, Angus', *ibid.*, 189–90.

1944
The Story of Tools; Cobbett Publishing Co. Ltd., London.
'The Cave of Parpalló and the Upper Palaeolithic Age in Southeast Spain', *Antiquity*, XVIII, 29–35.
'Archaeological Ages as Technological Stages: Huxley Memorial Lecture, 1944', *J.R.A.I.*, LXXIV, 7–24; (also published separately by the Royal Anthropological Institute, 19 pp).
'The Future of Archaeology', *Man*, XLIV, no. 7 (an address in the series, The Future of Anthropology, given at the Centenary Meeting of the Royal Anthropological Institute).
'Recent excavations on Prehistoric Sites in Soviet Russia', *ibid.*, no. 29.
'Historical Analysis of Archaeological Method' (review of *The Three Ages*, by G. E. Daniel), *Nature*, 153, 206–7.
'An Unrecognized Group of Chambered Cairns', *P.S.A.S.*, LXXVIII, 26–39.
'Newly-discovered Short Cist Burials with Beakers' (with A. J. H. Edwards, A. Low and M. MacDougall), *ibid.*, 106–20.
'The Bronze Blade from Craigscorry, near Beauly, *ibid.*, 138.
Memoir: Arthur J. H. Edwards, *ibid.*, 150–1.

1945
Progress and Archaeology; Watts & Co., London.
'Tripil's'ka Kultura' (review of *Tripil's'ka Kultura*, Tom. I, Akademia Nauk, Ukrainian SSR, Kiev), *Antiquity*, XIX, 203–6.
'Directional Changes in Funerary Practices during 50,000 Years' (complete text), *Man*, XLV, no. 4.
'The Huxley Memorial Lecture: Archaeological Ages as Technological Stages' (Summary), *ibid.*, no. 8.
'Archaeology and Anthropology in the USSR', *Nature*, 156, 224–5.
'Prehistoric Cereals in Scotland, *P.S.A.S.*, LXXIX, 167.

'An Unusual Cinerary Urn from Droughdool, near Dunragit, Wigtownshire', *ibid.*, 168–70.
'Rational Order in History', *The Rationalist Annual*, 1945, 21–6.
'Introduction to the Conference on the Problems and Prospects of European Archaeology' (16–17 September 1944) *University of London Institute of Archaeology, Occasional Paper no. 6*, 6–12.

1946
Doğunun Prehistoryasi; translation of the 1935 edition of *L'Orient préhistorique* by Ş. A. Kansu; Türk Tarih Kurumu Basimevi, Ankara; XX, 250.
Scotland Before the Scots: being The Rhind Lectures for 1944; Methuen & Co. Ltd., London; VIII, 144.
What Happened in History (new impression).
'The Significance of Cord-ornamented Bell-beakers'; in *Homenaje a J. L. Santa-Olalla*, I; Madrid; 196–201.
'Human Cultures as Adaptations to Environment', *Geog. Journal*, CVIII, nos. 4–6, 227–30.
'The Science of Man in the USSR' (summary of a Communication on 23 October 1945), *Man*, XLVI, no. 9.
'The Distribution of Megalithic Cultures and their Influence in Ancient and Modern Civilization', *ibid.*, no. 83.
'The Social Implications of the Three "Ages" in Archaeological Classification', *The Modern Quarterly*, NS, I, 18–33.
'A Bronze-Worker's Anvil and Other Tools recently acquired by the Inverness Museum, with a note on another Scottish Anvil', *P.S.A.S.*, LXXX, 8–11.
'Archaeology and Anthropology', *Southwestern Journal of Anthropology*, 2, no. 3, 243–51.

1947
The Dawn of European Civilization (4th edition, revised and reset), XVIII, 362.
History; Cobbett Press, London; 86.
Prehistoric Communities of the British Isles (2nd edition, revised).
'The Final Bronze Age in the Near East and in Temperate Europe', *Arch. News-letter*, 2, 9–11.
'Nuevas Fechas para la Cronología Prehistórica de la Europa Atlantica', *Cuadernos de Historia Primitiva*, II, no. 1, 5–23.
'A Stone Age Settlement at the Braes of Rinyo, Rousay, Orkney' (second report) (with W. G. Grant of Trumland), *P.S.A.S.*, LXXXI, 16–42.
'Megalithic Tombs in Scotland and Ireland', *Trans. Glasgow Arch. Soc.*, XI, 7–21.
'Archaeology as a Social Science: Inaugural Lecture', *University of London Institute of Archaeology, Third Annual Report*, 49–60.

1948
Man Makes Himself (new impression).
What Happened in History (reset), 288.

'Cross-dating in the European Bronze Age'; in *Festschrift für Otto Tschumi*; Verlag Huber & Co., Frauenfeld; 70–6.
'Sur l'âge des objets importés des Îles Britanniques trouvés en Pologne'; *Slavia Antiqua*, I: *Kostrzewski Volume*, 84–93.
'Megaliths', *Ancient India*, 4, 4–13.
'The Technique of Prehistoric Metal Work: a review' (of *Metallteknik under Förhistorisk Tid*, by A. Oldeberg), *Antiquity*, XXII, 29–32.
'Mesopotamian Archaeology: a review' (of *Foundations in the Dust*, by S. Lloyd), *ibid.*, 198–200.
'Palaeolithic Man in Greece', *ibid.*, 210.
'Cinerary Urns from Kirk Ireton' (with G. T. Warwick and G. S. Johnson), *D.A.J.*, 68, 31–6.
Archaeological Note, in: 'Ancient Mining and Metallurgy Group: Preliminary Report, Part I', *Man*, XLVIII, no. 3.
'Culture Sequence in the Stone Age of Northern Europe', *ibid.*, no. 44.
'The Final Bronze Age in the Near East and in Temperate Europe', *P.P.S.*, XIV, 177–95.
'The Culture Sequence in the Northern Stone Age: Revised after Twelve Years' Research', *University of London Institute of Archaeology, Fourth Annual Report*, 46–60.

1949
Prehistoric Communities of the British Isles (3rd edition, revised).
L'Aube de la civilisation européenne; Payot, Paris.
Človek svym tvurcem; translation of *Man Makes Himself* by J. Schránilová; Nakladatelství Svoboda, Prague; 199.
Progress i Arkheologiya; translation of *Progress and Archaeology*, by M. B. Sviridova-Grakova; Foreign Literature Publishing House, Moscow; 194.
Il progresso nel mondo antico; translation of *What Happened in History*, by A. Ruata; Einaudi Editore; 301.
A Szerszámok Története; translation of *The Story of Tools*, by S. Jolán; Szikra Kiadás, Budapest; 59.
Social Worlds of Knowledge: L. T. Hobhouse Memorial Trust Lecture, no. 19, delivered on 12 May 1948 at King's College, London; Oxford University Press, London; 26.
'The First Bronze Vases to be made in Central Europe', *Acta Arch.*, XX, 257–64.
'The Origin of Neolithic Culture in Northern Europe', *Antiquity*, XXIII, 129–35.
'The Sociology of Knowledge', *The Modern Quarterly*, NS, IV, 302–9.
'Neolithic House-types in Temperate Europe', *P.P.S.*, XV, 77–86.
'Organic and Social Evolution', *The Rationalist Annual*, 1949, 57–62.
'Great Science and Society' (Review); *Labour Monthly*, XXI, 221.
'Marxism and the Classics' (Review); *ibid.*, 250.

1950

The Dawn of European Civilization (5th edition, revised); Routledge & Kegan Paul Ltd., London; XIX, 362.

Prehistoric Migrations in Europe; Instituttet for Sammenlignende Kulturforskning; Serie A: Forelesninger, XX; H. Aschehaug & Co., Oslo; Kegan Paul, Trench, Trubner & Co. Ltd., London; IX, 249.

Skara Brae, Orkney: Official Guide (new Impression).

What Happened in History (new impression).

Jak Powstały Narzędzia; translation of *The Story of Tools*, by T. Szumowski; Warsaw; 52.

Magic, Craftsmanship and Science: The Frazer Lecture, delivered at Liverpool on 10 November 1949; University Press, Liverpool; 19.

'Kent's Cavern. 1949 Report of the Investigating Committee', *The Advancement of Science*, 7, no. 25, Sect. H, 98–9.

'La Civilisation de Seine-Oise-Marne' (with N. Sandars), *L'Anthropologie*, 54, 1–18.

'Cave Men's Buildings', *Antiquity*, XXIV, 4–11.

'University of London Institute of Archaeology', *Arch. News-letter*, 3–4, 57–60.

'Social Evolution in the Light of Archaeology', *Mankind*, 4, no. 5, 175–83.

'Comparison of Archaeological and Radiocarbon Datings', *Nature*, 166, 1068–9.

'Algumas analogias das cerâmicas pré-históricas britânicas com as portuguesas', *Rev. de Guimarães*, LX, 5–16.

'The Urban Revolution', *The Town Planning Review*, XXI, no. 1, 3–17.

'Axe and Adze, Bow and Sling: contrasts in early Neolithic Europe', *Jahr. Schwiez. Gesell. f. Urg.*, XL, 156–62.

1951

Man Makes Himself: Man's Progress through the Ages; American printing of revised English edition (1941); New American Library, New York; 192.

Social Evolution. Based on a series of lectures delivered at the University of Birmingham in 1947–8 under the Josiah Mason Lectureship founded by The Rationalist Press Association. Watts & Co., London; Henry Schuman, New York; VIII, 184.

'The Balanced Sickle'; in *Aspects of Archaeology in Britain and Beyond: Essays presented to O. G. S. Crawford*; ed. W. F. Grimes; H. W. Edwards, London; 39–48.

'La última Edad del Bronce en el Próximo Oriente y en la Europa Central', *Ampurias*, XIII, 5–34.

'The Framework of Prehistory', *Man*, LI, no. 119.

'Bronze Dagger of Mycenaean type from Pelynt, Cornwall', *P.P.S.*, XVII, 95.

'An Exotic Stone Adze from Tuckingmill, Camborne, Cornwall', *ibid.*, 96.

'The First Waggons and Carts—from the Tigris to the Severn', *ibid.*, 177–94.

Review: *Periodizatsiya Tripolskikh Poselenii* ('The Periodization of Tripolye Settlements', by T. S. Passek), *Soviet Studies*, II, no. 4, 386–9.

'Copper and Stone Battle-axes', *University of London Institute of Archaeology, Seventh Annual Report*, 44–5.
'30th Birthday Greetings', *Labour Monthly*, XXXIII, 342.

1952

New Light on the Most Ancient East (4th edition, rewritten); Routledge & Kegan Paul Ltd., London; XVI, 255.

Scotland: Illustrated Guide to Ancient Monuments in the Ownership or Guardianship of the Ministry of Works, Vol. VI (with W. D. Simpson); HMSO, Edinburgh; 127.

What Happened in History (new impression).

U istokov evropeĭskoĭ tsivilizatsii; translation of *The Dawn of European Civilization*, by M. B. Sviridova-Grakova; Foreign Literature Publishing House, Moscow; 468.

Stufen der Kultur, von der Urzeit zur Antike; translation of *What Happened in History*, by F. W. Gutbrod; Europäischer Buchklub, Stuttgart, Zürich, Salzburg; 348. Same edition also issued by W. Kohlhammer Verlag, Stuttgart.

L'uomo crea se stesso; translation of *Man Makes Himself*, by G. Gorlier; G. Einaudi Editore; 393.

Van Vuursteen tot Wereldrijk; What Happened in History translated, adapted and illustrated by R. Van Amerongen; N. V. Em. Querido's Uitgeversmij, Amsterdam; 323.

'Trade and Industry in Barbarian Europe till Roman Times'; in *The Cambridge Economic History of Europe*, II. *Trade and Industry in the Middle Ages*, ed. M. Postan and E. E. Rich; Cambridge University Press; Chap. I, 1–32.

'The West Baltic, Britain and the South: some new links'; in *Corolla Archaeologica in Honorem C. A. Nordman*; ed. E. Kivikoski; K. F. Puromiehen Kirjapaino O.y., Helsinki; 8–16.

Old World Neolithic. Inventory paper for Wenner-Gren International Symposium on Anthropology, New York City, 9–20 June 1952; Paper No. 10, 1–21; duplicated.

'Terminology in Egyptian Prehistory', *Antiquity*, XXVI, 149–50.

'Aims of Research'; in 'Report of Ancient Mining and Metallurgy Committee', *Man*, LII, no. 124.

'The Birth of Civilization', *Past and Present*, 2, 1–10.

'Re-excavation of the Chambered Cairn of Quoyness, Sanday, on the behalf of the Ministry of Works in 1951–2', *P.S.A.S.*, LXXXVI, 121–39.

1953

L'Orient préhistorique; translation of 1952 edition of *New Light on the Most Ancient East*, by A. Guieu; Payot, Paris; 322.

Progresso e Archeologia; translation of *Progress and Archaeology*, by G. Fanoli; Universale Economica, Milan; X, 128.

What is History?; American edition of *History*; Henry Schuman, New York; 86.

'The Middle Bronze Age', *Archivo de Prehistoria Levantina*, IV, Tom. II: *Homenaje a D. Isidro Ballester Tormo*, 167–85.

'The Significance of the Sling for Greek Prehistory'; in *Studies presented to David Moore Robinson*, ed. G. E. Mylonas and D. Raymond; Washington University; 1–5.

'The Constitution of Archaeology as a Science'; in *Science, Medicine and History. Essays on the Evolution of Scientific Thought and Medical Practice, written in Honour of Charles Singer*, I; ed. E. A. Underwood; Oxford University Press, London; 3, 15.

'Science in Preliterate Societies and the Ancient Oriental Civilizations', *Centaurus, International Mogazine of the History of Science and Medicine*, 3, 12–23.

'Model of the Chambered Cairn, "Egmond's Howe"' (with J. D. Akeredolu), *Museums Journal*, 53, no. 8, 197–9.

1954

What Happened in History (2nd edition).

History; Japanese edition; Tokyo.

Man Makes Himself; Chinese edition, translated by Chow 'Tsia-kai; Shanghai; 228.

Människan skapar sig själv; translation of *What Happened in History*, by A. Ellegård; Almqvist & Wiksell/Gebers Förlag AB, Uppsala; 310.

Postep a Archeologia; translation of *Progress and Archaeology*, by A. Ponikowski and Z. Slawska; Państwowe Wydownictwo Naukowe, Warsaw; 178.

Los orígenes de la civilización; translation of *Man Makes Himself*, by E. de Gortari; Fondo de Cultura Económica, Mexico; 291.

The Story of Tools; Chinese edition, translated by Chow 'Tsia-kai; Shanghai; 49.

The Artifacts of Prehistoric Man as Applications of Science; International Commission for a History of the Scientific and Cultural Development of Mankind, 2 February 1954; duplicated.

'Prehistory. 1 Man and His Culture', 3–10; 2. 'Pleistocene Societies in Europe', 11–27; 3 'The Mesolithic Age', 28–38; in *The European Inheritance*, I, ed. E. Barker, G. Clark, and P. Vaucher; Clarendon Press, Oxford.

'Early Forms of Society', 38–57; 'Rotary Motion', 187–215; in *A History of Technology*, I, ed. C. Singer, E. J. Holmyard, and A. R. Hall; Clarendon Press, Oxford.

'The Diffusion of Wheeled Vehicles', *Ethnographisch-Archäologische Forschungen*, 2, 1–16.

'Archaeological Documents for the Prehistory of Science (1)', *Journal of World History*, I, no. 4, 739–59.

'Documents in the Prehistory of Science (II)', *ibid.*, II, no. 1, 9–25.

Obituary of Prof. H. Frankfort, *Nature*, 174, 337–8.

'The First Colonization of Britain by Farmers' (review of *The Neolithic Cultures of the British Isles* by S. Piggott), *ibid.*, 575.

'The Stone Age Comes to Life', *The Rationalist Annual*, 1954, 1–7.
'The Socketed Celt in Upper Eurasia', *University of London Institute of Archaeology, Tenth Annual Report*, 11–25.
'Archaeological Notes in the U.S.S.R., 1953', *Bull. Soc. Cultural Relations U.S.S.R.*, no. 4, 7–8.

1955
'Dates of Stonehenge', *The Scientific Monthly*, 80, no. 5, 281–5.
'The significance of lake dwellings in the history of prehistory', *Sibrium*, 2, Part 2: Atti del Convegno internazionale di paletnologia, Varese, 29–31 Agosto, 1954; 87–91.
'The Sociology of the Mycenaean Tablets', *Past and Present*, no. 7, 76–77.

1956
Piecing Together the Past: The Interpretation of Archaeological Data; Routledge & Kegan Paul, London; VII, 176.
A Short Introduction to Archaeology; Frederick Muller Ltd., London; 142.
Society and Knowledge; Harper & Brothers, New York.
'Kostienki: "East Gravettian" or "Solutrean"?', *University of London Institute of Archaeology, Twelfth Annual Report*.
'The Past, the Present and the Future' (review), *Past and Present*, X, 3–5.
Man Makes Himself (3rd edition). London: Watts & Co.

1957
The Dawn of European Civilization (6th edition), XIII, 368.
'The Bronze Age', *Past and Present*, XII, 2–15.

1958
The Prehistory of European Society; Harmondsworth: Penguin Books.
'Retrospect', *Antiquity*, XXXII, 69–74.
'Valediction', *Bull. Lond. Inst. Arch.*, I, 1–8.

1962
The Prehistory of European Society; Cassells, London.

1963
Social Evolution (revised edition); Watts and Co., London.

1964
How Labour Governs (2nd edition); Melbourne University Press, Melbourne.

1965
Man Makes Himself (4th edition); Watts and Co., London.

1970
The Aryans (re-issue); Port Wash & Co.

1973
The Dawn of European Civilization (6th edition); Paladin, Frogmore, St
Albans.
What Happened in History (3rd edition); Book Club Associates, London.

1976
What Happened in History (revised edition); Penguin Books, Harmondsworth.

1979
'Prehistory and Marxism', *Antiquity*, LIII, 93–95.

Index